PRAISE FOR *KAPP TO CAPE*

*'A thrilling and beautiful book. The journey that Reza
undertakes – both physically and mentally – is astonishing.'*

Ed Stafford, explorer

*'A brilliantly candid, funny and thought-provoking escape to the wild.
Through Reza's unique cultural lens we are taken on the adventure of a
lifetime, and left reflecting on our own sense of purpose and adventure.'*

Mark Beaumont, author of *The Man Who Cycled the World*

*'It took me over a year to cycle to South Africa. Reza
managed it in just 100 days – that is extraordinary.'*

Alastair Humphreys, adventurer and author of *Grand Adventures*

*'I am literally lost for words at the scale of this heroic
achievement. To the benefit of his readers, Reza isn't.'*

**Tim Moore, author of *Gironimo!*, *You Are Awful
(But I Like You)* and *French Revolutions***

*'An absolute page-turner about Reza's courageous world-
record bid. The inner journey is every bit as fascinating as the
outer as he candidly shares his doubts, struggles, challenges
and triumphs while navigating some of the world's most
cyclist-unfriendly regions and roads. Recommended!'*

**Roz Savage, world-record ocean rower and
author of *Rowing the Atlantic***

*'A moment of self-realisation among the commuters on London
Bridge triggers a selfless and enduring determination in Reza
Pakravan, to live his own life in a way that makes a positive
difference to others. Kapp to Cape is the story of an epic journey of
self-discovery, self-discipline and triumph against all the odds. It
reveals the best of the human spirit and reminds us, yet again, that a
life well-lived is never about the destination: it's about the ride.'*

Deborah Bull, CBE, dancer, writer and broadcaster

KAPP
TO
CAPE

• NEVER LOOK BACK •

RACE TO
THE END OF
THE EARTH

REZA PAKRAVAN

summersdale

KAPP TO CAPE

Summersdale Publishers Ltd
46 West Street
Chichester
West Sussex
PO19 1RP
UK

www.summersdale.com

Printed and bound by CPI Group (UK) Ltd, Croydon, CR0 4YY

ISBN: 978-1-84953-967-8

Substantial discounts on bulk quantities of Summersdale books are available to corporations, professional associations and other organisations. For details contact general enquiries: telephone: +44 (0) 1243 771107, fax: +44 (0) 1243 786300 or email: enquiries@summersdale.com.

To my Mum and Dad

CONTENTS

PART THREE: LEG TWO

ANNAPURNA
RCUIT, NEPAL
DRAVAN

PART ONE

BEGINNING

CHAPTER 1

LONDON BRIDGE, FALLING DOWN

The revelation came at 8.45 a.m. one cold November morning. On London Bridge, beneath a canopy of low-hanging cloud, I stopped.

A man walked into my back. Others jostled on either side of me, shoulders connected with shoulders, elbows with elbows, and I was nudged and bounced in a chorus of grumbled complaints towards the railings. I clung to the concrete, standing firm, an immoveable object. The tide of commuters found its rhythm once more and flowed around me with no further contact, as if I was surrounded by some unseen bell curve of protection – a sheen of impenetrability: the physical space we afford those we do not trust. I was no longer perceived as trustworthy on this bridge. I had broken the rules. At this time of day, you do not stop. Those who do are inconsiderate or inexperienced or, worse, mad. Perhaps my fellow commuters thought exactly that: I was mad and therefore best avoided. I did not mind so much.

I looked about me. Down below, the Thames boiled and chopped, its thick and silty swells smacking wetly against the bridge's legs. It flowed relentlessly and without mercy, the same colour as the bulging clouds above. As I turned and rested my back against concrete, it struck me that these people, this river of suits and umbrellas, matched the waters below. Leaden and dreary, they stopped for nothing. If I had fallen, if I had dropped to my hands and knees at that very moment, if I had crumpled and landed spreadeagled on my back, would anyone have stopped? Or would the tide have merely pushed around me, even over me, and continued on? Perhaps. And, if so, you can't blame it. It's what a river does.

The revelation was a simple one. I was a part of this river – this surge of workers washing over London Bridge towards the City only to repeat the same in reverse 10 hours later and then continue the numbing exercise day in and day out – and I had been for almost a decade. This had never been the plan.

––––––––––––

Five months later, I found myself facing a different river. Unlike the Thames, which had flowed 30 ft beneath me from my London Bridge vantage point, this one was just a few centimetres away and all my energy was focused on keeping it from washing into my tent. Piling sacks of rice against the inside of the door flap and wrapping my scant belongings into plastic bags, I wedged my guitar against one of the bending tent poles as extra support and then lay on my back across the groundsheet, praying that my own weight would serve as ballast to keep the tent rooted to the muddy earth. The wind roared and howled outside as the tropical storm rose in pitch and intensity, whipping the thin canvas walls in and out.

The river was a new addition to a landscape I thought I had come to know. It had not been here yesterday. But the storm had raged mercilessly for hours now and, with nowhere to go, the rising rainwater had pushed up from the saturated earth and found its trajectory. My tent was still not quite in its path – it had not yet suffered the same fate as the fallen branches and ripped-up roots that sailed past me on the churning, blood-red tumult – but if the rain did not stop soon it, and all my belongings, would doubtless be swept away. I remained on my back, motionless, breathing slow and deep in contrast to the downpour that splattered against my tent in a deafening thunder. There was no sign that this storm would end. I had not been so happy in years.

The tent had been my home for the past two weeks: pitched in the small village of Agnena, deep in the heart of Madagascar. I was there as a volunteer labourer for a non-governmental organisation called SEED Madagascar, which built much-needed schools in rural areas of the country. The London Bridge revelation had left me hollow and bereft, desperate to find a way to bring a sense of purpose to my life, something noble through which I could prove to myself that I wasn't just a City-bound financial analyst contributing nothing to this world nor to myself. That desperation had led me here, to Madagascar, to this tent, to this storm.

I was exactly where I wanted and needed to be. Back in London, I rarely felt that way. As I lay in my tent, listening to the rain hammer its relentless tattoo on the canvas, I contemplated my life, the decisions I had taken that had resulted in the stable but soulless existence I no longer wanted a part of.

It had not always been this way. As a child growing up in Iran and then a young man taking his first few tentative steps into adulthood, when I thought of the future, if I ever did at all, it was filled with excitement and adventure. It was natural to believe that it would be, for my youth had been enveloped in much the same. An avid explorer of Iranian wildlands and mountainscapes – first with my father and then later with friends or alone – I cherished travelling and all the thrills and wonder that came with it. My life back then had been active and filled with adventure, and I found my recreation in demanding and competitive sports. It came as no surprise to me – indeed, it felt somehow pre-ordained – when I became a semi-professional basketball player. If anything can qualify, that was my first real job, and I played until I was 24.

University had been a natural next step and I chose a degree I knew I could excel at: mechanical engineering. Yet the more I studied it the more I came to understand that it held little appeal for me, and the prospect of immersing myself in an engineering career became anathema. The master's degree I chose, finance, was a step in an entirely different direction and it contained a potential future that I found alluring – the promise of work that was high-speed and international; the promise of a lifestyle that was seductive and enthralling. I moved to London, found myself a job in the City and began my new life.

There's something horribly glamorous about money and that only intensifies when you work with it on a daily basis. My new career as a financial analyst was a demanding one, but it suited my ambitious mindset and I slipped into it all with ease. Compared with friends who worked in stocks or hedge funds, my earnings were far from spectacular, but before long I was able to pay off my gargantuan student-loan debts and could even start saving. It all absorbed me with such immediacy and totality that there was no longer any space left for my real passion: adventure. Time and inclination dissolved, and before I knew it I was 35 years old and the past decade had slipped by in a haze, leaving me hollow and helpless on London Bridge, staring down into the grey waves of the Thames.

The rain began to lessen. I rose from my back, scrambled over the sacks of rice, unzipped the tent door and poked my head outside. The black clouds were receding, and patches of blue sky and sunlight sparkled through. The worst of the storm was over. I was glad. There was work to do.

I had not chosen Madagascar. Instead, I had chosen the NGO itself: SEED (Society for Energy, Environment and Development).

It was imperative to me that, should I make a change in my life, that change should contribute in some way towards the well-being of others. Though I yearned for a huge and immersive adventure, I was not ready. But I could still make a start. I estimated that I could spend one month abroad volunteering for a worthy charity or non-governmental organisation.

I began my research, studying the annual reports of myriad charities across the world. The results I accumulated made me sad. It seemed that almost every organisation I looked into channelled less than half of the donations it received into the causes it supported, with the rest spent on staffing and overheads. This was not what I expected, nor what I intended to contribute my own time and energy to. I continued my research.

After some weeks, I chanced upon SEED – a charity which aims to eradicate poverty, suffering and environmental damage in Madagascar – during a late-night online investigation. A perusal of its annual reports revealed that, for every £100 donated to SEED, £90 went directly to its projects. In this impoverished and disregarded island off the African continent, SEED was making a genuine difference: building schools, empowering the locals, conserving the environment and changing lives. I wanted in.

I made contact and within days was booking flights and time off work. The thought of this new adventure immersed me with far more intensity than my recent work ever had, and the intervening months flew by in a whirlwind of preparation and anticipation. Then, one grey evening, I left the office, caught the train to Heathrow and boarded my flight to Madagascar.

The touchdown filled me with exhilaration. This was my first time in Africa and certainly my first time in such a remote environment. The local airport was little more than a runway and a building no bigger than a London taxi depot. Palm trees ringed the terminal. The heat was astonishing. A minivan transported me to the nearest town where I met Lumba, the young and friendly Malagasy man who would take me to Agnena.

'So how are we getting there?' I asked as Lumba took my backpack from my hands and shouldered it himself. 'Is there a bus?'

Lumba laughed. 'There's no bus to Agnena, man. We'll drive some way, we'll pirogue the rest.'

'Pirogue?'

'You don't know what a pirogue is? Man, this will be some treat for you.'

He laughed again and then ushered me towards his old and rusting car, which he started in a series of cracks and pops. The heady scent of petrol fumes assaulted my nostrils and I wound down the window.

'Yes!' Lumba shouted over the engine, gesturing at my window and then winding down his own. 'Nature's air con, man!'

We pulled out into the sparse traffic and within minutes were beyond the limits of the town, heading out into a landscape devoid of anything except endless red earth. Deforestation was a serious problem in Madagascar and its unique flora had suffered perhaps irreparably. After a few hours in the car, bouncing along virtually impassable dirt roads, we pulled up and parked beside a river, where Lumba led me down to a long and decidedly flimsy looking canoe.

'*This*,' he said proudly, 'is a pirogue.'

'I love it,' I grinned.

'Good. Climb in, man!'

I did as I was told. Lumba pushed us out into the shallows of the river and then nimbly leapt into the pirogue, retrieving his paddle and gliding us off along the water. Another paddle lay across the floor of the boat and I picked it up, dipping it into the river in tandem with Lumba's strokes. Feeling the extra surge in our motion, Lumba turned his head and laughed once more. I loved that laugh.

'You like to get involved, huh? Man, you're going to fit *right* in at Agnena.'

And, so it seemed, I did. After just two days of orientation alongside my SEED compatriots, I was thrown into the work. My days began to take on a reliable and comforting routine: an early-morning rise, followed by a breakfast of banana and dough balls with honey under the fierce African sun, an hour's lesson in the Malagasy language, and then work – such long but such beautifully meaningful days of work – mixing cement, building walls, learning the intricacies of effective carpentry and joinery. At night, we were all so fatigued that the evening meal of rice and beans tasted sensational. It was a simple life and exactly what I craved. With no electricity, no phones, no relentless intrusion of media, when the sun went down there was little to do other than sleep, and I slept like a kitten each night.

Occasionally, and especially at weekends, we would treat ourselves to the luxury of a large, outdoor fire, which illuminated the otherwise all-consuming darkness of the night. These fires were not just for us workers, they were for the whole community of Agnena, and the villagers came out en masse to share their food with us and dance and sing. I became especially entranced by the songs the children would perform for us with barely concealed delight, and when I retrieved my guitar from my tent one night I was surrounded by giggling and fascinated youngsters, who urged me to play them a tune. We traded songs long into the night, taking it in turns to bellow out our favourites, until it grew so late that their parents had to drag them away to bed. It did not take long for this to become a regular occurrence.

Perhaps it would be too dramatic to state that those children saved me. In any case, they changed me. A week after the storm and just a few days before I was due to leave, I was woken at 4 a.m. by their singing. It was Easter Sunday. All the children in the village had converged around the still-glowing embers of the previous night's fire, coming together to sing a song woven from such intricate harmonies and delicate refrains that, as I lay there in my tent listening to them, what started as a simple prickle along my spine soon engulfed my entire body with such force that I could do nothing but weep at the sheer beauty of it all. I understood then that my life had to change. This was where I wanted to be. This was *who* I wanted to be.

———————

Exactly one week and one day later, I was back on London Bridge, on my way to the job I had come to loathe. I checked my watch. It was 8.45 a.m. I thought of those children, of those lilting melodies, of the tears they had engendered. I looked around me. These were the same faces, the same suits, the same umbrellas I had lived among for too long. I didn't recognise a single one of them.

Beneath the canopy of low-hanging cloud, I stopped. A man walked into my back. Others jostled on either side of me, shoulders connected with shoulders, elbows with elbows, but this time I would not let them push me to the side. I stood firm, resisting the shoves and ignoring the breathy obscenities. Slowly placing my bag on the ground and straightening my tie, I turned around to face the tide of faces.

The river swelled, banked and diverted around me.

CHAPTER 2

THE RISE

Madagascar began to infiltrate my dreams. I would wake and, in those blurry moments before consciousness and reality took hold, I believed I was still there, anticipating the dawn chorus of children's songs. When my mind cleared and I realised that the day ahead held spreadsheets and business meetings rather than Malagasy lessons and the laying of a floor, I often wished myself back to sleep so that I could experience that moment once more.

I remained in touch with SEED. I was so proud of everyone who worked for the organisation: together, they were doing some of the most important work of which I had ever been a part. I wanted to continue to help them. One month of voluntary labour each year was not enough; I knew I was capable of more. Even while I was in London, I could still fundraise for them and, the more I began to think about how, the more I realised that I could do so on a grand scale. I have, you see, a particular kind of talent, one I had not exploited for almost 15 years, but one which I still knew I was ready and willing to utilise. That talent lay in adventure travel.

And so I made my resolution. I knew that if I could set myself and then undertake challenges of truly epic proportions, I could fundraise and garner sponsorship for them, and I could donate every penny that I made to SEED, to Madagascar and to those children. They had changed my life with their magical songs. It was now my turn to change theirs.

I began in Nepal, cycling the entirety of the Annapurna circuit – a trail made for feet rather than wheels. The experience was a shock to my system. Cycling incongruous terrains and pathways had not been easy when I was in my twenties, but it had been a breeze compared with this. Thirty-six years old, overweight and far more used to my comfortable office chair than this chafing saddle, I was struggling, but I pushed on nonetheless. The physical turmoil was tough enough, but I was also weighed down by the fact that I hadn't raised as much money as I'd hoped. Indeed, I had invested more of my own finances into the adventure than had been returned through donations and sponsorship.

But then something miraculous happened. By chance, I met a hiker on the Annapurna trail who turned out to be a journalist for CNN. When she heard my story, she asked if she could write about it and her article was published on the CNN website soon after. Arriving back in Kathmandu – exhausted, weak, yet jubilant that I had seen the adventure through to its conclusion – I settled into an internet cafe for the evening, where I found that countless congratulatory emails from my friends had clogged my inbox. Almost all contained a link to the CNN article.

One particular email caught my eye. It was from a name I did not recognise. I opened it, read its message three times in a state of disbelief and then opened up the website I had created for those who wanted to contribute to SEED via my journey. The contents of the email were true, glaring up at me from the website's online counter. A representative for an American aid organisation had read the CNN article about my adventure. And they had donated $25,000 to my SEED fund.

———————

Things snowballed. With the SEED fund suddenly gargantuan, further donations poured in. It was enough for another brand new school in Madagascar, and the sheer delight I felt when I transferred the money to the charity took on a bright and new meaning. I was doing what I loved for the people I loved. And I could do more. So much more.

Using the fundraising template I had created with the Annapurna ride, I set out to cross the Sahara Desert by bike. I not only accomplished the expedition, I did it in record time: 13 days and 5 hours. That record was officially recognised by the Guinness World Records board. The acclaim fed my ego to some extent, but, more importantly, it helped raise the SEED fund to levels I had never anticipated. Over the course of two years and with two major expeditions under my belt, more than £50,000 had been raised. It all went to SEED and with it four new schools were built. It was thrilling, it was worthy and I had never been so exultant.

Exultant, yes, but not yet content. I wanted a greater adventure. I wanted more schools in Madagascar. I recognised that drive, recognised the ambition it fuelled. It was the same drive that had led me down the path of a career as a financial analyst, the same drive that had focused me on the accumulation of money to the detriment of anyone but myself, and perhaps myself as well. I was at the mercy of that drive, I always had been, but at least now I knew that I could channel it towards something worthwhile. A truly extraordinary adventure loomed.

I called my friend Arash. He had been instrumental in turning my Sahara expedition into a documentary. Before his input, I had only thought of taking on the journey to raise funds for SEED, but he had convinced me to record it on camera and together we had transformed my footage from the adventure into a short film. A tall and bearded man with thick glasses and perhaps the largest head I've ever seen, Arash was a cinematic *wunderkind* and, though he worked a full-time job in London, he still found the hours to help me produce my documentary and had even joined me for the final two days of the journey itself. His advice then had been invaluable and I craved it once more.

'Rather than looking for the route first,' he said over the phone, 'why not start by considering the areas of the world that you're most interested in and want to travel through? Once you know what they are, plan your route *around* them.'

'If I can figure out the journey,' I said, 'will you help me turn it into another film?'

'Sure I will,' he replied. 'But you need to work out what the journey's going to be first.'

And so, taking my notebook from my desk, I sat back in my chair, closed my eyes and tried to think simply of where I wanted to go.

Russia. That was paramount. I had always been fascinated by Russia, had read books and books about it when I was a child and still continued to. Russia would be an extraordinary country to witness from the saddle. I scribbled it down in my notebook and closed my eyes again.

Africa. I had fallen in love with the continent in Madagascar and then during my Sahara crossing. To return would make me deeply happy. It went in the notebook.

The Middle East. Though this was my birthplace, there were so many parts of it I had never seen and yet yearned to.

Scandinavia. Another long-held fascination.

I sat forward again. Those four entries were enough for now – each separate region was gargantuan and surely capable of myriad routes alone. I opened Google Earth on my computer and looked at each place in turn: Russia, Africa, the Middle East, Scandinavia. Seeing them together, the dots joined, and I realised that a single route could take me into and through every place I had noted. Moreover, if I started in Scandinavia at the northern tip of Europe – a place called Nordkapp in Norway, located in the Arctic Circle – and then followed a trajectory down through Russia, the Middle East and then to Cape Town in South Africa, I could cycle one of the longest continuous north to south routes on the planet. There was a pleasing poetry in those two names, too – from Nordkapp to Cape Town, from one cape to another – and, as I began to frenetically skip from website to website to see if and how it could be done, I came to a realisation. While a small number of people had cycled this particular route before, most had taken over a year to complete the journey and no one had done it in record time.

I made contact with Guinness World Records and they agreed that, if I could complete the journey in 100 days or less, they would grant me the record. Why 100 days, I asked. No one had attempted it before as a record, so there was therefore no record to break. Why not just give me the record, no matter how long it took me? The answers I received were vague and cloaked in obscure calculations I could make no sense of – something about similar journeys, other cyclists, other records, equivalent distances and times. It did not matter in the end: the 100-day target was set and inflexible. If the journey took me 101 days, there would be no record. I could take it or leave it. I agreed to the terms and, in truth, as I began to plan my journey, that 100-day benchmark, arbitrary as it was, gave me a demanding but achievable goal to work towards. There was a lure to it which appealed to my ambitious side and, the more I worked on my new adventure, the more I came to believe that I could do it.

In tandem with the project, something else had begun to build, something which would add a new and exciting element to the journey.

In Madagascar, I had learned something fundamental: the beauty of sharing. That was why I had cycled the Annapurna circuit and then the Sahara Desert, because I had wanted to share what I could create from those journeys (money) with others (the Malagasy children). But the adventures themselves had been singular and no one else's but my own. I had seen so much of the world that others hadn't and this began to strike me as selfish. Though others had shared in the results of my adventures, no one had shared in the actual adventures themselves. It was true that Arash and I had made a film of my Sahara crossing, and that some had shared my journey via that medium, but the film had only really come about as an afterthought and it was far from representative of the beauty of the world as I had seen it. *That* – the beauty of the world – was what I wanted to share with others, and as truthfully as I could.

One solution I thought of was to look for a travel companion, someone who could join me all the way from Norway right down to South Africa. But I could not quite dispel a certain amount of reluctance for this option. Could I really spend 100 days on the road with just one other person for company? Wouldn't we drive each other to insanity by being so close for so long? It was something I would need to dedicate more thought to, but while I did there was another option to consider. If I could not share this next adventure itself – if I could not find the right person to share it with – I could perhaps document it instead. Properly. Mine had become a blessed life, and if I could relay the things I saw and the situations I experienced on my adventures then it would make what I was prepared to do all the more worthwhile. This time, Arash and I would not make just a short film. We would make a TV series.

When, only a few weeks after these thoughts had run through my mind, Steve's email arrived in my inbox, it was perhaps less of a surprise than it should have been. I barely knew Steve. We both worked for the same company in the same building, but had only spoken to each other once or twice before. And yet here was his email, expressing his interest in my journey and asking if we could meet at a nearby pub to talk about it. I agreed, and I think I did so out of more than mere curiosity.

'I saw your website,' Steve said, taking a sip from his pint as we perched at the bar in the quiet and largely empty pub.

'How did you hear about it?' I asked.

'Actually, I saw the website before I knew you had anything to do with it. Then I looked into it a bit more, and I was all like – I know that guy! That's Reza! I had no idea you had done all that stuff, the charity work, the Sahara. It's pretty incredible.'

'Thank you.' I was fairly certain I knew why Steve had invited me for this drink, of what he was about to ask me. It all left me with a faint sense of unease, which I tried to quell with a glug of beer. It didn't work.

'So the reason I found the website is because I was looking for exactly the kind of thing you're doing – your Kapp to Cape project.'

'You want to donate?'

'Sort of,' he replied. 'I want to donate my time. I want to join you.'

There it was. A silence hung between us, a silence which grew increasingly awkward as I found myself lost for words. I knew I was going to make a film of my journey, but I had not yet resolved whether I was going to do it alone or with a companion. I thought briefly of the world record and realised that I wanted it for myself. It was selfish and arrogant and horribly egocentric, but that did not stop it from being true.

Steve broke the silence. 'Listen. I know you're probably reluctant. This is your thing and why would you want me tagging along? I get that. Plus, we hardly even know each other. But what you've already done is something I've been wanting to do for a while now. I need an adventure in my life, some big personal challenge that isn't work-related. Surely you can understand that.'

I could.

'And your Kapp to Cape, as soon as I saw the website it just made perfect sense to me. It's not just an adventure, it's raising money for a good cause, it's going for a world record and it even ends in my home town!'

I hadn't known that. With English as my second language and Steve's South African accent on the milder side, his heritage had eluded me. 'That's one of the places I'm looking forward to the most,' I said. 'I've always wanted to visit Cape Town.'

'See? Tonnes in common!' He laughed and I found myself laughing with him. Steve was, I realised, inherently likeable. Perhaps we could spend 100 days on the road together. I felt my scepticism begin to fade, but only a little.

'Most of all, though,' he continued, 'I guess I just want to share your journey. All of it. Share the ride, share the planning, share the experience. Would you let me?'

I considered his proposal. I had been looking for a way to share my journey and here was a man who had arrived as if from nowhere, offering to do exactly that. I could not shake the poignancy of it all.

'I don't know, Steve,' I said. 'I'll admit, I've been thinking about teaming up with someone for this, but I still haven't decided myself if it's the right way. It's going to be tough. *Really* tough. Are you sure you could cope with that? More importantly, are you sure you could cope with *me* for one hundred days? With no respite?'

'Absolutely!' he grinned. 'I'm a people person through and through!'

I thought for a moment or two. 'Look, I can't give you an answer right now. I can't just say, fuck it, why not? But I don't want to just say no, either. So how about this? Why don't you join me for a couple of rides and maybe help out a little with some of my planning? That way, we'll get to see how well we work together.'

Steve agreed and we began to meet regularly for long bike rides and even longer discussions about the how, the what and the where. With Steve assisting, the planning, organisation and structure of our journey sped up miraculously. Arash took over the filming side of things, and that freed up our time to enlarge our online presence, raise a sizeable amount of sponsorship and, above all, train mercilessly. It took me a long time – some three months – before I could finally give Steve a firm and definitive 'yes', but the moment I did I understood that it had been exactly the right thing to do. Everything was running so smoothly that we were able to set a date. It was all becoming tangible, substantive and very, very close.

And then the car hit me.

CHAPTER 3

THE FALL

I woke up in the hospital. Steve was sitting beside my bed. When he saw my eyes open, he grinned, exhaled deeply and rested his hand on my forearm.

'What happened?' I asked him. I had no recollection of the accident; I could not even remember precisely where we were. Steve carefully explained it to me.

It had been our last big training session. With just two months to go before our grand journey down the length of the world, we felt the need for one final mini expedition. We needed to get ourselves into the routine of cycling all day every day for a sustained period of time, and we needed to get ourselves into the mindset of being able to do it together. Steve suggested Paris to Rome and it appealed to me. At close to 1,000 miles, the route consisted of a selection of varying standards of terrain and it traversed three countries – France, Italy and Switzerland – which I had always wanted to cycle through.

Sadly, we made it no further than 100 miles. At the end of our first day, just 2 miles away from the stop off we had designated to spend the night, along the meandering turns of a quiet countryside B-road, a man drove his car into my bicycle from behind. It transpired that the tendon in my right leg had snapped. I left the local hospital on crutches.

We took a taxi to a nearby hotel and, while I changed my clothes, Steve went to retrieve my bike from the roadside. Half an hour later, as he carried it into the room piece by piece, nausea flooded my stomach. My bike had been obliterated. There was no point taking it back to London. It was beyond repair.

'We're going to have to postpone the journey,' Steve said.

'It's all right,' I remonstrated. 'I'll get a new bike. I can probably just about afford it.'

'It's not the bike that's the problem.' He gestured down at my leg and pointed at my crutches resting beside the bed.

'The doctor said I'll be walking again in six weeks,' I said. 'Then we've still got another two weeks after that before we go. It's plenty of time for me to get back on track.'

'Two weeks? Are you joking? Your leg is going to spend the next six weeks atrophying, just wasting away while the rest of you does the same because you can't keep up the exercise you need until your tendon has healed. It took us a *year* of training to get to this standard. There's no way, no way at all that you're going to be ready in just two weeks.'

'All right, all right,' I said, irritable now but willing to capitulate. 'So we'll put it off a couple of months, even three if we have to. It's not ideal, but we'll just have to get through it. Six weeks to heal, then two more months to train. Three months tops. I can easily get back in shape by then.'

Steve laughed a thin chuckle and cast a disconcerting gaze at me. 'You don't get it, do you? Can't you remember why we set our start date for August in the first place?'

The realisation hit and I suddenly understood exactly what he was getting at.

'Even if it takes you three months to get back in shape, it'll be November by then, November in the Arctic. Cycling's impossible in those conditions. We either leave in the summer or we don't leave at all. There's no question about it. We're not going anywhere for at least another year.'

The accident set off a chain reaction of misfortune. Our adventure was postponed for a full year. I developed a debilitating post-traumatic stress disorder which manifested itself whenever I was on a road. The notion that someone was going to hit me from behind was so powerful and unshakeable that it became a belief rather than a mere concern. I lost all my confidence and found that I could no longer ride my motorbike without anxiety attacks forcing me from the road to shudder and hyperventilate at the kerbside. I did not buy a new bicycle. I stopped exercising altogether and instead took to drinking heavily. Every day seemed to involve a new argument with my co-workers or my boss. My girlfriend and I broke up, and I moved from our house to a single rented bedroom on the other side of London. Arash called to tell me that he had been offered the opportunity to film for a more prestigious, more definite series and would not be able to join us for the expedition. Depression engulfed me.

At times, it could almost feel like I was somehow projecting my misfortune outwards, magically inflicting it upon the world of my postponed journey as portions of it crumbled into political disarray and civil war. Of the 20 countries I had hoped to cycle through, travel warnings were issued for four. In Syria alone, full-scale civil war had erupted as rebel groups, militias and government forces began to clash with ever-rising bursts of horror. It became clear that, had my accident not occurred and our journey begun as planned, we would never have made it into Syria, let alone across it. With the conflict escalating and world powers tentatively making their own involvements known, I understood there and then that we would not be able to cross it the following year either, nor perhaps for years to come.

I got in touch with Guinness World Records and explained the geographical predicament. After some back and forth, we came to an agreement: so long as we cycled to a point in Iran which lay on exactly the same latitude as Cairo, we would then be allowed to fly there and resume our journey, thereby completing it in two separate legs. This was the only concession they were prepared to make. We were offered no extensions on the original 100-day deadline, and we would still have to brave those countries and regions – such as Dagestan, Egypt and northern Kenya – which our governments were warning travellers to avoid. While the inclusion of Iran pleased me, for it offered the opportunity to cycle to and through my home country, I could not ignore the fact that this new route added a full 500 miles to our journey, and that the clock would not stop as we flew laterally from Iran to Cairo, so we would also lose 24 hours in the transition.

My leg had healed and physiotherapy had literally got me back on my feet. I could walk unaided and without a limp, though my legs seemed more inclined to take me to the nearest pub than to the gym. I was gaining weight and my eyes had begun to take on a curiously red hue. The original start date for our adventure had long since passed and I often found myself thinking: *I should be in Russia now… At this point, we would have made it to my home town… Right now, I could be swimming in a lake in Ethiopia.* But I was in none of those places. I was stuck in London, stuck at work, stuck in my cramped room.

I only realised much later that the email had arrived exactly 100 days after our agreed start date, on the very day we were supposed to have arrived in Cape Town at the end of our journey, setting a record, completing our adventure. Perhaps that was just a coincidence. Or perhaps not. Either way, I clicked on the email and read the opening lines:

Dear Mr Pakravan

We regret to inform you that we are no longer able to recognise your Kapp to Cape record if it is undertaken in two separate legs. In order for a record to be granted, your journey must be completed in one leg without any breaks of time or distance…

I slammed my laptop shut, grabbed a bottle of beer from the fridge, necked half in one gulp and then phoned Steve to tell him the news.

'Shit,' he whispered. 'What are we going to do?'

'To be honest, mate,' I replied, 'I don't really care any more.'

A long and morose autumn transformed into a darker winter. By December, I felt sick and listless. A deep malaise had taken hold, intensified by the polar wind and the drenching rain that never seemed to end. I dreaded the onset of Christmas.

I had begun to see a psychotherapist, and when she pointed out that my mood appeared at its lowest since our very first appointment, I told her that I felt no desire to celebrate, and that the festive spirits of my friends and co-workers had only sent me spiralling further down.

'Have you thought about taking a break from it all?' she asked. 'Going somewhere new and different for a while? Of all the things we've talked about from your past, you've never been more enlivened than when describing your adventures. Maybe you need another. An easy adventure, but an adventure nonetheless.'

I considered the idea. There was no denying that the prospect of taking some time out in a foreign land held its appeal.

'Let's say you did it,' she surmised. 'Just picked a place and went. Where would you go? Forget the cycling, forget going on an expedition, just imagine a place you'd like to spend some time. To relax. To enjoy yourself. Where would it be?'

'India,' I replied without thinking.

'That was quick,' she laughed. 'But maybe India is something you should give some serious thought to. It seems to me that a change could do you good.'

To this day, I'm still unsure why I said India. It was true that I had always wanted to visit the subcontinent, but why hadn't I picked those places which had always sat higher on my personal wish list? Russia, for example, or Scandinavia or the Middle East? Why not Africa again, which had absorbed me so completely during my time in Madagascar and then later during my Sahara journey? Perhaps it was the cycling itself. Those places had been earmarked for a long and ambitious bike ride, and whether it was because I wanted to save them for it or because the notion of cycling itself had started to bear negative associations for me following my accident, I couldn't say. All I knew was that spending Christmas in India was suddenly the only thing I wanted to do. As slavishly devoted to my impulses as ever, I bought a ticket that afternoon.

Two weeks later, I was in Calcutta, ready to travel up to the Ganges and then follow it as far as I could, perhaps even to its source if I felt so inclined. The freedom of such an itinerary-free route was heartening – my previous journeys had held so many determined timescales and destinations – and, shunning feet and cogs in favour of engines, I found solace in the trains, buses and boats that powered me forward. India was fascinating and startling in equal measures and, through and along and because of it, for the first time in nine months I felt the dissipation of my depression as it slowly lifted from my shoulders, back and legs, gradually replaced by the wonder and adoration of the world from which I had once derived such succour.

With Christmas and New Year passed in wilful ignorance, I found myself staying in a Hare Krishna ashram in a small town called Vrindavan in the lowlands of Uttar Pradesh early in January. My hosts and co-habitants never tried to convert me, but accepted me without any conditions or prerequisites. My days were spent wandering the streets of Vrindavan; my evenings returned me to the ashram, where the robed and shaven-headed gurus and disciples treated me to their joyful songs and dances, which they participated in ritually regardless of my presence.

And then, one night, reclining among a mess of pillows while the sonorous chants of the Hare Krishnas rebounded off the ashram's walls in an all-consuming resonance, I felt a prickle along my spine. It was both familiar and welcome. I closed my eyes and tried to recall when I'd first felt this sensation. The chanting intensified, as if it was meant for me, and for me alone. Keeping my eyes closed, I foraged along the walls of my memory. When had I felt that same prickle before? There was something in the music, something that induced that physical effect on my own body. The chants rose to and rested upon a chord, a specific tonic triad that was not typically Eastern or Western but somehow both and neither at the same time.

It was *tribal.*

A single memory flooded my senses, and all of a sudden I was back in and among its visceral sounds and smells. An Easter morning four years ago. The interior of a musty tent. My eyelids, crusty with sleep, opening in tandem with my consciousness. The trills and harmonies of a group of Malagasy children singing. The sinking in, the revelation, the epiphany, the concrete decision.

———————

I returned to London from India with a fresh resolve. Any remnants of my malaise had been shattered that night in Vrindavan, when the actualisation of everything I had done over the past four years presented itself to me on the tides of those ashram choruses, and when I remembered precisely why I had lived it all. Although there had been times when the depression following my accident had left me wondering if I could ever go through with the Kapp to Cape adventure – when I had come to envisage the whole expedition as a dead end, an unachievable pipe dream that was best left to the annals of my own regret – I was tearfully grateful to find that Steve had never lost faith in me and had kept things ticking over during my emotional absence.

Nevertheless, there still remained much to be done. We had no tickets, no visas and no stores of foreign currency. Our travel-kit repository was virtually non-existent. Our website needed days and days of work, as did our social media reach. Sponsors remained few and far between. Still reeling from the physical consequences of my accident, I needed to commit to serious training if I was ever going to get back to the levels of fitness the journey demanded.

Although there was a full seven months left before our start date, both Steve and I had to fit everything in around the 50-hour weeks our respective jobs demanded. Every spare second was filled with preparation, preparation, preparation. And, perhaps as a match to our resolve, things began to work. Sponsors trickled in, slowly at first but then exponentially as the months passed. Friends volunteered their free time to help us with our online pursuits. Arash, apologetic that he would not be able to join us on the road but still maintaining his belief in my expedition, appointed three separate cameramen to take his place at varying stages: Peiman in Norway, Kamyar in Iran and Grant in South Africa. Steve and I trained whenever and wherever we could, and in our freewheeling moments we would coast alongside each other and debate the best and fastest possible route, the one that would get us to Cape Town in 100 days or less. I had still not given up on the promise of that record and I challenged my Guinness World Record contacts with such relentless fortitude, holding them accountable for our original agreement, that they finally gave in and once more agreed to recognise the record in two legs, providing we could still do it in 100 days.

Their decision proved to be both validation and consolidation for us. The journey was finally set and inexorable. With money from our new sponsors now available, we bought our tickets, quit our jobs and purchased our equipment: a tool-bag kitted out with everything we'd ever need for the road; a GPS and a tent; a tiny stove and an even tinier fuel bottle; sunglasses and knives; helmets; sun cream for us and gaffer tape for our bikes; zip ties; a medical kit filled with pills ranging from paracetamol to doxycycline; salt and pepper; tea and coffee; shorts and thermals; 12 spare tyres and 12 spare inner tubes; weatherproof matches and water filters; a universal adapter to charge our iPods and video camera, our sound equipment and tracking device.

And then, finally and crucially, we received our new bikes. Sponsored by Koga, they were World Travellers: splendid, state-of-the-art examples of Dutch engineering, individually custom-made and sumptuously designed to meld with our bodies. These two bikes were the last and definitive piece of the puzzle.

All was ready.

I woke up at 6.45 a.m. It was far later than we had intended to rise. The alarm had sounded, that I knew, but who had turned it off remained a mystery to me. We had fallen back into our slumber without a word. Groggily pulling myself from my bed, I parted the curtains. A wash of sunlight flooded the small room. Francesca issued a curse and then buried herself beneath her blankets. Peiman, Paula and Steve barely stirred. I padded into the adjoining bathroom and opened the small window. A blast of fresh Norwegian air sent me into a paroxysm of shudders, pimpling my skin as if the outdoor frost had settled on to my naked torso. I closed the window, lifted the lid on the toilet and vomited into it for several minutes.

I towelled down, took six deep breaths and re-entered the living space of the Honningsvåg cabin we had booked for a single night. My companions were out of bed and readying themselves for the day ahead: Paula had stepped outside to start the van and warm its engine; Francesca – already my digital 'Base Camp' though we had barely started – was fielding emails, enquiries and donations on her laptop; Peiman was simultaneously taking light readings and polishing lenses and trying to film everything we were doing; Steve was assembling his bike which we had shipped over in a large cardboard box of cogs and wheels, brake pads and bars. I joined him, ripping open the box with my own bike inside, a library of bubble-wrapped segments, the disassembled pieces of a whole, which, once crafted, would transport me from this Norwegian wasteland down through one hemisphere and then another to a point on the southern tip of Africa, which, as far as I was concerned, could have been as far away from my present location as Saturn. We all worked in silence.

With the bikes assembled and tested, with our stomachs full and the GPS localised, with the panniers packed and then unpacked and packed again, we bundled everything into the back of the van and set off for Nordkapp.

The drive took less than half an hour and before we knew it we were there. Nordkapp. Our starting point. The bikes were pulled from the van, looking so fresh and untarnished in this Norwegian light. We climbed on to them, testing their weight and then melding feet with pedals. We wrapped bandanas around our heads, laid sunglasses across our eyes. Francesca hugged me and then moved over to enfold Steve in the same embrace. Paula did the same, in the same order. Peiman filmed it all.

There was nothing left to do but begin.

Steve and I clutched hands – his right in my left – and then we simultaneously pushed down with our feet. Cleats clicked, wheels turned and we were off. Cape Town was only 11,000 miles away.

PART TWO

LEG ONE

CHAPTER 4

THIS IS IT

Distance remaining: 11,000 miles
Time to record: 100 days

———————

Behind us, our beginning was the world's end. The Nordkapp peninsula
stared out on to the wide and stark Barents Sea, beyond which Svalbard
island formed one last desperate punctuation mark of land before the
seemingly endless Arctic Ocean consumed all. At that hour and at that
latitude, sunlight was weak and insubstantial, yet it found its way through
the low-hanging mists to play and bounce off the gentle rippling waters
that lapped at the edge of Europe. The cold penetrated through my
clothing, sending ripples of shivers down through my body and towards
my stiffening fingers and toes. I took it all in, absorbed my environment
through each and every sense and stored it within the part of my brain
reserved for extraordinary memories, filing it somewhere between the
view from Iran's Mount Sabalan's peak and the sound of Malagasy
children singing.

I turned to Steve, whose hand I was still holding. Behind him, the
Nordkapp Globe Monument – a majestic spherical skeleton that presided
over the end, or beginning, of a landmass – sailed by. There was a 360°

webcam lodged permanently inside the globe, and I knew that, at that very moment, there were people dotted across the world watching us through their computer screens. I considered releasing Steve's grip and raising my hand to the globe, casting a wave to the webcam to say hello and goodbye simultaneously, but it felt inappropriate. This moment was for me and Steve alone. I pulled him slightly closer towards me.

'Mate, this is it,' I said. My voice, tremulous with excitement and adrenaline, had fractured and warped, sounding as if I was on the verge of giggles or tears or both.

'This is it,' Steve rejoined. 'Enjoy.' It pleased me to notice that he had fallen victim to the same vocal twinges.

We laughed at ourselves, feeling overwhelmed by the moment and understanding it was perfectly natural to be so. And then we let go of each other's hands and cycled on.

There was nothing spontaneous or impromptu about our holding hands. Indeed, it was all for the camera – not to create an enforced and erroneous impression of our friendship, but as evidence for Guinness World Records. The criteria we had to follow to the letter required that we begin the journey in some form of attached position: by joining hands we created our attachment; by filming it we created our evidence.

This was just one of the many hoops we had to jump through in order to merit the record. Another, which was tough to document and even more so to enact, was the rule that we had to remain no more than five bike-lengths apart at all times. With this in mind, as we relinquished our hold on each other's hands, Steve pushed on to take the lead while I made sure to maintain the correct distance behind him.

Though we were now fully on the road, Steve and I were still not alone. The same van that had brought us to Nordkapp continued to hold pace with us, sometimes falling back and sometimes speeding ahead, like a loyal but easily distracted dog. Inside the van were our 'crew': Paula, Francesca and Peiman. They sat in their respective and by now well-maintained positions: Paula at the wheel, perfectly matching our speed and ready to swoop about us as required; Francesca in the passenger seat, dividing her attention between three different screens as she fielded emails, tweets and phone calls on an array of devices; and Peiman in the back, his face invisible behind the camera which pointed ever outwards, filming every possible detail.

My adventures and expeditions – to Madagascar, along the Annapurna circuit, through the Sahara – had always divided the opinions of my domestic social group, and none more so than this journey.

'What if you get hurt and there's no one around to help?' had been Brian's concern.

Rassa had said: 'You don't own a house, you're not even in a relationship. Shouldn't these be your priorities?'

Justin had been a little more blunt. 'You're too old, mate. Far too old for this nonsense.'

But both Francesca and Paula, two of my oldest friends, had been immediately and immaculately positive.

'That sounds *amazing*!' said Paula.

'How can we help?' said Francesca.

There is no hyperbole in stating that without the help of these two wonderful women, the journey might never have come to fruition. As well as being instrumental in helping us get to Nordkapp, they were – along with Mark from SEED and my friend Andy, who managed our daily blog – key members of our digital Base Camp, a collection of individuals who voluntarily organised packages of supplies to be sent to us along the way, managed our website and social media, and posted online edited highlights of the footage we shot each day. Francesca became our logistics manager and, like a whirlwind of productivity, she designed our route, mapping out all the stops we should take with daily distances and timings in between. As our point of contact during each day of the journey itself, she was our link to the rest of the world – if anybody wanted to communicate with us and offer us help, they did so through Francesca; and if we had a particularly challenging day ahead, Francesca would warn us of exactly what elevations or varying road surfaces or potential obstacles we should expect.

It would have pleased me to have Francesca, Paula and Peiman follow us all the way to Cape Town. They weren't just good company; they also constituted a safety net, which, during those early planning stages, I had not realised I would come to value so highly. The risks of the journey, from the far-away menace of Dagestan to the immediate dangers of road accidents, were only just beginning to truly sink in, and a readily available van stocked with first aid kits, food and friends would have proved a welcome addition to the adventure.

Sadly, it was an impossibility and far too much of an expense for any of us to afford or justify. Francesca, Paula and Peiman had arranged to accompany us only as far as the Norway–Finland border, at which point they would have to turn back, leaving us finally and truly alone.

Norway was good practice for the solitude our crew's departure would cause. Its roads were almost entirely devoid of any traffic save ourselves and, if anything, this added to the exhilaration of those first few miles. The road from Nordkapp began as a downhill, and we coasted it leisurely, free from the petrol fumes and sudden swerves of overtaking cars, our feet barely moving as we let gravity do the work for us.

In fact, when there was other traffic on the road, it tended to be fellow cyclists. 'Where are you going?' we called to those we passed. The responses were long and in Norwegian, incomprehensible to us. We hoped they would ask us the same, so that we could reply, 'Africa', but they never did.

In just over an hour, we had reached the Honnigsvåg cabin where we had spent the previous night, 16 miles south of Nordkapp. Already, I felt hungry. It was a consequence of our preparation. We had steadily begun to increase our daily calorie intake as the expedition neared. This had the benefit of building up our stores of body fat in readiness for the 7,000 calories we would be burning each day as we cycled. On the downside, my appetite had grown along with my eating habits, so that by 10.15 a.m. I already felt inclined to tackle a hearty lunch. We stopped at the cabin for a quick coffee and snack break, and then pressed on.

Perhaps the caffeine in the coffee re-ignited something inside me, or perhaps it was simply our making it past that first milestone – either way, rushes of adrenaline surged through me once more as we left Honnigsvåg. We had everything the cyclist craves: good roads, strong tailwinds, and new and thrilling landscapes. Reindeer stood, immoveable, at the roadsides, their jaws working away at tough knots of vegetation, their eyes implacable and indifferent to the two men who skimmed by on their thin and noiseless machines. Sometimes, we would see them far ahead, gathered in twos or threes in the middle of the road. We expected them to flee from us as we neared, or at least trot out of our paths, but it was invariably us who slowed and veered, altering our trajectories to avoid a collision, which, both they and we knew, we would come out of worse.

The road began to drop further towards sea level to ultimately push below it as we neared and then entered the Nordkapp tunnel. Since it was summer, the anti-freezing gates – which, during the winter, keep the entrance and exit closed until a car approaches to prevent water leaking in and freezing – remained perpetually open and we glided through with ease. Once inside, it was a tunnel like any other – straight as a Roman road, walls and ceiling a seamless semi-circle, perfectly spaced electric lights the orange of burning embers – but it still made my skin prickle and my heart accelerate. We were, I knew, 700 ft below the Magerøysundet strait, and the sheer weight of all that water above brought glimpses of claustrophobia, compounded by the fact that this was not a tunnel one entered and left in a matter of seconds. Almost 4½ miles in length, with the second half a strength-sapping uphill push, we were left with plenty of time to think, wonder and, worst of all, imagine. When we re-emerged into the daylight, it was not without a sense of relief.

Our plan for that first day was to make it to Lakselv, 118 miles south of Nordkapp. We hoped to arrive in the late afternoon, have our last dinner with Francesca, Paula and Peiman, and then get an early night. In anticipation of that meal, I was growing hungry again. I cycled up alongside Steve who admitted the same and we agreed to stop at the next cafe or restaurant on the road for lunch. Yet, for the next 50 miles as we rode down the west coast of the Porsanger fjord, there was nothing at all. We were passing through one of the most sparsely populated areas of one of the most sparsely populated countries in the world, and aside from the occasional cyclist, the only life here seemed to be the ubiquitous reindeer, which had begun to look increasingly delicious.

Opting for the role of gatherer rather than hunter, I dug some nuts and dried fruits out of my panniers and munched on them as I rode. The going was flat and the wind was still behind us. Steve and I rode parallel to each other, talking about food, concocting fantasy menus for the lunch, which seemed to be pulling further and further away from us, a heady cocktail of four different meats and 12 different vegetables and a bucketload of pasta.

'Wait!'

The voice was a shocking intrusion to our shared daydream, startling us both for, in our ecstasy of culinary imaginings, we had entirely forgotten the presence of the van beside us. We turned around to see Peiman leaning out of the window, his camera down, his left arm gesturing in a circular motion.

'Wait!' he shouted again. 'That conversation was gold! But I couldn't record it. The wind was drowning out the audio. Can you do it again?'

'Sure,' I said, turning back to Steve. 'Right, for the starter I'd like…'

Steve interrupted me with a snort and looked over at Peiman. 'You want us to have a conversation we've already had again? What's the point in that?'

'It'll look good on the film,' Peiman replied.

'Right, the film.' Steve looked agitated, and I noticed he was beginning to cycle slightly faster. 'And what if the wind drowns us out this time? Would we have to do it again?'

'Would that be all right?' Peiman asked.

'No, mate, it wouldn't be all right!' Steve laughed. It was a laugh which held little mirth. 'Because if we don't get that right we'll have to do it again, and before you know it we'll be spending all day saying the same shit over and over again and again.'

Peiman was quietened by Steve's outburst and I decided to attempt a conciliatory approach. 'Steve's got a point,' I said. 'The wind could get in the way again. How about we stop for a minute and shoot the conversation with us standing still? We'll definitely get it in one take that way.'

'I'm not stopping,' Steve growled. 'How about this? How about we get on and find somewhere where we can get some lunch.' With that, he pushed down on to his pedals, inched himself up from his saddle and transitioned into a sprint away from us.

I mouthed a *Sorry* at Peiman, who shrugged his shoulders and hitched the camera back up. Steve had flown ahead, and it took all my focus to try and maintain the five bike-length distance, so much so that, by the time we reached the town of Olderfjord and found a cafe, I had forgotten my hunger.

———————

My appetite returned with a vengeance the moment I entered the cafe. It was largely empty, more staff than customers. Steve had found a table and was sitting alone. He looked sullen and grumpy as he perused the menu. Peiman, Francesca and Paula were still in the van sorting equipment, and I desperately wanted Steve to snap out of his dark mood before they came back in so we could all enjoy our late lunch together. I tried a light approach.

'Don't bother showing me the menu. I'll take the sixty-four-ounce steak, a whole roast chicken and five-dozen napkins.'

Steve didn't laugh, but continued to stare down at the menu. 'You'll have what I'm having,' he grumbled. 'The plain burger.'

'You're joking, right?'

'No. I'm not.' He held the menu up for me to see. 'It's all we can afford. The cheapest thing on the menu. And it's still twenty quid.'

The five of us ate our miserable burgers in a miserable silence. Mine settled uneasily in my stomach, a ball of undercooked meat which I fancied I could feel rolling to and fro in my belly as I lurched to the toilet. When I returned to the table, Steve had left. I could see his helmet bobbing up and down outside the window as he readied his bike to leave.

'Peiman wanted to get a few shots of us eating,' Francesca explained.

'Didn't even get a chance to take my camera out,' Peiman said. 'Steve just got up and left.'

'He took his burger with him,' Paula added.

I left some money for the crew to pay and went outside. Steve's bike was ready and he was sitting atop it, chewing the last of his burger.

'What's up?' I asked.

'We need to head off. Now. No more pissing about filming. We need to start riding.'

'A couple of minutes here and there to get some footage isn't going to hurt.'

'Mate, this isn't a joke, this is a world record attempt. That's my priority. Not a film.'

Deep in my stomach, somewhere next to that burger, I could feel my own stirrings of anger. 'You knew that we would be making a film of this. It's one of the first things I told you. And you agreed to it. You said it wouldn't be a problem.'

'Well, maybe it's becoming a problem, mate.' He had, I noticed, that aggressive habit of using the word 'mate' when he meant it the least. 'Because it's holding us up. It's slowing us down. There's a daily distance we have to maintain. Look at us right now – it's already five-thirty and we've still got another forty miles to go before Lakselv.'

'All right, I understand that, I do, but we still have to get footage where we can. We need it for the film and we need it as evidence for the record.'

'Fair enough if we need it for the record. Because that's what's important. And I'm not going to lose out on it just because we need to reshoot some stupid conversation or photograph a tomato.'

With divine timing, Steve's rant was concluded by a heavy burst of rain. There was no gradual transition from dry to wet, no interim spits or drizzles, no turning up of the volume: quite simply, one moment it wasn't raining, the next it was. The droplets were fat and loud, bouncing off our waterproof jackets and already puddling around our feet.

'Fucking perfect,' Steve shouted above the roar, before climbing on to his bike and pedalling out on to the road. I hopped on my own and followed. The crew were still eating, but they could catch up. I had to stay close to Steve, even if I didn't particularly want to.

The rain blasted us in a relentless wash for the next hour and we pushed on with grim fortitude. The argument with Steve had shaken me. I had anticipated conflicts and confrontations with him along the way – the conditions of our adventure would be, I knew, conducive to short tempers and frayed nerves – but I had not expected it to happen so quickly, and certainly not on the first day. As the rain continued, I had little to do other than ride and think, and my thoughts centred on Steve, throwing up a wave of questions. How well did I really know him? Had I made the right decision to bring him? If we had argued over something as inconsequential as filming, what if something truly serious happened? What would we do then? Scream? Fight? Kill each other?

I considered the next 99 days, the next 99 days with Steve for every second and every minute, both of us inextricably tied to the other. The prospect of those 99 days was suddenly a deeply alarming one and I felt the first drops of anxiety as they percolated into my brain. How on earth were we going to cope with each other for that long? It would have been hard enough with my best friend, but with Steve, a man who had flared up because he was asked to repeat himself, was it even possible?

A thought occurred, a thought so vivid and potent that I felt it had been stamped on to my retinas, and that if I closed my eyes I could see it, written in my own handwriting.

I've made a mistake.

Once the thought arrived, it refused to leave. It deepened and darkened, filling my mind so that all other thoughts bounced off it before they could be recognised.

I've made a mistake.

The floodgates opened, and the anxiety tumbled in, substantive and nauseating. I remembered it well. After being hit by the car in France, this anxiety was the aspect of my PTSD that I feared the most. And here it was again.

I've made a mistake.

It wasn't just the thought of the 99 days with Steve. It was the thought of the 99 days themselves. What had I let myself in for? There was no possible way I could cycle 11,000 miles in one go. It was a fantasy, and a ludicrous one. There was a reason nobody had set this record before. It was far too easy to fail.

I've made a mistake.

And what if I did fail? I had given everything up. I had no job to return to, no desk to hide behind, no salary to get me back on my feet, not even a home – just a friend's spare bedroom if I was lucky. My mother had told me not to do this. She had understood that I would fail, and she had been right. I could not do this. I simply could not do this.

I've made a mistake.

There was nowhere to stay in Lakselv, but we pressed on and finally happened upon a campsite 15 miles further south. The anxiety had exhausted itself a few hours earlier, but it had left its impression. When I dismounted my bicycle, I felt weak and dizzy. Those 99 days left, those 11,000 miles ahead: it all still seemed insurmountable.

As we hung our soaked clothes up to dry in the campsite's sauna, I noticed Steve looking over at me. 'You know how much we did today?' he asked.

I shrugged.

'One-hundred-and-thirty-three miles.' He let the number land before repeating it with a wide smile. 'One-hundred-and-thirty-three miles, Reza! How amazing is that? That's the longest distance we've ever done with our bikes fully loaded. In one day! And I'll tell you what, if we can keep this up, one-hundred-and-thirty-three miles every day, we'll smash that record!'

His eyes were blazing with triumph and I didn't have the heart to dampen his spirits. 'We've done well,' I offered.

Steve laughed, hung up one of his socks, and then turned back to me. 'Listen, Reza – sorry about today. I was out of order. I've apologised to Peiman, too. I know you told me about this, about how a trip like this is an emotional rollercoaster and you need to try and keep a grip, but I guess I didn't expect it to hit so hard and so soon. So yeah, you know, my apologics.'

With no energy left to pitch our tent, we took a room at the campsite. Francesca, Paula and Peiman sequestered the beds while Steve and I collapsed on to our Therm-a-Rest (our camping mattress) on the floor. By midnight, the room was filled with the soft snores of my companions, but I remained awake. I was thinking about Steve, about the things he had said. I was grateful for his apology, but even more so for his reminder of how adventure travel can reduce one's emotional state to that of a troubled teenager. I had perhaps forgotten my cycle across the Sahara, which had been as demanding psychologically as it had physically.

Yet there was something else Steve had said, something which was working its way through my delicate nerves, soothing and calming them. It was the way he had broken the journey down. We had covered 133 miles today. If we could cover 133 miles every day, we would get to Cape Town in 100 days.

In fact, and this was what was really working its charm on me and making me feel better with every passing second, if we covered 133 miles every day we'd get to Cape Town *before* the 100-day limit. We only actually needed to cover *110* miles each day. And we had done that, had done it so well that, arguments and anxiety aside, we had carried on and covered another 23 miles on top of it.

I realised then that I needed to change my mindset. I had to stop thinking about the journey as a whole, as a non-stop narrative which spanned 11,000 miles. To do so was unhealthy and overwhelming. Instead, I had to think smaller and approach each day as a discrete entity. I wasn't cycling 11,000 miles, I was simply cycling 110 miles each day. At the start of the day I would think only of those 110 miles. And then, at the end of the day, I would think only of the following 110 miles. Nothing more.

So let's try this out, I thought. *Tomorrow I have to cycle 110 miles. Am I up for it?*

The answer was so immediate it almost made me laugh out loud.

110 miles? I thought. *Piece of piss.*

CHAPTER 5

NIGHT RIDER

Distance remaining: 10,867 miles

Time to record: 99 days

———————

Another late night meant another late start. We did not set off until 11 a.m. This put Steve into another poor mood, especially when our departure was delayed yet further by mine and Peiman's desire to film as much as possible.

Finland, the second of the 13 countries we hoped to cross, was 46 miles away and, as soon as we hit the road, we began to make good progress. We arrived at Karasjok, a small town close to the border, in the early afternoon and decided to break for lunch. It was our last meal with our crew and possibly our last meal with anyone we knew for the next 98 days.

As per the previous day, Steve found the restaurant first and was already sitting at a table and reading the menu by the time I entered. This time, however, his mood had lightened and he was chuckling quietly to himself.

'You're going to love this,' he said. 'Check out number fifteen on the menu.'

I picked up one of the laminated menus from the Formica table top and scanned down until I found number fifteen. '*Reindeer!*' I looked up at Steve, who was grinning back at me. 'I've been wanting to eat one of those for the past twenty-four hours!'

'Tell me about it,' Steve said.

'But it's thirty-five pounds a portion,' I faltered. 'Can we afford that?'

'Ah, so what – I reckon we deserve it.' He laughed once and then marched up to the counter to order for both of us.

I began to remember why I had first liked Steve.

The reindeer meat came on a thick bed of mashed potatoes and was dripping in cranberry sauce. It was extravagant and outstanding, and it tasted of Christmas. We left the restaurant glowing and gleeful, and remained so all the way to the border.

Once there, we all indulged in the usual rounds of handshakes and hugs. It somehow felt that Francesca, Paula and Peiman were the ones who were leaving, but of course it was the other way round. While they remained in Norway, albeit temporarily, it was Steve and I who were departing, crossing a border, entering a new country. That's one of the strange things about continuous long-distance travel. It can often seem that it's not you moving but the world. The wheels of your bike do not push you forward, they merely move to maintain your position as the planet spins beneath you, sending you new countries and new people to meet, and pulling those you've come to know back and away from you. It was a strange image I sometimes entertained myself with when my mind drifted after hours of riding: the whole earth, seen from space and about the size of a fist, and then a tiny me riding a tiny bike on the very top, pedalling furiously to keep the world spinning, like a hamster in its wheel.

Steve checked his tyres, Paula climbed back into the van and Peiman set up his camera on a tripod at the best vantage point to catch us when we crossed our first border. Francesca and I were left alone.

'Will you be able to meet us in Cape Town?' I asked.

'Wouldn't miss it for the world,' she replied. 'The question is, will *you* be able to meet *me* in Cape Town?'

'Definitely.'

'When?'

'In ninety-eight days. And a half.'

'Good.' She smiled, and tucked a loose strand of hair behind her ear. 'Looking forward to it.'

Our crew gone and any semblance of immediate support gone with it, we were alone. The few shivers of fear I felt as we crossed the border were immediately outweighed by the tangible thrills of adventure. That adventure no longer loomed on the horizon or hovered before us: with the departure of our crew, the adventure was now wholly and irrevocably here, coursing through our veins and pushing us to cycle harder and faster – both a delight and a necessity, for with our entrance to Finland we had entered a new time zone and needed to make up for the lost hour.

Finnish Lapland was a long and gruelling stretch of wilderness. As the hours and miles passed, the days began to collapse into one, and we seemed to spend all our time cycling down the same endless straight road in the middle of the same endless pine forest. The highway cut through the trees like a tunnel, and looking down it was like peering down a telescope, vainly searching for the Great Bear, Russia, at the end of it.

The monotony could be maddening at times and was broken only by the sporadic appearances of reindeer. Finnish reindeer were bolshier versions of their Norwegian cousins, perhaps even deliberately mischievous. They didn't just block the road with stubborn obstinacy, instead they seemed to purposely move towards you as you approached, as if they *wanted* to knock you off, as if they took delight in watching your face contort with terror and your frame wobble as you wildly swerved out of the way. I swear that one waited at the side of the road, watching me all the time as I neared, and then at the very last moment stepped out towards me with his head dipped so that I only just managed to avoid catching his antlers in my spokes.

We had hoped to finish each of our days during the early evening, but this, it seems, had been ambitious. Instead, in order to meet our daily target, we cycled long into the night, and sometimes into the following morning, before we were able to stop. This night riding had a knock-on effect the following day: the later we cycled at night, they later we would wake and set off in the morning, and the later we would end up cycling the next night to compensate.

Our slow progress was not helped by the relentless cold and rain of Finland: the cold rendering us numb and sluggish; the rain reducing visibility and, despite our waterproofs, soaking us within minutes. We were grateful that a common feature of all Finnish campsites and guesthouses appeared to be a sauna room. Empty at the late hours of our arrivals, we colonised them, hanging our wet clothes and kit wherever we could across the rooms and then stopping for a few moments ourselves, resting, allowing the heat to percolate back into our frozen bones. We grew to love those saunas deeply for, without them, we never would have been able to dry our clothes in time for the following morning.

We began to look forward to Rovaniemi. The capital of Finnish Lapland (and, according to its tourist board, the 'official home town of Santa Claus'), its significance to us lay in the fact that it was situated in the Arctic Circle and, therefore, marked the end of the Arctic portion of our journey. We had known from the start that entering Rovaniemi would be a watershed moment for us and as we neared the excitement for that moment built, but we also looked forward to the prospect of civilisation. Steve and I had been getting along well throughout Lapland – I had made a conscious effort to focus more on the miles than the filming, which he had appreciated – but we still yearned for a little more variety to the patterns of our days: someone different to talk to, perhaps; or a restaurant that sold food other than burgers and reindeer meat.

We were delighted to discover that Rovaniemi had both: friendly locals who were more than happy to sign our evidence book (another Guinness World Record stipulation, we were required to obtain signatures from police, border guards, hotel and restaurant employees and anyone else we could think of as evidence that we had passed through the places we had agreed to pass through), wish us luck and recommend to us their favourite restaurants from the wealth that Rovaniemi offered. An all-you-can-eat Chinese came high on most lists.

'All you can eat?' Steve asked. 'I'll take that challenge.'

We gorged ourselves on Chinese food until we could take no more and then, sated and spent, we fell back into our chairs with languorous sighs. Outside the window, it had grown dark. Sheets of rain hung in the glow of the street lights. We toyed with the idea of spending the night in Rovaniemi.

'I could be up for that,' Steve said.

'Me too,' I replied. 'I could just pass out beneath this table right now, wake up in the morning, have another all-you-can-eat breakfast and then set off.'

'It'd be easy to find somewhere to stay here. We could be in bed in less than an hour.'

'Don't tempt me,' I laughed.

'So why don't we?'

I looked up at Steve and, to my surprise, he was being serious. If either of us had voted to keep pushing forward tonight, I would have placed my bets on him.

'We can't,' I said. 'We've still got another forty miles until we reach our daily target.'

He mulled it over for a while. 'Yeah, I guess you're right. We meant to get to Ranua tonight, didn't we? We should. I'm just getting sick of the night riding.'

'Me too,' I agreed. 'But if we don't do it tonight we'll have to pull one-hundred-and-fifty miles in one go tomorrow.'

That was motivation enough for Steve – indeed, any mention of mileage was always a sure way of motivating either of us. He stood up, stretched, announced: 'Right, come on, then. Let's smash this forty!' and strode out to his bike. I paid the bill and followed him, pleased that we could work things out so rationally. We had not argued again since that first day and, as we clambered on to our bikes and pushed out into the rain with Steve taking the lead and me following no more than five bike-lengths behind, I suddenly felt a great warmth for Steve. I was glad he was there, on the road to Ranua with me.

We awoke at 10 a.m.: cold, damp and headsore after a poor night's sleep. On arrival in Ranua the previous night, we had lurched through a string of rejections. Every campsite was shut and every hotel closed. By 4 a.m., desperate with fatigue, we stole inside a campsite, testing each of its cabin's doors in case one had been left open. None had but, by luck, Steve spotted the barbecue room and gave the door handle a cursory twist. It opened, and we had never been so grateful. We collapsed on to the Therm-a-Rest and were asleep within seconds.

In the morning, we were both quiet, wrestling with our individual exhaustion hangovers. I retrieved my camera to capture some footage of the barbecue room and gently persuaded Steve to say a few lines. He was reluctant, but acquiesced. I understood his reluctance: after such a draining night and little sleep to recuperate, my brain felt like it was made of wool and I could barely string a sentence together.

'We need food,' I said. 'Breakfast. Sort us out.'

'Definitely,' Steve agreed. 'But let's make it a quick one. It's late already.'

We mechanically packed our bikes and rode the short distance into the centre of Ranua. The cafes and restaurants open were limited and expensive, and I had begun to prepare myself for yet another bland hamburger when I spotted the four words that were becoming my favourite four words in the English language.

'All you can eat'.

I called Steve over, energised by the prospect. 'Steve! All you can eat! *All you can eat*! It's a full buffet, only twelve euros each. Let's do it!'

Steve nodded, not quite as excited as me, but keen nonetheless.

It was a veritable feast. We exchanged not one word but a considerable amount of grunts as we ploughed through slabs of salmon; mounds of rice and potatoes; eggs fried, boiled, scrambled or poached; a rainbow of vegetables; litres of coffee; and, finally, fistfuls of tiny, delicious cakes. It was a Nordic bargain.

Satisfied at last, I took my camera out and laid it on the table so that its scope encompassed the mess of plates and Steve and I sat either side of them. 'Last night,' I said to the camera, 'I wished for an all-you-can-eat breakfast. My wish came true.' I left a pause, hoping Steve might fill it, but he remained silent. I continued. 'Last night was one of the toughest yet. Did you think we were ever going to find a place to sleep, Steve?'

Without answering, Steve reached across the table and turned the camera off. He looked at me for a long while and then finally sighed: 'Not now, mate.'

'Okay, you're not in the mood, that's cool, I'll just film myself,' I said, picking up the camera and angling it towards my face.

With a sudden lunge, Steve grabbed the camera from my hand.

'What are you doing?' I shouted.

'I said, not now. We haven't got time for this shit, mate. It's almost midday already! We should be on the road, we should be on the road right now.'

'But I need to say something about last night, to get a document of it while it's still fresh. If I do it later I'll forget and it could be an integral part of the film.'

'A much more integral part of the film would be us getting on our bikes and covering some miles. I'm sick of having to wait around all the time for you.'

It was the same argument we'd had on the first day and I was loath to repeat it. 'We've been hitting our daily target each day,' I said, trying to maintain my calm. 'Sometimes we've exceeded it. We can afford a couple of minutes here and there to film. I won't be longer than that now. I promise. It's a late start anyway. But we'll do the miles. Even if we have to cycle through some of the night.'

I hoped this would assuage Steve's mounting anger, but it had the opposite effect. Incensed, he slammed his palm on to the table. '*That's exactly what I'm talking about!*' he hissed. Other people in the restaurant were turning to look at us. 'I don't *want* to cycle through the night. I was trying to tell you yesterday in Rovaniemi. I *knew* you weren't listening to me.'

'I was,' I protested. 'I hate it, too! But what choice do we have? We have to meet our daily target.'

'Of course we have a choice! We can *choose* to wake up earlier. We can *choose* not to spend two hours getting ready to leave and eating breakfast. We can *choose* not to waste time by filming every single fucking thing.'

At the back of my mind, a small and nagging voice told me that I should be filming this argument. I briefly entertained the idea of turning the camera on, if anything just to see Steve's reaction, and perhaps I would have, but then I realised it was still in his hands.

'So what do you suggest?' I asked. 'You think there was any possible way we could've got up earlier today? We need our sleep, too, you know.'

'Maybe, but we could have got ourselves sorted and back out there a lot quicker. Half an hour max, not two hours.'

'Are you dreaming?' I had begun to allow my own anger to surface, my voice had raised, and I didn't care that everyone in the restaurant was now looking intently at us. 'In what world could we possibly get our stuff packed up, our bikes ready *and* eat a decent breakfast in half an hour? You're not being realistic, Steve, that's your problem.'

'That's my problem? No, mate, my problem is that I'm trying to set a world record while my partner is doing everything he can to fuck it up.'

This infuriated me. 'Number one,' I said, 'without me, there wouldn't even *be* a record to set. And number two, if you hadn't started this whole stupid argument, I would have already finished filming and we'd be on the road right now.'

With this in mind, I rose from the table and stormed out of the restaurant before another word could be uttered.

———————

The cycle was long, wet and lonely. Steve pushed ahead of me, fuelled by vitriol, and I struggled to maintain the necessary proximity to him. We rode in silence, stopped once for a late lunch – more burgers, more chips, more Coke – ate in silence and then rode some more, always in silence. Rain beat down incessantly and when night settled it was almost impossible to tell at first. It had been a dark day. It was to be a dark night.

The need to hit our daily target propelled us forward. We were night riding again.

There is something about cycling through darkness that heightens the senses. Perhaps it is the absence of the visual, like the blind man with the olfactory capabilities of a bloodhound. With my bike's headlight an ineffective beam illuminating only the sheets of rain a few feet ahead of me, with Steve a tiny red dot faintly winking in the distance, I was cocooned inside a world that seemed to stretch no further than my own skin.

The lack of traffic enhanced the cocoon effect, and when the sporadic cars and trucks passed, they ripped into my consciousness like the sting of a wasp. They came on hellishly, brutes of the night that soaked me with road water and left me rocking unsteadily in their wake. Those that blared their horns did not do so out of warning, but out of sheer sadistic delight, or so I fancied at the time.

The most common vehicle of all was the lorry transporting its tonnes of pine logs south to the rest of Europe or Russia. Out of boredom, for there was little else to do but ride and then ride some more, I began to count them, stumbling over numbers once I hit triple figures, for that train of thought had led to another. Loggers. They were everywhere in the world, but I knew of them most intimately in Madagascar, where their exponential deforestation over the years had cleared vast swathes of land that might never be recovered. Madagascar came back to me then, a welcome cerebral diversion from this interminable ride, and I imagined myself there, at this very moment... what time would it be?... perhaps just before dawn, that magical time when light crept in with the softness of footsteps on orange earth... and the children would start singing soon, their Malagasy lilts and harmonies framing the sunrise... me in my tent... warm, comfortable, smiling... the taste of dough balls and honey... the smell of frying bananas...

I awoke the second my shoulder connected with the road. My bike lay on top of me, its wheels spinning silently in the air. There was no physical pain, only the jarring emotional discomfort of a sleep interrupted. Groggily, I pulled myself to my feet, shaking my head to dispel the thunderous roar which assaulted my ears. It had no effect, if anything the roar grew louder and more insistent, and had I not pushed my bike back to the side of the road, the lorry that sailed past me might instead have sailed over me, and I would never have seen, as I did now, those logs bumping up and down upon its rear.

I called out to Steve, but he was far ahead. So I clambered back on to my bike and pedalled, deciding not to count anything any more, and instead singing a Red Hot Chili Peppers song as loud as my watery lungs could muster.

'You're right,' I said.

'What's that?'

'I said you're *right*.'

'That's music to my ears.' I could see the smile play about Steve's lips by the faint torchlight. 'But what, exactly, am I right about?'

'The night riding,' I sighed. 'We need to cut it out. I can't do it any more. I fell asleep back there.'

Steve laughed. 'You fell *asleep*? While you were cycling? Is that even possible?'

'Trust me,' I muttered. 'It's possible. I'm your living proof. Just.'

It was 4 a.m. We had found the campsite over an hour earlier, but the ritual of erecting the tent, recording the day's events in the logbook and sending our daily email to Francesca and the Base Camp had meant we were only just climbing on to the Therm-a-Rest. My eyelids were swollen and heavy, and as Steve talked I felt myself drifting away.

'We need to change our strategy,' he was saying. 'Sacrifice tomorrow, do just a hundred miles or maybe even less, finish early, then start early the next day...'

I blinked, and suddenly it was morning.

The tent was empty save for myself. I rose unsteadily to my feet and unzipped the door flap to poke my head out. Steve had already packed his bike and most of mine.

'I'm sorry…' I faltered.

'No worries,' he said. 'You needed to sleep.'

'What time is it?'

He checked his watch. 'Ten. All's done here. We just need to pack the tent, eat some breakfast and then we can hit the road. Do you remember what we agreed on last night?'

I did, albeit vaguely. 'Change strategy,' I mumbled.

He nodded. 'I've been working it out in my head. We're ahead of our target. We can afford to do less today.'

'But we've been building up those miles for later. To compensate for the African roads. We won't be making one-hundred-and-ten miles a day on them.'

There was a silence as Steve stared at me. 'Do you want to fall asleep on your bike again tonight?' he asked.

I shook my head.

'I don't want you to, either. So today we have a new target. Not miles this time. However far we get, we stop at six p.m. And we stop for the night.'

'Thanks,' I said. 'I mean it. Thanks, Steve.'

He was right, and I knew he was right all the way until 6 p.m. when, according to our new resolve, we stopped. To negate the time and energy spent erecting the tent and cooking for ourselves, we checked into a hotel with a restaurant. All that was left to do was eat, fill in the logbook and email our daily update to Andy at Base Camp. I fell into my bed at 8 p.m. and slept without interruption until 6 a.m., and it may well have been the most gorgeous sleep I've ever had.

CHAPTER 6

THERE MAY BE TROUBLE AHEAD

Distance remaining: 10,200 miles

Time to record: 93 days

Russia was close: 130 miles away lay the border town of Imatra and I felt strong enough after my solid 10 hours' sleep to make it in one day. Steve concurred. The last of Finland passed in a blur of pine forests and reindeer, and my feet were powered by the impending thrill of Russia, that great and mysterious country I had always longed to see.

Lunch was a petrol-station pizza and we made use of the free wi-fi to catch up on emails we had ignored throughout our night-riding bonanza. Most were missives which delighted in our progress so far and encouraged us on to make the record, although here and there a more pejorative theme began to surface. There was trouble ahead. We knew that already. Norway and Finland are some of the most stable countries on the planet, but we were under no illusions that the upcoming lands would be so safe. Friends and family members had peppered their emails with warnings embedded in the news-website links they attached, sometimes as a by-the-way or did-you-know afterthought, but more often as their first paragraph or, in the case of my mother, the entire body of an email.

Egypt was a recurrent trope. Just five days earlier, the military had declared a national state of emergency and the UK foreign office had issued a statement advising against all travel to the country. I clicked on the links embedded in the emails to read reports of how the Muslim Brotherhood were responding. They were, in a series of reactive measures, burning police stations and churches, and above all looting. I perused it all with a curious interest at my own disinterest. I knew the reality of the danger and knew I would soon be among it, but it all seemed too far away to bear contemplation. The change in my mindset I had wrought back in Norway – to preserve my mental health by taking each day at a time rather than surmising the entire journey as one long and overwhelming punishment – still held fast, and before the prospect of Egypt I had first to deal with Russia, Azerbaijan and Iran.

It was the former of those countries, Russia, which predominantly occupied my headspace. All going well, we would be there the following day, and the thought of that both elated and terrified me. On the one hand, I would finally visit St Petersburg, a city that had fascinated me since I was a child, when I would borrow books from my father's library and read about the cultural and architectural wonders of Leningrad, a stronghold deep inside the Soviet Union, which back then seemed as impenetrable as it was otherworldly. On the other hand, I knew too well what was waiting in the darker, south-western pockets of Russia we needed to strike through to reach Azerbaijan. There lay Dagestan: a republic in name only; littered with separatist ideologies and ethnic tensions; the source of frequent and often bloody conflicts as those who lived there wrestled with their place in the greater Russian state.

One email, from Andy at Base Camp, captured my attention far more than the others. Within it, he detailed the *Shahidka,* or 'Black Widows', whose terror attacks were growing ever more prolific in Dagestan. The Black Widows were female suicide bombers, and their colloquial name derived from the fact that many were widows of men killed in Chechnya by Russian forces. While earlier assaults by these *Shahidka* had largely been localised to Chechnya and Moscow, they had recently become prominent in Dagestan, and in the past year alone three separate suicide bombings by Black Widows had between them killed 15 people and injured 20 in that region. Andy explained that, among the darker places of the internet, there were rumblings that a new attack was imminent in Dagestan, perhaps to mark the anniversary of the suicide bomb that had claimed the life of the Sufi leader Said Afandi on 28 August the year before. The anniversary was only nine days away and I realised with some dismay that it was possible we would be in Dagestan then.

I showed Andy's email to Steve, who grimaced as he read it. 'I got something similar from my dad,' he said. 'It's scaring the shit out of me.'

'Me too,' I replied. 'But what can we do? Just hope for the best, I guess.'

'Can't we go around it? Avoid it altogether?'

We opened up Google Maps. It was possible to skirt around Dagestan, but that meant travelling through Chechnya, which we fancied even less, and then Georgia, and without even calculating the distance we could see immediately that it would add too many miles to our journey and render the record unattainable.

'Like I said,' I shrugged. 'Hope for the best.'

The ride to the Russian border helped to dispel the dark thoughts that had clouded my mood over lunch, although it was clear that Steve still harboured them. A strong and vigorous cyclist, Steve had enjoyed taking the lead and setting our pace since Nordkapp, but this afternoon he lagged behind me, as if taking things slower would keep him from ever reaching Dagestan. I eased off my pedals and coasted until we drew level.

'I've got an idea,' I said.

'Oh yeah?'

'For Dagestan. How about we ride only at night? It might be safer that way. All the Black Widows will be in bed.'

Steve laughed. 'Only you could try to cheer me up by suggesting *more* night riding.'

Arriving in Imatra at 9.30 p.m. raised our spirits. A local bed and breakfast took us in for the night and, as we set about the nightly routine of logbooks and emails, we did so happy in the knowledge that we had another good night's sleep ahead. Talk of Dagestan would have spoiled our cheery moods, so we chose not to mention it, instead chattering gaily about the prospect of St Petersburg, which, all being well, we would reach the following afternoon.

And perhaps we would have, were it not for the explosion.

It happened the following morning, on the bridge leading out of Imatra. Traffic was light and so Steve and I were cycling level with each other. Still afraid to raise the topic of Dagestan, its impending threat had nonetheless inspired our conversation, which was about Egypt, about the Muslim Brotherhood and about the prospect of a gunshot, perhaps stray or perhaps intended, flooring one of us in the dust of North Africa. Our repartee was deadpan but not sombre, and we hid our genuine fears beneath jokes of how we might react if the other was shot.

'I'd leave you behind. No question. Gotta get that record.'

'I'd cauterise your wound with a stormproof match and slap you if you cried.'

'I'd call Francesca and tell her to send the chopper.'

'I'd kick you to the side, show the shooter my knife and put on my best Cockney accent. *You like my knife? It's a big, fuck-off shiny one.*'

'I'd tell them you're American and I'm their Iranian brother. I'd tell them I was leading you to them so we could all beat you down together.'

The jokes took on a more and more politically incorrect tone, but we could not help ourselves, and had begun to laugh hysterically at each one.

'I'd—'

The crack of the explosion was so violent that it resonated through my entire body in a series of shuddering echoes, sending me coursing towards the side of the bridge where I detached from my bike's handlebars and grabbed the railings to steady myself. It was no gunshot, I decided with some relief, it had been far too loud for that, and I swung my blurred gaze from side to side, searching for the source, imagining some sort of nuclear attack, at the border perhaps, Russia's attempt to isolate itself from the West in one fell swoop by irrevocably dismantling any passage to and from Finland.

I looked back towards Steve, who remained on the road and, to my dismay and confusion, was laughing and pointing at something just behind me.

'Look!' he guffawed. 'Look!'

'Did you see it?' I gasped, still reeling with shock. 'What was it?'

'Reza,' he managed between giggles, 'it was your tyre. Your back tyre. Look at it. It blew.'

'My *tyre*?' I struggled to comprehend. True, my back tyre was flat, but there was no possible way it could have made such a noise. 'It was so loud!'

This made Steve laugh harder.

'Stop laughing,' I remonstrated.

This made Steve laugh harder still.

'I thought it… I thought we…' I managed to stop myself from spouting my nuclear theory. 'My *tyre*?'

'I told you!' Steve had begun to punch the air with his fist, and I do not doubt that, had he not been on his bike, he would have hopped from one foot to the other. 'I *told* you! Don't overfill your tyres! But did you listen? Did you fuck! *I'm Reza Pakravan, I've cycled the Sahara, I know how much a tyre can take.* I told you it was too much!'

I didn't know what I was angrier about: that Steve was right; that I had just mistaken a simple blowout for full-scale war; or that his impression of me had been somewhat competent.

The mockery persisted throughout the puncture repair and then all the way to the Russian border. I bore it with a self-conscious grin and let Steve revel in his righteousness. At least, I thought, it stopped him thinking about Dagestan.

Entrance to Russia meant entrance to a new time zone, but while we lost an hour we gained a new country. The record was a driving force and the further I rode the more I wanted it, but often it could seem a hindrance, which propelled me forward with too much momentum, weighing time over space, a ticking clock that favoured the accretion of numbers and disavowed the impact of experience. How pleasant it would be, I thought, to spend all those 100 days just here in this one vast country, cycling from city to settlement, learning the land rather than racing for its border. Russia seemed to demand more: the moment we left Finland and entered it, the exclusivity, the unique otherness of it, was immediately apparent and I yearned to immerse myself in it rather than just scratch the surface. Russia was a continent to itself. Behind us was Europe and before us the Middle East and Africa, but between them was this: the largest nation in the world and the longest single-country ride we would have to endure.

The roads were not as well-paved as those in Finland, but they were smooth enough and with the wind on our side and the sun warming our backs we made superb progress. In Vyborg, we celebrated our Russian arrival with a beef stroganoff lunch and then gulped water in the shadow of Lenin's statue in the town's picturesque square.

St Petersburg was less than 100 miles away. Though we still hoped to shirk night riding wherever possible, we were buoyed up by the thought of reaching the famous city and reasoned that, if we followed the A-road that connected it to Vyborg, we could get there before midnight. Our plans were shattered after just 5 minutes on the road. Strewn with potholes so deep that a single miscalculation could bend a wheel, our progress slowed to a winding meander and we both understood without discussion that we would never reach St Petersburg in time if we continued along it.

There was another option. The motorway. It was a dismal prospect. We both disliked motorways and had been careful to avoid them wherever possible when planning our route back in the UK. It was not just the fact that riding a bicycle on motorways is illegal in most countries, it was the fact that it is illegal for a reason. Any motorway is incredibly dangerous for

the cyclist and any Russian motorway is more so. These are the roads upon
which accidents are so common that the dashboard camera has become a
nationwide bestseller. Yet we knew that it would get us to St Petersburg
far faster than this crumbling A-road. The record made our choice for us
and we approached the motorway with extreme caution.

We were relieved to discover a hard shoulder and for the first 70 miles
we cycled well, spurred on by the tailwind and deriving pleasure from
the cloudless sky. It was still cold, but an invigorating cold, no longer the
deep piercing chill of the Arctic. It was impossible to cycle side by side,
but when my odometer clocked 1,000 miles I pulled up as close to Steve's
back tyre as I could and shouted the news to him. His whoops were audible
even above the thunder of the passing traffic.

Twenty miles from St Petersburg, conditions changed. Roadworks
sprung up with increasing regularity, forcing all traffic on to our hard
shoulder, the only lane left open. We shared the narrow aperture with
vehicles driven with a reckless abandon and little regard for the reduced
speed limit and ourselves. Cars didn't swerve to avoid us, they simply
powered forward as if we were invisible, compelling us to hug the very
edge of the shoulder – a steep bank of ballasted earth or concrete – as
wing-mirrors threatened to catch our handlebars and send us careering to
our deaths. Worst of all were the lorries, so many lorries that, in the rare
moments when I allowed my focus to drift from the raw self-preservation
that encompassed my attention, I decided with absolute surety that I had
never before seen so many in such a short period of time. Juggernauts
of impending doom, they came on with relentless fortitude, transforming
atmospheric pressure as they passed, pushing me away and then sucking
me back into their slipstream.

When we finally left the motorway, veering on to the dual carriageway
that would lead us to the heart of St Petersburg, we were exhausted, our
lungs clogged with diesel fumes. The orange glow of the great city on the
horizon cheered me somewhat, but then the rain started, a thick Russian
storm that seemed to saturate my bones, and we were forced to take shelter

beneath a flyover on the outskirts. I looked over at Steve. He had taken off his sunglasses after the sun had set, and I could now see the day-old tan lines, which took a pencil-straight line from his ears to the pale circles around his eyes. Beads of rain dripped down his cheeks, tracking fresh rivulets through the grime and soot that darkened his face.

'Well, we made it,' he said. 'St Petersburg. Is it everything you dreamed it would be?'

I coughed, hacking up a thick wad of dark, diesel-infused phlegm. 'No,' I said. 'Not yet.'

We cycled back and forth across St Petersburg's myriad bridges, island-hopping the city's fractured topography, knocking on the doors of hostels and bed and breakfasts and finding not a single available room anywhere. It was growing late and the burgeoning cold left us shivering in the rain as we rode. Desperate to find somewhere, anywhere, to sleep, we came to a corner shop, and I signalled to Steve to stop so that we might go in and inquire about any likely accommodation in the area. A young couple were leaving the shop as we climbed off our bikes and the woman cradled an enormous watermelon in her arms as if it was her baby.

'Excuse me,' I said. 'Could you tell us if there are any hostels near here?'

The man's eyes lit up at the sound of my voice, as if he had been waiting for this very question all his life. 'Yes! I know a hostel. The *best* hostel! In all St Petersburg. In all Russia, perhaps!'

'Brilliant,' I said. 'So... err... where is it?'

Flicking the blond hair from his eyes, he proceeded to spin off a dizzying list of directions, which I hoped Steve had kept track of, for I had not. 'So where are you men from?' he asked after he had repeated the directions twice more. 'English?'

'Iranian,' I said.

'South African,' Steve said.

'An Iranian and a South African walk into a St Petersburg hostel. Sounds like a joke, no?' Perhaps he knew what the punchline to the joke was, for he laughed hard for a solid 10 seconds. Whatever it might have been, he did not divulge it. 'And what are you men doing in St Petersburg?'

We explained our adventure and he took a keen interest in every word.

'This is a good thing,' he said when we had finished. 'A very good thing. I applaud you.' And he did, too. His girlfriend tried to do the same, but almost dropped her watermelon in the process and instead hugged it to herself tighter. 'We wish you the very best of luck.'

We thanked them both, mounted our bikes and set off, aware that we had no idea where we were going. Just 5 m later, we heard the shout of '*Stop!*' and turned around to see them both bounding towards us. It was the woman who had called and, as she neared, watermelon bouncing precariously in her arms, she asked us when we were leaving St Petersburg.

'Tomorrow,' Steve said.

'Then we would be honoured if you would spend the night with us. We have a spare room at our house. It is yours if you would like it.'

We were too overcome with gratitude to reply and the woman seemed to mistake this for reluctance.

'Ivan and I have been drinking tonight,' she said. 'We finished some wine and we thought, you know, we would like something different. Something unusual. I suggested a watermelon. So we came to buy one. And look what we found! Two men cycling the world! There is nothing more unusual than that. Except this watermelon perhaps. Look at it. Don't you think it's unusual?'

'What my beautiful girlfriend is trying to say,' Ivan chipped in, 'is that we have been having a wonderful night and we think it would be even more wonderful if you would join us. Join us and our watermelon.'

It was an offer too surreal to refuse.

Ivan and Katya's apartment sat halfway up a majestic and gorgeous old building and, as we locked up our bikes in the courtyard and removed the panniers, they helped us carry all our belongings inside. While Ivan went to open a fresh bottle of wine, Katya showed us our room for the night, gave us clean towels and directed us to the shower, insisting that we take as long as we like getting clean and dry, and that a dinner of meat stew with berries and rice would be waiting for us once we were ready.

'And do you know what we will have for dessert?' she asked.

'Watermelon?' I hazarded.

She grabbed my shoulders and beamed into my face. 'Yes! Watermelon! Ha!' And then she left us alone, closing the door behind her.

The shower was sensational, the meat stew delicious, the watermelon perhaps a little underwhelming and the company spectacular. Ivan and Katya were in their late twenties, fiercely in love with each other, fiercely welcoming to us and fiercely drunk. Katya was the more intimate of the two: she liked to lean in and talk one-on-one, exploring concepts and ideas long-form in rambling but never incoherent detail. Ivan, on the other hand, was the class clown, jumping up from his seat to act out his stories and one-liners, holding court with impressions and expansive gesticulations, and while we all laughed at his gambolling antics, none of us laughed as loud or as hard as he did. They were a wealth of infectious glee, and often Steve and I would exchange glances with each other, silently communicating our good fortune at having been taken in for the night by this beautiful pair.

'We're so grateful to you,' I said. 'Thank you so much. I don't know what we would have done tonight without you. We're really happy to be here with you.'

'*We're* really happy to be here with *you*!' Ivan shouted, pouring out another round of wine into my and Steve's glasses. He had that particular inclination of the inebriated, to ensure that anyone not quite on his level of drunkenness would get there soon.

'Do you know why we offered you to stay tonight?' Katya asked. 'Last year, I was driving through Lithuania. I got to this town – I can't even remember which one now – and I must have visited every single hotel looking for a bed for the night, but there was nothing. Then I met this guy, just on the street. I had stopped the car and asked him if he knew anywhere, and he offered me to sleep at his place for the night, without even thinking about it! I was a little cautious, but he seemed nice and I had no other option, so I went. And do you know what he did? He slept on the floor so that I could sleep in the bed. It was so kind of him, and when you asked us about hostels tonight, it reminded me of that guy, of how he had been so nice, and I wanted to pass it on.'

'You wouldn't have liked that hostel I told you about anyway,' Ivan said.

'You said it was the best hostel in St Petersburg,' I replied. 'The best hostel in Russia!'

'Yes, I did, didn't I? But I was drunk.'

'Aren't you drunk now?'

'No. Now I am pissed. And what about you? Are you pissed?'

I assessed my internal state. There was no denying that I was, in every conceivable way, pissed. A thousand miles of cycling had taken its toll, and the few glasses of wine I had imbibed had exploded into my bloodstream with the numbing efficiency of morphine. At least, I thought I had only had a few glasses. I could not be sure. Ivan's habit of topping up one's drink before it was finished meant that for all I knew I could have downed two bottles. It felt like it.

'Ivan,' I said, 'I'm absolutely smashed.'

'Liar!' Ivan shouted. 'You have pants! And they are on fire!' He leapt from his chair to grab another bottle of wine, which he made a show of uncorking with his teeth, grunting and groaning with the faux machismo of a wrestler.

'I'm not sure we would have found the hostel anyway,' I said. 'That was a lot of directions to take in and I wasn't even pissed then.'

'You insult me, sir,' Ivan cried, spitting the cork into his palm. 'I challenge you to a duel.' He waved the wine bottle around like a rapier, spilling half of it down his T-shirt and then sucking it out of the fabric like a starved puppy.

'Another reason to ask you to stay with us,' Katya said. 'If you had not found that hostel, you would have been trapped here, on this island, on Vasilyevsky. They close all the bridges at midnight.'

'It's a police state,' Ivan said. 'At night, I am literally stuck here. But at least I am stuck here with Katya.' He lurched forward to wrap her in a hug and plant a kiss on the top of her head, then swung the bottle over the table towards our glasses. I held my hand over the top of mine, but he knocked it aside with the neck of the bottle and refilled my glass regardless. 'We must drink more. *And...* we must eat more watermelon!'

The semi-demolished fruit still sat as the centrepiece of our table, a symbolic reminder that it was this that had brought us all together. Ivan secured a knife and set about carving into it with lustre. Feeling light and merry and far beyond pissed, I waved a hand at the watermelon and attempted a joke of my own.

'That's what they're going to do to us in Dagestan.'

The change in atmosphere was as tangible as it was sudden. Katya looked down at her glass of wine and began to drag her fingers along the beads of perspiration. Ivan back-stepped from the table and leaned against the cooker, tapping the knife nervously against his thigh.

'You are going to Dagestan?' he asked.

'Yes,' Steve said. 'We need to pass through it to get to Azerbaijan.'

'You should not,' Ivan said. 'You should not go to Dagestan.' Gone from his voice was the jokey warmth and ribald humour we had grown used to. Now, he spoke quietly and with certitude.

'We have to,' I said. 'To go around it would take too long.'

'I would prefer to take too long rather than to go to Dagestan.' He placed his wine glass on the worktop at his side. It was the first time he had relinquished it all night.

'To be honest, so would I,' Steve said. 'But Reza's right. If we want the record, there's no choice but Dagestan.'

'Do you know what happens there? In Dagestan?' Ivan asked, his face serious with concern.

'We've been reading about it. The Black Widows. The *Shahidka*.'

'Yes, the *Shahidka* are bad, but that is only what you will read in your newspapers. People die every day in Dagestan. Russian people. All

73

the time. But you won't see that in your newspapers. Only last week, a Dagestani man here crippled a Russian police officer in the vegetable market. Did you read about that?'

'No,' I said. 'And I'm sure there's a lot we don't know. There's a lot of tension between Russia and Dagestan. We know that. But we are foreign guys. They don't have a reason to hurt us.'

'They don't need a reason,' Ivan said. 'You will cross the Russian border. Be prepared. People die. Men die. I strongly – *strongly* – advise that you do not go.'

The air had grown thick and muggy. Ivan went back to carving the watermelon and we watched him in silence. I felt the familiar surges of fear that had accompanied any thought of Dagestan over the past 24 hours, though they were outstripped by the sense that I had ruined an otherwise perfect evening with my tactless joke. Katya, perhaps aware of my awkward shame, changed the subject and Ivan returned to the table to eat the watermelon with us. Soon, the quips and impressions and stories returned, and I chose to listen and laugh rather than reciprocate with any further potential faux pas.

The evening lasted perhaps an hour longer. I had grown drowsy from the copious wine and no further offerings of watermelon could arouse me, and so I drunkenly stumbled to my feet and explained my absolute need to go to bed. Steve stood up with me and Katya hugged us both, promising a hearty breakfast in the morning.

'It is very beautiful of her,' Ivan said, shaking our hands but looking at his girlfriend. 'This is why I love her. Me you will not see in the morning. I like my sleep. So I will say goodbye now. I will thank you for your company. And I will say just one last time. Avoid Dagestan.'

As we lurched towards our room and our beds, I looked over at Steve. His eyes were glazed and his arms hung limply. He was clearly every bit as pissed as I was. He seemed to be muttering something to himself, and when I wrapped my arm around him in drunken solidarity and said, 'All right, mate?', his only reply was a repetition of Ivan's parting words.

'Avoid Dagestan.'

CHAPTER 7

ZEN AND THE ART OF PUNCTURE REPAIR

Distance remaining: 9,941 miles

Time to record: 91 days

———————

Despite Katya's breakfast of fresh bread and omelettes, despite her heartfelt but encouraging farewell and the sound of Ivan's muffled snores from the bedroom as we left, despite the cessation of the rain, I was immaculately hungover, and it was horrible. This was St Petersburg, the city I had looked forward to above most others on our journey, and all I could focus on as we cycled through it were the queasy rumblings of my stomach, the throbbing headache diverted only by sporadic flashes of white-hot panic and the meandering wobbles of my front wheel. I was disgusted with myself.

It seemed to take forever to find our way out of the city. Hunting down a bike shop to stock up on inner tubes, we became lost in a maze of cobbled streets, then labyrinthine one-way systems, then an industrial estate the size of Heathrow airport and finally another busy, horrific motorway. The city map on our GPS was not detailed enough to rely upon and, as we bumped along the hard shoulder while a never-ending fleet of lorries blared past, I prayed that we were on the right road to Moscow.

The hangover persisted long into the afternoon, rendering me sick and anxious. The never-ending rain – indeed, the never-ending cold and grey darkness of Russia – did little to help. It had rained every single day since the journey began and my shoes felt like paddling pools strapped to my feet. With some force of effort, I managed not to think about Dagestan and Ivan's sombre warnings, but my brain seemed determined to berate me for the poisoning I had subjected it to, and instead of Dagestan I began to obsessively recall the accident in France. The injuries I had sustained from that had only been from a car on a country road. What if one of these 80 mph lorries on this motorway swerved just slightly? What then? The end of the journey. Perhaps the end of me.

The misery was all-consuming, and I struggled with the idea of whether I should share my feelings with Steve. On the one hand, he could help talk me out of my mounting depression; on the other, such a conversation could serve to bring him down to my level. I glanced over at him, cycling beside me. He looked in even worse condition than me. I decided to keep quiet.

I was ripped from my vicious psychological circle by another puncture. In contrast to the last, this one was inaudible, but the sudden shudders of my front tyre as the air left it in less than a second reverberated through my wrists and forearms with a violence as tactile as the last was auditory. I careered to the very edge of the hard shoulder and planted my feet on the ground, gulping in the diesel-fogged air, my entire body a shaking, sweating frame.

I called ahead to Steve, who turned around and rode back towards me. 'All right?' he said.

'Puncture. Another. Shit.' It was impossible to formulate a complete sentence.

'You okay?'

'No,' I admitted. 'I'm freaking out.'

'About Dagestan?'

'Not even. Just this. Fucking horrible.'

Steve dismounted his bike and helped me with the repair. Perhaps the most significant lesson I learned that day was that, if you ever want to placate your nerves, fixing a puncture on the side of a Russian motorway is the least likely way to do it.

With my tyre patched up and re-inflated, we set off again. Mile by mile, the hangover began to dissipate, exhausting itself and the veins of panic it had caused. The puncture on the bridge was the first of the day, but not the last, and we soon came to realise that our tyres were unsuited to the Russian roads, most of which seemed to be strewn along the sides with broken green glass, which, we later discovered, came from the Russian drivers who happily chucked their empty beer bottles from the windows of their cars. A tailwind rose to spur us on and the gentle drizzle that came with it was a welcome relief, washing the grime-clogged perspiration from my eyes and soothing my overheated limbs.

We did not get so far that day, just 87 miles, but even that had been an ordeal, and as we bore down upon a service station complete with a motel and Burger King, I knew I could go no further.

'Food, a place to sleep, stunning views of the motorway, it's a one-stop shop!' Steve grinned.

'You don't need to convince me,' I groaned. 'I'm done. We're stopping.'

After a tasteless dinner at the Burger King, we pushed our bikes to the motel and entered. The receptionist explained in faltering English that they were full. I felt like I was about to cry.

'No worries,' Steve said to me as we stepped back outside. 'Let's ask if we can put up our tent behind the petrol station and camp. All these Russian petrol stations have twenty-four-hour security guards on duty. We'll be safe enough.'

We crossed the forecourt and entered the petrol station. Steve asked the lady behind the counter if we could camp there for the night.

'Not allowed,' she said. 'I am sorry.' To her credit, she did seem to be.

'Please,' I said. 'We won't be any trouble. We're desperate. There's nowhere else. Please.'

'Not allowed,' she repeated, looking like she might apologise again, but then she stopped herself and turned to the security guard who stood next to her. They began to converse in rapid and incomprehensible Russian, punctuating their sentences with pointed fingers which jabbed towards the CCTV monitor. Then, with a booming laugh and a knowing wink, the security guard marched out of the door and disappeared around the side of the building. We watched as he popped up on each of the tiny squares that filled the screen, waving his arms at the cameras and sometimes performing little jigs which would send the lady into peals of laughter.

'They're taking the piss,' I whispered to Steve. 'They're taking the piss out of us.'

'Hang on,' Steve replied. 'I think—'

He left his thought unuttered as the security guard disappeared from the monitor, returning to the building two minutes later. He held the door open and ushered us to follow him. I looked back at the lady behind the counter.

'Yes, yes,' she nodded. 'Go with him.'

The security guard led us to a small patch of grass, where he opened his arms and then performed a rather passable mime of erecting a tent. I suddenly understood the purpose of the elaborate show. They had found the one space both suitable for camping and out of sight of the CCTV cameras, thereby ensuring that we could spend the night without detection. It was a clandestine and generous gesture, and it softened the end of an otherwise dreadful day.

We awoke the next morning, relieved to be entirely free from the previous day's hangovers, and so enlivened that we covered 60 miles before lunch. The motorway remained perpetually busy but was no longer perpetually terrifying. We were getting used to it. The one solace of fear is that it has a limited shelf life.

A small cafe with an outdoor barbecue stood on a slip road from the motorway. A stout man with gold teeth and a tight black vest rushed between the barbecue and the cafe, carrying fistfuls of skewered meats inside. Seeing us approach, he waved frantically at us, beetled back inside the cafe with his latest consignment of kebabs and then reappeared, smiling and wiping his hands on his vest.

'Shashlik?' he asked, pointing at the roasting meats.

I nodded with excitement, recognising the word. Shashlik is a traditional kebab in Iran. I asked for two and he guided us into the cafe. We seemed to be the only customers, and it transpired that all those other kebabs we had seen him shuttling inside were for his family, who huddled in the kitchen out of sight.

Our shashliks came to us on a bed of rice and onions and were delicious. He left us to eat, and when he returned later with the bill he sat beside us and began to point at our chests.

'Italian? English? Spanish?' he asked.

'South African,' Steve said.

'Siff iffrin?' He frowned in puzzlement, shook his head and turned to me. 'Italian? English? Spanish?'

'Iranian,' I said. 'I'm from Iran.'

'*Irani hasti? Farsi harf mizani?*' The vocabulary of my mother tongue was as unexpected as it was delightful. *You're from Iran? So you speak Farsi?* he had asked.

'Of course!' I replied. 'How do *you* know Farsi?'

'I'm from Tajikistan,' he said proudly. 'It is also my language.'

Steve looked back and forth between us, bemused and uncomprehending. I explained the revelation to him. The man, hearing us speak English and keen to be involved, pointed at Steve and asked me in Farsi whether he was Christian, Muslim or Jewish. My role, it seemed, was translator.

'I'm an atheist,' Steve said.

The man laughed, his gold teeth glinting in the reflections from the cafe's single flickering lightbulb. Then he held his arm above his head and pointed at the ceiling. 'I believe in God,' he said. 'Mohammed is my prophet.'

'That's cool,' Steve replied. 'I learn from all religions.'

This pleased the man greatly, and he jumped to his feet to give Steve a rough and noisy shoulder massage, chattering away at me in Farsi while he kneaded. 'Did you enjoy my shashlik? I am very proud of it. Do you like my cafe? I am very proud of that, too. It is open twenty-four hours every day. I run it during the day and my son runs it during the night. His shashlik is not as good as mine. So why are you here? Where are you going?'

'We're cycling from Norway to South Africa,' I explained. 'In a hundred days.'

He cooed with disbelief and left Steve's shoulders alone to sit back next to me. 'One hundred days? From Norway to South Africa? Oh, you will see so many things. I am jealous. I would love to see all those countries.'

'You want to come?' I joked. 'You would be welcome! Come with me!'

'Me?' he said, pointing at his vest. 'Why don't you come to my place?' The gold teeth came out again, the shining sentries of his infectious laugh, but then he pulled his phone from his pocket and began to flick through photos of his 20-year-old daughter, and the notion that he might not be joking after all began to bubble. 'This is my daughter. She is very beautiful, isn't she? Would you like to marry her?'

'I'm thirty-nine,' I laughed. 'Probably a bit too old.'

'No, no, this is absolutely fine.' He was still flashing those teeth and belching out laughter, but he had clutched my elbow and held on to it as he continued. 'And I have not even told you the best part! You can have this beautiful girl as your wife and you can also have her house! It is my family house in Dushanbe. Huge! Do you want it? You can have it! You will be very happy there and so will my grandchildren!'

Everything about his demeanour suggested he was joking, but I could not eradicate the idea that, had I said yes, I would have been whisked away to Dushanbe and married in an instant. There was a pleasant whimsy to the thought and I allowed myself a few seconds to entertain it before bursting into a fresh bout of laughter, which my new friend reciprocated with chortling warmth.

'You want more shashlik?' he asked.

'I wish I could, but I'm so full.'

'Okay, but please wait for one minute while I take some more to my family,' he said, slapping my thigh and then using it as an anchor to push himself to his feet.

'Reza,' Steve said as he left. 'When he comes back, find out from him what he thinks about Dagestan.'

I did, and while I hoped with every ounce of my will that his impression would be favourable, it was as dark and foreboding as Ivan's.

'Maybe I am being unfair,' he concluded. 'I have never been to Dagestan. But we hear a lot of things here, a lot of unpleasant things. I am from Tajikistan, so I am no stranger to troubles.' He sighed deeply and his gold teeth were nowhere to be seen. 'But I will tell you this. If you did marry my daughter, if you were my son-in-law, I would forbid you to go to Dagestan.'

The vastness of Russia was incomprehensible, even from inside it. Our ride from its border with Finland to its border with Azerbaijan crossed nearly 2,000 miles: more than a cycle from Land's End to John o'Groats and then back again twice over. And yet those 2,000 miles were a paltry sample of this immense land mass. Had we chosen to transform our journey south to a journey east, we would have had to cross twice that to reach Russia's Pacific coast. Moscow itself had seemed so close to St Petersburg on the map, yet almost 500 miles separated the two cities, and we endured four long days of brutal motorway cycling, most of it under a thick veil of rain. Here and there we stopped in provincial towns and gridlocked cities – Krestetsky, Valday and Klin, among others – as monotonous as they were uninspiring. The Soviet Union cast a long, posthumous shadow in these places, the Socialist Classical architecture still abundant and domineering with its right angles, its hyperbole of stature, its 50,000 shades of grey. Campsites were few and far between, but hotels were cheap and invariably empty, and we were given our pick of the rooms. Wandering down windowless corridors lit by fluorescent bulbs and so long we fancied we could see the curvature of the earth, we ducked our heads into and out of the vacant dormitories, singles and doubles, all of them much of a muchness. Tiny windows, giant radiators, which we dried our perpetually soaked kit on, plastic floors and wallpaper so old Stalin himself could have designed it were the key features, and often we chose our room on the basis of one rare distinction – that it had a plug socket. Once, we found a room with two, and were so overjoyed we celebrated with a high-five, the resounding pain of which caused us instant regret.

Something odd had begun to happen to our fingers. I had first noticed it the night before, while trying to email Base Camp from the hotel. To move my fingers was no longer automatic, it seemed to require a conscious effort of will. They were slow and sluggish, like tiny drunk men who wouldn't listen to me unless I repeated my command five or six times and who, when the message finally got through, set about their task with lacklustre inefficiency. I had remarked upon it to Steve, who concurred that his fingers were behaving in the same way.

'When I went to pay at the supermarket this afternoon,' he said, 'it was virtually impossible to get the money out of my wallet. Counting it was even worse. Felt like I had Parkinson's. The cashier ended up serving three other people while she was waiting for me.'

We concluded that it was nerve damage, caused by 10–12 hours each day hunched over our handlebars. Our fingers at least tended more towards numbness than pain, although they transformed a simple puncture repair into a task Herculean in scale.

'You know what we should get in Moscow?' Steve asked. 'Finger massage.'

It was as tempting as it was ludicrous and became a recurring joke between the two of us as we neared the Russian capital. One afternoon, following three punctures that came one after the other and left our fingers raging when we repaired them, we pulled into a layby for a much-needed break. I lifted my hands up to inspect them, these two misshapen claws that twitched and spasmed involuntarily. I flexed my fingers one by one and then all together, sighing as waves of relief spilled over the tortured muscles.

'*Da?*'

I looked up. There before me stood a huge Russian man, smoking a cigarette with one hand and gesturing at his stand of pumpkins and berries with the other. I realised that he had mistaken my wiggling fingers for a beckoning gesture and had approached me to see what I might like to buy. He grinned through gold teeth and blinked through thick glasses. The cigarette was finished and thrown to the ground, and his hand rested itself upon the vast belly which protruded out from a T-shirt many sizes too small.

'I'm sorry,' I said. 'I was just stretching my fingers. I don't want anything.'

It was clear he spoke no English and could not understand it, for he continued to talk and to gesture, describing perhaps the firmness of his pumpkins or the sweetness of his berries, and soon he was joined by his son, a man of equal size, though his stomach did not flow out from beneath his T-shirt quite so luxuriantly.

Suddenly remembering that, back in London, I had asked a Russian colleague to scribble some key Russian words on to a piece of paper for exactly this kind of situation, I dug around in my panniers – no easy task with my fingers still sore and cramping – until I located it. The single sheet of A4 was creased and already partially torn, but it remained legible enough for me to falter through an approximation of: 'Hello. I am from Iran. I am going to Moscow.' My stammering attempt at their language caused a sensation with the two men and they began to jabber excitedly.

'I'm sorry, but we really have to go,' I said, pointing at the road, at myself and miming cycling.

'*Nyet, nyet,*' the father said, grabbing me by the arm and issuing a series of commands to his son, who in turn ran over to the Lada car parked behind the fruit stand, searched for a few moments in the boot and then came back bearing a large, black plastic bag. He held it out to his father, who let go of my arm, took the bag and offered it to me.

'Present,' he said.

'*Present?*' I asked, in disbelief that he was giving me a gift, and in further disbelief that, of all English words, 'present' seemed to be the only one he knew.

'*Da, da,*' he said. 'Present.'

I took it and he beamed with delight as I opened the bag to reveal a gigantic smoked fish. Reeking odours poured from the bag, assaulting my nostrils, and I fought the urge to retch. Both father and son seemed so pleased to be giving me this huge, foul-smelling lump of meat, and I did not have the heart to upset them by refusing it, so I tied it carefully on to the back of my bike, where it lazily emitted its invisible and offensive fumes.

The two men took further delight in signing our evidence book and posing for a number of photos with us, and when we wheeled our bicycles away they mimed eating and then rubbed their bellies with satisfaction.

'Steve,' I said. 'Any chance you like smoked fish?'

He grinned at me. 'Can't stand it.'

'Me neither,' I said miserably.

The father and son looked by no means rich, they had probably been looking forward to feasting on the fish for dinner that evening, but they had given it all away to a foreigner just because he had uttered a few Russian words. The thought made me want to sob with gratitude and then sob some more for the fact that I found the fish repugnant.

A few miles down the road, we stopped at a petrol station to buy water. An old man worked the petrol pumps, his movements slow and arthritic. He was doubtless somebody's grandfather, was old enough to be a great-grandfather, and had he been mine, I would have loathed the thought of him working in this cold. I resolved to give him the fish.

He did not look up as I approached, and I had to tap him on the shoulder to gain his attention. Ignoring the plastic bag in my hands, he instead looked either side of and then behind me. 'No car?' he asked in English.

'No,' I said, pointing at my bike. 'Bicycle.'

'Ah,' he said. 'So no petrol?'

'No, thank you,' I replied, holding out the bag with one hand and opening it with the other so that he could see the fish.

'Oh, nice fish,' he said. 'You very lucky.'

'I would like you to have it.' I held the bag out to him, but he did not take it and instead started to look either side of and behind me again.

'So,' he said, 'no car, no petrol. You want something else?'

'No,' I asserted. 'I don't want anything else. Except to give this to you. Here.' I took one of his hands and placed the bag into it.

'Oh,' he said, feeling the contours of the fish inside the bag. '*Very* nice fish. Maybe two, maybe three kilograms. Expensive. You *very* lucky.'

'No,' I said. 'Please, look, it's... I want you to have it. *It's yours.*'

He finally grasped my intention with those last two words. He said nothing further, no questions, no remonstrations, not even a thank you. But the smile which swelled across his face, squashing his nose down and illuminating his eyes: that smile remains one of my most memorable images from the entire journey.

As we neared Moscow, the frequency of punctures heightened and in the space of one day alone we endured eight. They left us jarred and out of flow. To long-distance cycle requires a rhythm, one you can fall into and suspend yourself inside. That rhythm, that flow, is crucial to good mileage, for it provides a harmony between mind, body and bicycle. Punctures interrupt that rhythm and, with it, they interrupt that harmony. The endless stopping and starting meant that we were unable to find our rhythm and had begun to lose miles; and fixing each puncture under a barrage of freezing rain at the side of a dangerous highway riddled with broken glass was causing us to lose our sanity.

Steve muttered something behind me as I knelt on the ground searching for the latest tear.

'What was that?' I asked, turning around.

'I said we need bloody mountain bikes for these roads.' I could only just make out his voice above the roar of the traffic. He was speaking softly and staring down at the ground. Rather than displaying the risible anger I expected of him at this point, he instead appeared as deflated as my tyre.

'Let's stop at the next service station,' I said. 'We could do with a break.'

Steve did not reply, but nodded slowly. He avoided my eyes and, once I had fixed the tyre, he followed me towards the next service station. This in itself was unusual. Steve always liked to take the lead.

A few miles later, a service station appeared, with a McDonald's at its rear. We ordered food and took it to a free booth.

'Another McDonald's, so nutritious,' I said. Steve did not reply, but picked sullenly at his fries. I tried again. 'It's better than the local meals we've been having, though – all those boiled meats, all that mince and mashed potatoes. That's something that I never thought I'd say – that I'd *rather* have a McDonald's!'

Steve remained silent, and it was beginning to unnerve me. I hated it when we argued, but at least there was communication in that. This overbearing silence was awful. I needed to confront it head on.

'Is it the punctures that are getting to you?' I asked.

Steve sighed, and finally began to speak. His voice was low, flat, devoid of any emotion. 'The punctures, the rain, the road, the lorries, the glass, the food, the cold, all of it. I hate it. I hate this. It's too much. I'm sick of it.'

'Things will be better once we get to Moscow,' I ventured.

'Why? How? Moscow's not even halfway through Russia. We've got days of this kind of riding left, *weeks* maybe. And what do we have to look forward to once it's over? Dagestan. *Dagestan*! Where it'll be just as bad only there will be people trying to kill us, too. What's the point, mate?

Honestly, what's the point in all this? Some stupid record? If this is what it takes to get it, I don't want it any more.'

I didn't know what to say and let his words hang in the air between us as the atmosphere grew increasingly uncomfortable.

'This isn't just a bad mood, Reza,' Steve said. 'I've been thinking about this for days now. I'm not sure I'm cut out for this. I think I might have to go home. You'll be all right without me, you don't really need me. I'm just bringing you down. I think it'll be better for both of us if I just give up.'

'You're wrong, I *do* need you.' I was not just trying to make him feel better. I was speaking the truth. 'We've planned all this together, as a team. We've organised it all, right down to how we pack and share our kit, as a team. If you want to give up, that's on you, but don't think you'll be doing me a favour. Quite the opposite.'

'But I just don't think I can do it any more.' He took a sip from his drink and even that action seemed half-hearted. I could see that he wasn't being melodramatic. The journey was crushing him, forcing him to question his capacity to continue and endure. I recognised that feeling; indeed, I knew it intimately. I had felt it myself in the Sahara Desert and, before that, on the Annapurna circuit. When it came, it felt insurmountable and it made continuation appear impossible. But it wasn't impossible. All you had to do was push through it, for on the other side lay renewed hope. I understood that getting Steve out of his self-doubt would require me to step up, to take charge and lead him through it and towards that hope.

'It's the punctures,' I said with conviction. 'All that other stuff – the rain, the food, the roads – you can cope with all that easily. Trust me. But these punctures are killing us. That's why you're feeling like this. So I'm going to sort this out in Moscow. I'm going to get us some better tyres more suited to these roads. Once we get back to uninterrupted riding again, you'll feel much better. Trust me. And then, once we leave Moscow and head south, it'll start getting warmer and the roads will start getting quieter. All we need to focus on now is getting to Moscow. Once we've done that, everything will get better.'

Steve looked at me and nodded slowly. 'We've just got to get to Moscow,' he repeated.

'Trust me,' I said.

He did and, although a few more punctures still stood between us and Moscow, we both made it to the great city intact. Ghazal, an old Iranian friend of mine, came to meet us on the outskirts and led us to her home. She and her South African husband Chris had offered to put us up for the night when I told her of our plans, and seeing her once more was a tonic. The matching of nationalities made for a beautiful and relaxed evening, as Farsi and English rang out over the sumptuous spaghetti bolognese dinner. It was all so splendid and heartening that it felt almost decadent: great food and company; soft, snug beds; and even the next day arrived with a blue and cloudless sky.

Over breakfast, I explained to Ghazal our need for new tyres. It took her a matter of seconds to locate exactly the kind of bike shop we required online, and soon we were in her car bumping along Moscow roads towards it. The shop was professional and well-stocked, and we bought brand new Finnish touring tyres, puncture patches and inner tubes. Ghazal drove us back to her apartment where we fitted and tested the tyres. They were perfect. As we rode away from Ghazal and from Moscow, I felt revived and enlivened.

'How are you feeling?' I asked Steve as we coasted towards the highway.

'Much better,' he said. 'These tyres were a great idea. You can feel already how much tougher they are.'

'So are you ready for the rest of Russia?' I asked.

'Absolutely,' he replied.

'And then Dagestan at the end of it.'

I did not phrase it as a question, and maybe that's why he did not reply.

———

When your headspace is clear and your resolve firm, long-distance cycling can engender and then maintain perpetual contentment. One good night with friends in Moscow had restored my factory settings, and I felt almost as if we were setting off from Nordkapp all over again, buoyed up by the same excitement and the same heightened sense of self-worth. Life became automation as we powered down through Russia, and the days blurred as we continued to clock our daily quota, continued to finish and start early, continued to live and feel and cycle well. I had never ridden so far in one journey before, and I began to experience a curious thoughtlessness, something meditative and perhaps even Zen-like, as we wended our way from Tambov to Borisoglebsk, from Mikhaylovka to Volgograd. Hours passed devoid of any kind of inner monologue; emotions dulled and levelled to a neutral baseline; my breathing synchronised with the revolutions of my pedals, rising and falling in accordance with the changing gradients; and even my fingers no longer bothered me. In short, I was filled with peace.

Five days after leaving Moscow, we arrived in Volgograd. I was overjoyed. This was another place I had dreamed of visiting since I was a boy, fascinated by its history of wars and name changes. Known first as Tsaritsyn, it became Stalingrad in 1925, its famous and eponymous battle one of the turning points of World War Two. Entering from the north, we pushed down into the city centre and then followed the curve of the Volga as it led us gently south, Mamayev Kurgan towering majestically above us. How I longed to stop for three, four days, perhaps even a week, to take my time here, to visit the museums and the memorials, to gaze out over the river with a cold vodka in hand, to put all I'd read about the city into a tangible perspective. But, as ever, the record dictated we keep moving and I had no choice but to adhere to it.

The Republic of Kalmykia, the only majority-Buddhist region in Europe, was close. Steve had grown quiet again over the past few days and when I asked him if he was as excited about Kalmykia as I was, he replied that he was not. He had, he revealed, been cycling towards it with an ever-mounting dread. For Kalmykia bordered Dagestan. And Dagestan had occupied his thoughts for some time now, heightened especially when we received an email from Andy at Base Camp informing us that the two brothers implicated in the Boston Marathon bombing just a few months earlier had lived for some time in Dagestan.

We reached the Kalmykian border after dark and were stopped by the local police. Unable to speak English, they signalled for us to hand over our documents. Once they had checked them through, they did not give them back, but went inside their office to make a telephone call. Before long, an interpreter appeared at the border, her eyes bleary as if she had just got out of bed. The larger of the two officers asked her a question and nodded his head at us.

'We would like to know where you are going,' she translated.

'First, Kalmykia,' Steve replied, 'and then we're going down through to Dagestan and to Azerbaijan to Iran.'

The interpreter turned to translate his words to the officer, who stood back with his arms folded across his portentous belly, and we listened as they both repeated back the place-names Steve had mentioned.

'Dagestan?' the officer said again.

'You say you are going to Dagestan after Kalmykia?' she asked Steve.

'That's right.'

At this, the officer burst into a long and heated rant. The oft-repeated word 'Dagestan' was the only I could understand, though it was difficult to misinterpret the finger he slowly drew across his own neck.

'What's he saying?' Steve asked impatiently.

'He is saying you must not go to Dagestan. It will be very dangerous for you. We strongly advise that you do not go.'

'Why?' I asked.

When my question was translated for the officer, he grew even louder, even more animated.

'People in Dagestan are violent barbarians,' the interpreter finally translated once his impassioned speech had come to a close. 'And if you go, they will kill you.'

We made it to Sadovoye and found a guesthouse in which to spend the night. Steve had not spoken to me since leaving the border. It was clear he had much on his mind and I wanted to give him the time to process it.

'We shouldn't be doing this,' he finally said as we perched opposite each other on the beds in our room. 'We should reconsider. It's too dangerous.'

'But the record—'

'Fuck the record. It's not worth it. If it's go on and risk it or it's expedition over, for me it's expedition over. I'm not going to be stupid about it.'

'Think about it rationally, though,' I said. 'People just don't stand on the side of the road, waiting for two strangers to come.'

'Some people are militant – they *are* waiting, they *are* doing stuff, they *are* causing trouble, they *are* walking into restaurants with bombs. That's what happened in Dagestan a couple of months ago. There are fucking bombings, mate – there are indiscriminate bombings. We could just be sitting in a cafe at the wrong place having lunch. It just takes one incident, that's it.'

'And how likely is it that that one incident is going to happen to us? We'll only be there for four days.'

'In any other country, sure, I'd say the chances are low. But in Dagestan, there are incidents every single day. Bombings, drive-by shootings, kidnappings, just constant violence and chaos. We'd be stupid to go there. Actually, no, we'd be suicidal.'

The following day, as we cycled to Elista, the capital of Kalmykia, Steve trailed listlessly behind me, pedalling slowly, his mind elsewhere. I thought of our journey between St Petersburg and Moscow, of how he had nearly lost it then and how I had had to motivate him into continuing. I wondered if this might happen again as we cycled through Dagestan and Iran and Egypt and the Sahara and all the wild places below. I did not like the idea.

Elista was warm, pretty and completely anomalous. I had seen cities before which blended both East and West, but there was something oddly specific about Elista with its temples and tower blocks, its *stupas* and statues. This was not so much a place where all-East met all-West, but rather a place where Buddhism met socialism, where Siddhartha met Stalin.

We found a guesthouse and settled into it. I pulled the logbook from my bag and was about to begin noting down the day's events when Steve announced: 'I'm not going to Dagestan.'

I put the book down and looked over at him.

'And,' he continued, 'I don't think you should, either.'

'So that's it, then?' I sighed. 'You're giving it all up because of some horror stories we've been told?'

'I'm not going to argue about this, I've made up my mind,' he said. 'But I'm not giving up the whole journey. Just Dagestan. I can meet you in Azerbaijan.'

'That'll disqualify you from the record.'

'I know.'

'I'm not going to lie to GWR on your behalf. I'm not going to pretend that you came to Dagestan with me.'

'I know. I wouldn't want you to.'

There was a long silence.

'I can't believe you're doing this,' I finally said. 'Dagestan is tiny, we'll be there for less than a week. Never mind all the time it took us to cycle here, what about all the time we spent planning and preparing for this? You're just going to throw all that away?'

'My safety is more important to me than any of that,' Steve replied slowly. 'Yours is as well, you know. Don't go to Dagestan. Please. I'm worried about what's going to happen to you. You heard what they told us at the border. You've heard everything we've been told all the way here. It's too dangerous.'

Perhaps he saw in my eyes the same obstinacy I saw in his, for that was the last time he tried to talk me out of continuing on to Dagestan alone. Our communication soon diminished altogether, and we set about splitting our equipment in silence. The whole structure of our journey was organised around two people carrying two sets of bags rather than one person carrying one set. We did not each bear our own belongings but shared everything between us, so that while I carried the tent Steve took an equal measure of food, and while he carried the toolbag I loaded up on extra water. As I tried to pick out only what I needed, I soon realised I did not have enough room. Steve looked guilty and shameful, but I did not try to comfort him. I could understand his reasons for skipping Dagestan – it was a matter of his life and I did not want to be responsible if something happened to him; I could only be responsible for my own decisions – and, although I sympathised with him, I still felt betrayed. When we went to bed that night, the air was thick with animosity.

The next day, he organised transport back to Volgograd. From there, he hoped to catch a train down to Azerbaijan and meet me in its capital, Baku. I could not believe how quickly he had organised it all and when it came time for us to say goodbye, I was not ready. I was suddenly overwhelmed with a tremendous urge to beg him to stay, to not leave me on my own, but I kept it at bay.

'I hope I see you in Azerbaijan,' Steve said, enfolding me in a long hug. 'I really do.'

And then he was gone. And I was back on my bike. Riding towards Dagestan. Alone.

CHAPTER 8

DAGESTAN

Distance remaining: 8,538 miles

Time to record: 78 days

───────────

I was pedalling reluctantly and progressing slowly. Four or five times I stopped on the side of the road to check my panniers and the air pressure of my tyres. They were always fine. I knew exactly what I was doing: stalling, procrastinating, like a child concocting suddenly crucial activities out of thin air to avoid the dreaded homework. Anything to keep Dagestan on the far side of the border.

I stopped for breakfast at a small, roadside coffee shop. It was another excuse to delay the inevitable: I had already eaten my first breakfast two hours earlier. The waiter took my order of strong coffee and a pastry, and I noticed that the Kalmyk man on the next table turned his head in my direction.

'Are you English?' he asked.

'Yes,' I lied. There was something suspicious about the man and I felt no inclination to reveal any truths to him.

'And where are you going?'

It was a stock question, one I had answered scores of times already. But my suspicion (or paranoia) was beginning to intensify – *why did he want to know? What was he planning?* – and I decided to continue my false replies. 'Georgia.'

'But you are on the wrong side of the country for Georgia. You must go in the opposite direction.'

'Thank you,' I said. 'I'll do that.' The waiter brought over my coffee and pastry and I tucked into them, hoping the conversation with the man had reached its natural conclusion. But, when I looked up from my plate, beard flecked with beads of coffee and shards of pastry, he was still staring at me, hoping to talk more. With anybody else, I would have delighted in the conversation, but my suspicion kept me quiet.

'And why are you going to Georgia?' he asked.

None of your business! I wanted to scream at him, perhaps flinging the boiling coffee in his face and fleeing from the cafe, pedalling as hard as I could to outrun his co-conspirators who were surely waiting for his signal to take me out.

'Hmmm?' he added, now looking somewhat unnerved himself, for, I realised, I had been staring at him with wide, unblinking eyes for the past 20 seconds while the ludicrous fantasy played itself out in my head. It was time to snap out of it. I was letting Dagestan get the better of me before I'd even reached it.

'I'm on my way to Iran,' I said, the first truth of the conversation.

'Ah, Iran,' he sighed. 'A beautiful, beautiful country. I would visit when I was a boy. And, tell me, will you travel through Azerbaijan or Armenia?'

I cursed myself for my bigoted first impression of this man. There was nothing wrong with him at all, nothing whatsoever to be suspicious of. He was just a friendly and curious middle-aged man, offering a foreign guest the kind welcome of conversation. Perhaps this is how Dagestan would be, I thought. Perhaps all my impressions of it were wrong. Perhaps, once I entered, once I got beneath the surface of things, I would see the region for what it truly was – kind, curious, peaceful, just like this man.

I was interested to unearth his thoughts about Dagestan and, knowing my earlier lie had backed me into a corner, considered how I might secure them. A solution presented itself. 'I'm travelling through Azerbaijan,' I said. 'The shortest route is through Dagestan. I meant to go there originally, but then I heard some things about it and changed my mind.'

There was a pause then, a short and unpleasant pause, and when the man finally spoke again his voice had risen by half an octave. 'You were right not to go to Dagestan. Understand? You were very, very *right*.' An ugly leer began to usurp his countenance. 'All Dagestanis – *all* of them – are aggressive barbarians. My friend was in Dagestan last year. In Makhachkala. On business. And do you know what they did to him? *Do you*?' He pounded his fist on the table with that last word, sending the salt shaker toppling to the floor. 'The bastards attacked him with a knife and cut his ears off. *His ears*. He nearly bled to death, understand?' A trace of spittle flew from his mouth and landed somewhere just below my right eye. 'All Dagestanis are evil, understand? All Dagestanis are killers, understand? All Dagestanis are *bastards*! Understand?' Each rhetorical 'understand' was hacked out in pure anger and the last sent him into such paroxysms of rage that a coughing fit temporarily paralysed him, lending me the opportunity to pay my bill and flee from the cafe, no longer paranoid that he might have friends out here, but paranoid that he himself would chase me down the street with further curses.

And I was likewise paranoid, of course – in fact, more so now than ever – about Dagestan, which lay just 40 miles away.

There was little on or beside the road to distract me from my thoughts: a few pylons, a few more rusting signs, the occasional sputtering Lada – all of it drained of colour by the grey, overbearing sky.

The coffee sloshed about queasily in my stomach, which growled and popped with sharp sparks of pain. A similar turmoil raged in my head. I was angry, frightened, cautious, irritable, dismayed, insecure and reticent all at the same time. All the fear was reserved for Dagestan, but I found myself growing angry with Steve, as if the realisation that he had truly left

Left: My first bike touring experience – I was carrying a kettle and a rucksack (Northern Iran)

Below: Cycling the Sahara Desert in 2011 – my first world record attempt

Bottom: Kids in Agnena village (Madagascar)

Right: Our cabin in Nordkapp – discussing last details with Steve on the day before we set off

Below: Nordkapp sunset

Above: Nordkapp – there were a lot of reindeer hanging around

Left: Steve cycling in Norway

Below left: The beginning of the Arctic Circle

Below right: Drying out our clothes in a sauna in Norway after being soaked every day

Above: Posing with a Russian police car

Right: Me and Lenin (Russia)

Below: With Ivan and Katya and the watermelon in St Petersburg

Top: Our first encounter with Dagestani people

Above left: Puncture drama – we had eight punctures in one day (Russia)

Above right: Russian war memorial

Left: The Republic of Kalmykia – the only Buddhist-majority region in Europe

Above: Dagestani police

Right: In Dagestan I slept in a prayer room, because I was scared

Below: Dagestani ladies (Adabiat is on the far left). They were so kind to me and gave me a bag of food as a present

Top: North of Iran – Gilan Province

Above: Soaking wet in Northern Iran

Left: Persepolis (Iran)

Above: The infamous Naqsh-e Jahan Square (Iran)

Below: Posing with Iranian police

me to tackle Dagestan alone had only just sunk in. As I neared Artezian, the small border town that connected Kalmykia to Dagestan, I prayed I had not left anything crucial behind with him.

Sometimes logistics helped to take my mind off the fear, though they were inspired by it. From border to border, from Kalmykian Artezian to Azerbaijani Samur, was 290 miles. I hoped to do that in three days. I would reveal my itinerary to no one. I would keep my knife within constant easy reach in my front bag. I would stop as little as possible, cycle long into each night, and then camp as far away from any cities, towns or villages – in effect, from any semblance of civilisation – as I could. Solitude would be my mainstay.

One sensation and one sensation alone kept me from turning around and pedalling furiously back to Elista and Steve. It was the smell of the sea – specifically, the Caspian Sea – which lay just a few miles away. I could not yet see it, my first sight of it would arrive in Dagestan, but its very proximity evoked much-needed thrills of delight that helped to counteract the incessant worries. The smell of the Caspian: that was the smell of my childhood; my companion on so many bike rides of my youth. I latched on to the smell like a sniffer dog, changed up a gear, and pushed on to the border, grimly determined.

At Artezian, the surging machinations of my stomach had become excruciating, and I elected to find a toilet before crossing into Dagestan, a place where I did not relish the idea of, quite literally, getting caught with my pants down. The local petrol station was the only likely venue, and so I locked my bike up and began my circumambulation of the building, searching out its facilities. When I found them, I opened the door to the single squatter. It was a vile scene. A pool of thick, miry liquid bubbled up from the hole in the floor to cover the tiles in an inch of syrupy gore. The squatter itself was almost entirely submerged and, as I opened the door, the smell that assaulted me – followed closely by a battalion of flies – was so nauseating that I retreated on instinct alone, back-stepping so quickly I almost tripped over myself.

There was no question that I could not relieve my bowels in that dungeon, though there was also no question that my bowels had to be relieved somewhere soon. I walked behind the petrol station, where a large fenced-off enclosure led to an open field of scrub. Jogging out into the field until I was far enough from the road to avoid detection, I rolled my shorts down and squatted above the dusty earth with an exultant sigh.

Looking back on it now, I cannot quite recall if I heard the howls or the footfall first. Whichever it was, it alerted me enough to swing my head around and look behind to see, speeding across the field towards me, a 12-strong pack of wild dogs. They were still some distance away from me, but close enough for me to see their bared teeth and raised tails as they snapped and howled and pounded forward.

The sudden onslaught of terror worked liked a charm on my insides, which set about finishing their business in less than a second so that I could pull my shorts up and sprint back to the petrol station. As I pelted forward, it became clear that the dogs would reach me before I reached the petrol station and so, as I neared the fenced-off enclosure behind it, I increased my strides and sprung into an unwieldy vault that carried me sailing over the wooden fence to land in a crumpled heap among a dozen perplexed chickens. One waddled over, looked me calmly in the eye and began to peck at my knee.

I brushed it aside, amazed that the dogs could growl so loud. Though they were on the other side of the fence, it sounded almost as if they were in the enclosure with me, and when their growls grew louder still as I began to pull myself to my feet, I wondered if they could somehow see me. The ferocious barking set me straight. It did not come from behind the fence, it came from behind *me*, and as I turned around, there, standing at waist height, were three snarling, slavering guard dogs, as unimpressed by my obliviousness as they were by my treatment of their chickens. I pushed my back up to the fence: the 12 dogs behind it audibly frustrated; the three dogs before me visibly galled. I wondered which would take the first lunge and considered offering whichever it would be the sacrifice of my fingers, as useless as they had become.

Rescue came in the form of a 12-year-old girl: a diminutive and scrawny little thing who seemed to be all hair and eyes. She appeared from the door that connected the enclosure to the petrol station, swinging her arms above her head and bellowing at the guard dogs with such a strident roar that they, as surprised as me, immediately supplanted their growls for compliant whimpers. Then, squaring her little shoulders and straightening her little back, she marched across the enclosure, dogs sniffing and licking at her bare ankles, and took my hand in hers, guiding me out of the enclosure, through the petrol station and back to my bicycle. Then she clapped her hands, chuckled mightily and began to chase a butterfly across the forecourt.

I considered asking her to join me all the way through Dagestan. I figured I could do with her protection.

———————

The Dagestan border lay on the far side of Artezian, though it was difficult to tell exactly where. There were no border offices or guards to be seen, just the road and then emptiness, an emptiness that was to characterise much of northern Dagestan. Here and there graves peppered the roadside, something I had observed throughout Russia, though these were marked not with crosses but with green-painted crescents.

The first major settlement I had to pass through in Dagestan was Koktyubey. I would have preferred to have continued cycling, but the hour was growing late and I needed to stock up on food and water so that I could spend the night out in the wilderness, far away from any people and the potential threat they posed. With this in mind, I chose to pull into the petrol station on the outskirts so that I would not have to stop in the midst of the town itself.

'*Salaam alaikum,*' the attendant muttered from beneath her hijab as I entered.

'*Alaikum salaam,*' I replied, closing the door behind me.

I was the only customer, and was momentarily taken aback by how well-lit and well-stocked the garage was. The bread was fresh, the fridges were brimming with soft drinks and the variety of snacks on the shelves re-ignited my appetite with a vengeance, reminding me that all I had eaten today had been summarily discharged in flight from a pack of hounds. Choosing crisps, cakes, bread and bottles of water with care, I suddenly thought of Steve. He would have loved this petrol station. He loved *all* petrol stations and I could almost hear him proclaim: 'You can go to the bathroom, you can eat, you can drink, you can buy supplies. It's a one-stop shop!' I was filled with an overwhelming urge to speak to him. Was he still in Volgograd? Had he managed to secure a train to Baku? Was he cycling every day, or spending his time binge-eating and watching movies? It was with some sadness that I realised I had no means of contacting him. I hoped he was doing well. I missed him.

On the other side of Koktyubey, I was stopped by the police. Five of them stood by the side of the road, and as they waved their arms for me to halt, I noticed the thick bulletproof vests tied about their waists and at least two visible guns per officer.

'Passport,' one of them demanded. I retrieved it from my bag and held it out to him. He took it, examined each separate page in turn, looked at my photograph, looked at me, looked at my photograph again and then looked at me again, and then repeated the whole routine once more before passing it to his nearest colleague, who did exactly the same, and then passed it to the next, and so on until all five of them had undertaken the wearisome exercise. Finally, the passport was handed back to me.

'Okay?' I asked.

'No,' replied the same officer who had asked for my passport. 'Off bike.' He gestured for me to step a few paces from the road with him and then proceeded to search me with a slow and invasive thoroughness. The other four officers focused their attention on my bike, opening my panniers and bags, dipping their hands in and pulling out my tracker, GPS, camera and phone, then passing them between themselves and inspecting them with the tenacity of a bomb-disposal team. One was paying particular attention to my camera, pressing buttons and tapping the screen. I was glad he could not work out how to turn it on, for if he could he may have seen the footage I had taken of Dagestan and confiscated it.

Finally satisfied, they returned my goods, and me, to my bike. 'Where are you going?' the first officer asked.

'Azerbaijan.'

This seemed to cause some merriment among them: a few sniggers and smirks. 'Azerbaijan? Tonight?'

'No,' I said, deciding not to explain where I was going tonight, partly because I did not exactly know myself.

'You stop now. Dark.' He pointed at the police station. 'Stay with us.'

'No, thank you,' I said. 'I have to go.'

'No. No go. Stay. Sleep here.'

'I can't.'

'It dark.'

'I'll be fine.'

The officer sighed, exasperated by my stubbornness. 'Okay,' he said. 'Maybe we find you later.'

Whether it was a threat, a warning or a mistranslation, I did not want to ask, and pedalled away from them as briskly as I could.

The officer was right about one thing: it had grown dark. There was little traffic on the road, and this made me feel all the more conspicuous. The most prominent noise was the sound of my cleats rattling over my pedals, caused by my shaking legs. The land was wide and flat, and black thoughts began to worm their way into my consciousness. Surely I could be seen, a moving pinprick of light, from miles around. How easy it would be for someone to track me in their car, headlights off, perhaps even those police officers. *Maybe we find you later*. And if I was taken or murdered in cold blood in the middle of the road in the middle of the night, who would ever know? I would simply vanish. Forever. I could see the headlines. *Traveller disappears, family fears. Adventurer missing in Dagestan, GWR unconcerned.*

At least I was moving. Camping was out of the question. Pitching my tent anywhere here would have left me exposed and insecure, and I did not dare stop and attempt it. By 11 p.m., I could feel the onset of exhaustion, that familiar, sinking malaise, which did not start in one single place but burgeoned slowly in every limb and every organ with perfect synchronicity. A town was nearby, a small settlement called Kizlyar, and as I approached I paid heed to the roadside cafes on the outskirts, stopping at the one with the least trucks parked outside.

Putting long trousers on over my Lycra shorts, I entered. I was glad I had elected to don extra clothing since, for the first time on this journey, I noticed that the ladies behind the counter had their heads covered. I was unmistakeably in the Muslim world, where modesty was key. The ladies were quiet but polite, and after a meal composed of six parts rice and one part fried fish, I asked them if there was anywhere nearby where I could sleep. One of the ladies motioned for me to follow her outdoors, where she pointed at the small building beside the cafe.

'I can sleep in there?' I asked her.

She nodded.

'Is it a hotel?'

She shook her head and then performed a brief mime indicating that it was a place to pray.

'A mosque?' I asked. '*Masjid?*'

She smiled and nodded, then opened the door for me and pointed inside, nodding all the time. I stepped in, allowing my eyes to grow accustomed to the gloom. The mosque was a single room divided in two by a sheet of curtain: one side for men and one side for women. Three men were already asleep in the male half, sprawled on their backs atop the hard carpeted floor. Sequestering the corner opposite them, I unfurled my sleeping bag and crawled inside with my knife clutched in my right hand. And then I closed my eyes.

The scant sleep that came that night was shallow and interrupted. Some people came in to bed down alongside me and my three neighbours, but most were drivers coming in to pray, wash their hands and faces, and leave again.

All, I knew without opening my eyes, spent a minute or two hovering over me, studying my face and my pannier bags. I did not need to see them. The approaching footsteps followed by the soft grunts of breath were enough to identify each new curious onlooker. I gripped the knife tighter and kept my eyes closed.

I had finally managed to drift off for a full hour when I was awoken by the feeling of a large hand curling around my ankle and shaking me roughly. I opened my eyes. A filthy man in torn pyjamas with bloodshot eyes and rotting teeth stared down at me. He began to hiss something in Arabic and waved his hand wildly, pointing first at me and then at the door. It was clear he wanted me to leave.

'Okay,' I muttered, pulling myself to my feet. 'I'll go.'

He hissed the same words again, and then turned and marched outside. I looked about me. The three men I had seen when I entered had all left. Now the only other person in the mosque was a teenage boy, fast asleep and tucked up inside his Manchester United jersey. I packed my gear and stumbled outside into the bright morning. The filthy man was waiting for me. He looked infuriated.

'*Haram!*' he squealed, pointing at my bare legs, for I had removed my long trousers during the night. '*Haram! Forbidden!*'

Feeling ashamed at my show of disrespect, I sheepishly dug the trousers out of my bag and put them back on. This did not seem to assuage the man, for he moved between me and the mosque's doorway and then stood with feet firmly planted and arms crossed, staring at me with undisguised hostility until I climbed back on to my bike and cycled away.

Kizlyar marked the end of northern Dagestan and, below it, following the road that began to arc out away from the Chechnyan border towards the Caspian coastline, I entered the heart of Dagestan. Changes in landscape and demography were not immediate – they rarely are when seen from the saddle – but the transformations, as slow as they were, came on so assuredly that by noon I felt like I was in another country. Gone were the arid wastelands of Kalmykia: Dagestan was green, fertile and washed with stout trees and untamed bushes, its roadside stalls bursting with a rainbow of succulent fruits. The people, too, were recognisably different, darker of skin and hair, as if this were not the last frontier of Russia but the first of the Middle East. In fact, I thought, they looked a little like me.

Perhaps they disagreed, for in every village and town through which I passed, people from the youngest children to the oldest seniors would never fail to point at me as I cycled along. Those outstretched fingers were neither accusatory nor mocking, they did not even seem to be especially curious, but were instead more a simple knee-jerk reaction to the sight of something unusual, but only marginally so, as one might point out a flock of birds or smoke in the distance or a flag in a window. Maybe they were not even pointing at me but at my bike – I had seen no other bicycles as yet in Dagestan – and it may well have been this rather than myself that was the oddity in these hinterlands.

A headwind rose, impeding my progress, but the sun was out and I was grateful for its warmth. I was sick of rain and sick of the cloying sensation of riding in perpetually wet clothes, so the cloudless sky gave me an extra boost. It also offered, when it came, a supreme first view of the Caspian, its hazy azure reflected down and up and then back down again, a shade I remembered so well from childhood. Back then, the words 'holiday' and 'Caspian' were synonymous, and I returned to the sea each season with the euphoric glee of a soldier back from war and in his lover's arms once more. I would become amphibious, a frog-boy who kicked and splashed with regard for nothing save the setting sun, and when that came I would sulk, for it meant a return to the land. As the road skirted the coast, I felt an irresistible urge to stop, to strip and to swim. But Dagestan kept me moving. I feared the theft of my belongings should I leave them on the shoreline while I plunged; I feared far worse should I not make it beyond Makhachkala when night fell.

And so I pushed on, keeping the Caspian firmly to my left rather than all around me. A swim would have been sensational, but it would also have slowed me, and the police were already doing a fine enough job of that. It was impossible to ride 20 miles without the obligatory stops and searches from the roadside officers who waited for me with an implacable resolve, as if their comrades had called ahead and told them I was on my way, which they may well have. The routine never varied: each had to check every page of my passport; each had to empty my panniers and bags and analyse my electronics; each had to frisk me with the same systematic grapples and pokes. It was invariably an ordeal, but I somehow grew used to it, and between each I would assess the remaining hours of daylight and the remaining miles I hoped to cover, taking into account the remaining officers I would surely encounter on the way. I let them revel in their officiousness, for there was no use in protesting, and they rarely took more than 20 minutes before waving me on with a terse and dissatisfied grimace. Only once did I complain, when one particularly studious officer retrieved my iPod from my pocket and set about listening to the first bar of each song in turn. What he was hoping to hear I could barely imagine – spoken instructions on how to build a bomb vest, perhaps – and it took all my will, after 10 minutes of his relentless skipping and shuffling, not to rip the iPod from his hands and beat him around the face with it. Instead, I helped him navigate to the harshest Metallica track I could think of, turned the volume up to full and then let it resound through the headphones he had tucked into his ears. He handed it back to me immediately.

As the afternoon turned to early evening, and with Makhachkala still miles away, the rising headwind and my rising hunger forced me to stop at a cafe for a late lunch. The cafe was run by four women. They wore no hijabs and were instead characterised by flirtatious smiles and roving eyes. I was guided and petted towards a large square table where, after bringing out a delicious mound of fried chicken and chips, they sat down themselves and watched me while I devoured it all.

'Where are you from?' one asked me as I sucked the grease from my fingers. She was in her late 40s, with thick glossy hair and piercing eyes.

'I'm from Iran,' I said, concealing an unseemly chicken-laced belch beneath my palm.

'Iran? *Farsi hasti?*' she asked in Farsi. *Iran? Are you Farsi?* Elbows on the table and hands in her hair, she made it clear that she knew Farsi because her ex – her *ex* – husband was from Tajikistan.

'I like your accent,' I said in our shared language. 'It's not like Iranian Farsi. It's sweeter. Like you're reading from a book.'

This caused a bout of coquettish laughter which, when she translated my words to her friends, ricocheted around the cafe. 'I like that,' she said. 'I sound to you like I'm reading from a book. That's appropriate. My name is Adabiat. Do you know this word?'

'I do,' I replied. *Adabiat* was Farsi for literature.

Again, she translated. Again, her friends burst into peals of mirth, goading her on with nods and nudged elbows. She turned back to me. 'So,' she said, 'do you have a wife?'

'I'm single.'

'Good,' she replied. More laughter from her friends, and one of them took Adabiat's hand, mimed placing a ring on the fourth finger and then pointed at me.

A gulp of tea was already halfway down my throat when I understood the nature of the gesture, and it was impossible to supress a choke of surprise, which elicited yet another fresh explosion of laughter from the ladies. Adabiat looked at each of them with a cautioning disdain and then turned her gaze back to me.

'I am sorry,' she said. 'But do you have a ring? I *would* like one.'

'Sorry, I don't,' I spluttered out between hiccups, incredulous at my second marriage proposal of the week and, it would be remiss to neglect, rather flattered, too.

'I suppose you want to leave now,' she sighed. 'They always do.' There was a mischievous glint in her eye. A teasing sparkle.

'I do have to leave,' I said. 'But you can come with me. There's plenty of room on the back of my bike.'

She translated again. Her friends laughed once more, and this time she did, too.

After I finished my meal, despite my protestations, they refused to accept any money from me. I insisted to my potential fiancée that I could and should pay, but she was having none of it. Instead, I was handed a plastic bag filled with fresh tomatoes and cucumbers: a present to see me on my way to Azerbaijan. I asked if I might take a photograph of them and, when they hurried from the cafe after Adabiat's translation, I feared I had offended them. Minutes later, they returned, clad in what I presumed were their finest, most colourful clothes, their headscarves exquisite, the angles of their cheeks highlighted with subtle makeup. They were beautiful.

As I left, each of them wished me good luck and then returned to the shadows of the cafe. I was left alone with Adabiat, who slipped a thin piece of paper into my hands. 'My phone number,' she whispered. 'Call me when you finish your adventure.'

I cycled to Makhachkala, pleasantly surprised by their kindness, high on life. Perhaps, I thought as the wheels revolved beneath me, Dagestan wasn't so bad, after all.

And, I can tell you now, it wasn't.

Makhachkala was far from the anarchic dystopia I had imagined. As I breached its limits, there were no bomb craters or bullet-ridden walls or collapsing tenement blocks, no hobbling amputees or famished children with distended bellies, no guns or grenades, no impassioned screeches of extremists or fundamentalists anywhere. Instead, the cafes and restaurants that lined the roadside were lit in twinkling neon and thumped with the bass lines of loud disco rhythms; every tree seemed to be wrapped in fairy lights, which flashed in accordance with the music; and the smell of meats roasting on barbecues only just outweighed the laughter, shouts and catcalls of the myriad locals who thronged the streets. This was not the Dagestan of my nightmares; it was the Ibiza of my dreams.

I pulled my camera out and switched it on, determined to document my revelation. This was precisely the reason I had wanted to film this journey. My preconceptions of Dagestan had scattered and I wished to share that with the world, to show them that, despite what the media insisted, this region may well have been dangerous but it was not characterised by it. There were young people everywhere on these Makhachkala streets, and rather than guns and knives and bombs they carried food, bottles of juice and loud radios; rather than army fatigues, they wore ironed shirts or long dresses; rather than blood, joy poured from them.

The camera must have loaned me an air of importance, for girls appeared from doorways and corners, wrapped their arms around my neck and flashed grins and pouts at the lens. They were followed with sure inevitability by the boys, as if the girls had broken down an invisible barrier that their male counterparts could now happily stream across, who came at me without hostility but with playful curiosity. 'What's up, man?' was the standard catchphrase, as unchanging from person to person as the handshakes were diverse and variegated, and I received more invitations to meals than ever before, in any country.

The pure, untarnished joy that bounced around the streets of Makhachkala was infectious, and I left it feeling light-headed and relieved. The weight of all that fear I had harboured over Dagestan had broken and dissolved, leaving behind in its place a warm emptiness, like a headache finally cured. I was glad to be in Dagestan.

That night, in a motel not far out from Makhachkala, I slept for eight wondrous and uninterrupted hours, aided by the fact that my phone was switched off. In the morning, I turned it back on to be presented with a series of text messages. *Reza, where are you? Reza, we're worried. Reza, are you okay?* Resolving to answer them all after breakfast, I then walked over to the cafe on the other side of the road and promptly forgot.

The lady who worked there spoke no English, but she fussed about me with maternal indulgence, replacing the stale slices of bread on my table with a warm and fresh loaf, topping up my cup of tea at regular intervals and deluging me with more food than I could possibly eat. When she seemed content that I was sufficiently fed and watered, she began to point at my camera on the table and asked me something I could not decipher.

'Would you like me to take your picture?' I asked.

'No,' said the man sat three tables away from me, who was munching his way through a mound of doughnuts. '*She* would like to take *your* picture.'

'Of course!' I nodded, and she clapped her hands with enthusiasm, hurrying back to her kitchen and reappearing moments later with a disposable film camera. Carefully winding the film forward, she raised the camera to her eye and then held it there for 15 seconds while I awkwardly maintained a smile, and then finally the loud click revealed that the deed was done. Placing the camera into her apron, she laid one hand on my shoulder and the other on top of my head, laughed once and then skipped off to the door to greet the latest customer to enter.

'Are you famous?' the doughnut-muncher asked.

'Absolutely not,' I said.

'You will be,' he replied. 'You will be in here anyway. She will put that photograph up on the wall so everyone can see it.'

'I'm flattered,' I said.

'You should be. I've been coming here for eight years, and she's not taken my photo once!' He rose from the table and came to sit at mine, making sure to bring his remaining seven doughnuts with him. 'My name is Adnan,' he said.

'Reza,' I replied, shaking his proffered hand.

'And what do you think of Dagestan, Reza?'

'I love it,' I grinned.

This pleased him immeasurably. 'Wonderful!' he cried. 'It *is* wonderful. But people only know that when they come here. Otherwise they think it is a terrible place.'

'That's true. The only things you ever hear about Dagestan in the news are negative. I dreaded coming here, but I'm so glad I did.'

'Things are not nearly as bad here as they were a decade ago. Militant and jihadist attacks are still a part of life, but they are usually against the police or against government targets. Civilians are much safer now than they were before.'

'That still sounds pretty frightening to me,' I said. 'Whether or not jihadist attacks are aimed at the police and the government, I don't think I would like to live in a country where they are regular.'

'Of course, it is not a perfect situation,' he countered. 'But what I am saying is that it is better than it was before. And, although I do not agree with the people who make the attacks, I understand them.' He went on to explain the deep historical issues embedded in Dagestan, of a people struggling to retain an identity distinct from Russia and of Moscow's refusal to address these issues, instead implementing harsh measures that only pushed Dagestani radicals even further from allegiance. I could have sat and talked with Adnan for hours, whiling away the morning over bottomless tea and fascinating conversation. But, as always, I had the record to consider, so with a heavy reluctance I bade him farewell and walked to the counter to pay for my breakfast.

The lady watched me produce my wallet, shook her head, giggled and pointed at Adnan. I turned to him in confusion.

'Ah yes,' he said. 'I forgot to mention. I have already paid for your meal.'

'Adnan,' I remonstrated. 'It's incredibly kind of you. Really it is. But I can't accept such generosity. You've only just met me. Please, I must insist that I pay.'

'Sorry, it's too late,' he laughed. 'We may have only just met, but you are my guest. You are the first foreigner I have seen in many years and I am grateful that you have come to visit Dagestan. Perhaps, if you would like to return the favour, you can do one thing for me.'

'Of course,' I said. 'I'd be happy to.'

'You told me you love Dagestan. Now tell others.'

'I will,' I replied. And I did.

CHAPTER 9

QUARTER OF THE WAY
AROUND THE WORLD

Distance remaining: 8,205 miles

Time to record: 75 days

A snaking and stationary queue of motorists, who clambered from their vehicles to squeeze my tyres and spin my pedals to validate the bike's quality as I passed, led to an immense iron gate: a fittingly symbolic entrance and exit point for the great state of Russia. Two-hundred metres of no man's land separated it from Azerbaijan and, as my passport was stamped at the exit and I mounted my bike, ready and excited to cycle into the next country, I was stopped by a large hand on my shoulder. It was a border guard.

'No cycling allowed,' he intoned.

'How am I supposed to get across?' I asked.

'Take the bus.' He pointed at a wheezing, decrepit minivan which, for a fee, shuttled pedestrians back and forth between the two border posts.

'That's ridiculous,' I said. 'The border is right there. I can see it. It'd be quicker for me to cycle than to get on that bus and wait for it to fill up with passengers before it even leaves. It'd be quicker for me to walk!'

'No walking allowed.'

'No, that's not what I meant. I don't want to walk. I want to cycle.'

'No cycling allowed.'

'Look at that!' I cried, pointing at a motorbike as it sailed past on its way to Azerbaijan. 'He's going across! Why can't I?'

'Motorcycling is allowed.'

'I'm not going on the bus,' I affirmed, resolving to stand my ground.

'Okay.' He shrugged and turned to wave through a Lada which edged forwards.

Taking this as an implied blind eye, I placed my feet back on the pedals and was ready to push down when I felt the same large hand on my shoulder.

'No cycling allowed.'

'Please,' I said, 'I haven't got time to wait for that bus. I need to get to Azerbaijan as quickly as I can. It's late and I need to find somewhere to stay for the night.'

He sighed for a long time, expressing within it every ounce of his disdain for me, and then stopped the van that had just appeared, ordering the driver to step out and open the back doors. 'He will take you,' he said to me. 'Now get in the back and leave me alone.'

While the Azerbaijani customs and border control lacked the baffling bureaucracy of the Russian side, it made up for it with boundless mayhem. There were no queues, merely a scrum of men and women who screamed, pushed, shoved and fought with each other, viciously jostling for position around the single turnstile that would lead us all out and away from this chaos forever. Beside me, a stooped and haggard octogenarian lady moaned and wailed, looking as if she might fall to the ground at any moment and be trampled to death. I muscled my way forward to clear some space for her, and she immediately straightened her back and leapt into the space with surprising agility, delivering a sharp elbow to my stomach in the process and kicking two other people aside, before bending over once more and returning to her moans. She was through the turnstile in minutes. I, on the other hand, was not. I had left Russia at 7 p.m.; I did not enter Azerbaijan until 11 p.m.

The Azerbaijani border town of Samur was a dank and hostile hole filled with touts and hawkers trying to sell me local currency or drag me into their restaurants and hotels. With no wish to remain, I launched myself into the darkness of the road ahead, the only light my own. Few other people used the road and the only other life present was the packs of wild dogs who took it in turns to chase me as I rode. I tried to scare them away with my dog whistle, but it had little to no effect and so I resorted to cycling faster.

I managed 30 miles before exhaustion forced me to stop in Quba, and I spent the night in a rough $2 guesthouse, which smelled of rust and rat shit. I awoke irritable and snappish, cursing the border guards for their ineffectual management of a relatively tiny strip of land that had waylaid me so notably, and cursing the owner of this guesthouse who would have been better suited to the role of prison warden. Currents of anger rippled through me, and as I stomped out of the guesthouse I made sure not to utter a word to the receptionist for fear that, if I did, the word might erupt into a slew of splenetic vitriol.

On the way to Baku, I stopped for a bottle of water and checked my phone. There were more messages like those I had received in Dagestan asking where I was and if I was okay. About to answer them, I was distracted by the arrival of Ali and Samir: two mountain bikers riding in the opposite direction, and whom I waved to purely out of the novelty of seeing fellow cyclists. I could not remember the last time I had seen another bicycle, and wondered if it could perhaps even have been as long ago as Norway. Ali and Samir stopped beside me, introduced themselves and invited me to join them for breakfast. Realising all of a sudden how famished I was, I accepted and followed them away from the main road, down a dirt track and then into a leafy garden with an old and charming restaurant as its centrepiece. We ate kebabs: an exquisite breakfast.

'Samir and I are a couple,' Ali said, firmly and with dignity.

'Congratulations,' I replied, finishing one kebab and pouncing directly on to the next.

'Does this bother you?' Ali asked.

'Of course not. Should it?'

Ali laughed and turned to Samir with what seemed like gloating pride. 'See? He doesn't care! I told you!'

'Ali wants us to tell everyone,' Samir confessed to me. 'I disagree.'

'Of course I want to tell everyone,' Ali said. 'I *should* be able to tell everyone.'

'Homosexuality is no longer illegal here in Azerbaijan,' Samir said. 'But many people act like it still is. Being gay has a very strong, very negative stigma here. Things are getting better, but they will take a long time.'

'Samir is right. I hate having to keep our relationship private, but it would be a mistake to tell most people. A big mistake. But when we met you and you spoke to us in English, I knew you were a foreigner and I knew I could tell you. And I enjoyed it! It is a wonderful thing to be able to declare your love to others. You are one of just a few people who know about us.'

'I'm honoured,' I said.

'Even our parents don't know,' Samir continued. 'Only a few of our close friends, and only the gay ones. Keeping our secret is very difficult, although I think Ali finds it harder than me.'

Ali nodded vigorously. 'I do, I hate it, I do. We almost moved to the UK, so that we could live and be openly gay. But we had visa problems.'

'Isn't it a ridiculous thing?' Samir said. 'To move a quarter of the way around the world, just so you can be yourself?'

Our breakfast finished, I thanked Ali and Samir for their company and conversation. It had given me a vital perspective and left me feeling petty at my earlier tantrum. Here I was, a guest in this new country, and a mere 3-hour delay and some excrement-stained carpets had moved me to apoplexy; while Ali and Samir lived under such perpetual fear of, at best, ridicule and, at worst, violence that they had to hide what they should have been celebrating even from their parents. Samir's closing words haunted me – *to move a quarter of the way around the world, just so you can be yourself* – and I understood that I had journeyed a quarter of the way around the world not just to be myself, but to be the best possible version of myself that I could be. And that version was not one that got distracted by resentment or sidetracked by spite. Instead, that version made the most of life and it made the most of this world: this world of which there was still so much to see.

With that in mind, I moved forward and the solipsism of anger fell from me like an old cloak, my consciousness redirecting itself back to my senses as I cycled. The sun beat down ferociously, heating the headwind that blasted the sweat from my forehead. The sky was vast and cerulean and, as the road veered back towards the coast beyond Shabran, the Caspian reappeared to shimmer and sparkle beneath it. There was little between the road and the sea, little save the desiccated fields of a roasted wasteland, here and there a solitary house that leaned into emptiness, but more often piles of rubble and cracked brick, which I imagined would crumble to scree at the slightest tap. Colossal, skeletal arms began to appear along the coastline, bobbing their angry red heads up and down as if drinking from the sea and loathing every fresh taste. They were oil pump jacks and as I progressed further south their numbers swelled until they blotted out the shoreline altogether. Somebody here was growing prodigiously rich.

Perhaps the most noticeable thing about Azerbaijan was its diminutive size. It was the smallest of all the countries I was to cycle through between Nordkapp and Cape Town, and its capital Baku – the halfway point of the Azerbaijani portion of my journey – was almost upon me. The road to Baku began to run parallel to a railway and the occasional train ambled past, so slowly I could look through the windows and discern the expressions on the passengers' faces. I thought of Steve. Perhaps he was on that very train. If he was already in Baku, he would have travelled along this same railway. If not, he would be travelling along it soon – assuming, of course, that he still intended to meet me. I did not know. I had not heard from him since our split in Kalmykia.

I contemplated the possibility that he might have gone home. To my surprise, the notion did not bother me so much. My last few days, alone in Dagestan, had been spectacular, perhaps even the most adventurous part of the journey so far, where I had still succeeded in completing my daily distances and dealing with each problem and obstacle single-handed. Added to that, I had been able to take my camera out and film whatever I wanted for however long I wanted. I had come to despise the look Steve affected when I took the camera out in his presence; the look that was simultaneously condescending, bitter and disapproving; the look that, had it been decoded and transliterated, would have said '*Not again*' or '*Waste of time*' or '*There goes the record*'.

A sudden image of Ali and Samir checked my negativity and suggested I search for an alternative perspective, for the bright side. Perhaps, I thought, I was being unfair. Since he had skipped Dagestan, Steve was no longer eligible for the world record and maybe this would dilute his obsessive drive somewhat. Maybe it would remove that GWR-weighted burden from his back. Maybe he would come to perceive the journey in the same way I now did: not as a record attempt to be endured, but as an adventure to be enjoyed.

I would find out soon. A text message from Francesca informed me that Steve had arrived in Azerbaijan and was waiting for me in Gizildash, less than 30 miles away.

'Mate, we need to get out of here.' Steve held me by the arm and spoke quietly but urgently. 'It's not safe.' I had been there for less than 2 minutes. Gizildash was a small and dusty village devoid of streetlights and cavernously dark. The largest building in the vicinity was the local mosque, and Steve had been sitting outside it when I arrived, nervously picking at his bare feet and avoiding eye contact with the five or six conservatively attired men who lurked about him.

'What's the problem?' I asked.

'It's these guys,' he said, gesturing almost imperceptibly at the nearby men. 'They don't trust me. They think I'm American. I've tried telling them I'm South African, but they don't seem to understand. They keep saying Bush, Bush, George Bush.'

'What are you even doing here anyway?' I said. 'I thought we were meeting in Baku?'

'It was Francesca's idea. She said if I met you here we could bypass Baku and save some time.' He scratched at his head and glanced back over his shoulder. 'I shouldn't have listened to her. I should have just gone to Baku. It's not safe here, not safe at all.'

'Is there a hotel here? It looks pretty small. Where are we supposed to stay?'

Steve laughed at that. 'We're staying here, mate. In a *mosque*! Is that even allowed?'

'Sure, it's allowed if you're invited,' I said. 'I stayed in one in Dagestan. But you can't just turn up.'

'Those two over there invited me,' Steve said, tilting his head at the two gentlemen who stood slightly apart from the rest, and who must have noticed his subtle nod, for they began to approach us. 'They're called Ali and Rashid. They were the ones who kept talking about George Bush.'

As Ali and Rashid reached us I stuck out my hand.

'*Salaam alaikum.*'

'*Alaikum salaam.*'

They looked at me suspiciously and so I tried some Azeri – '*Chokh mamnoon*' ('*Thank you*') – and they brightened instantly with recognition. Through an amalgamation of English, Russian and Azeri words, we managed to establish a common ground upon which we could understand each other. They were convinced that Steve was American, so I told them he was from South Africa.

'Africa?' Rashid said, pointing at Steve. 'He African? He *white*!'

'*South* Africa,' I repeated. 'Nelson Mandela.'

'Oh! Nelson Mandela!' Both Rashid and Ali laughed and took turns shaking Steve's hand with newfound respect.

They invited us inside the mosque for a dinner of bread, cheese, tomato and cucumber.

'I've been getting all these text messages over the past few days,' I said to Steve as we walked towards the mosque. 'People asking me if I'm okay.'

'Didn't you know?' Steve replied. 'While you were crossing Dagestan, Andy disabled the live tracker on the website for your safety. He didn't want anyone to know your exact location.'

'That's a bit of an overreaction. I was fine in Dagestan. In fact, I loved it and felt completely safe. I'm so happy that I decided to cross it.'

'Andy didn't know you were safe. None of us did. We were all genuinely concerned.'

Steve relaxed over the food and, once we were finished and our hosts had left us to pray, he showed me to our accommodation for the night: a small side room just off the main hall. With our Therm-a-Rest laid out on the floor and our bags on either side of it, the room took on a homely air and I sprawled out on my back, tensing and relaxing each of my muscles in turn as Steve soliloquised about his journey from Kalmykia to Azerbaijan.

'… so I had to go all the way back to Volgograd, and I got in touch with Ghazal and Chris and they managed to sort a ticket out for me, but then the guard wouldn't let me on the train at Volgograd unless I bought an extra ticket for my bike, and I had forgotten to bring any food and it turns out that the train didn't have a restaurant car or anything, and it was going to take thirty-five hours to get to Baku, but this guy in my carriage shared some of his food with me, and if he hadn't I reckon I could have starved to death I was so hungry, and dehydrated too, so when we stopped at Makhachkala station, which was only supposed to be for two minutes I was so thirsty that I actually left the train to buy some water, and the guard blew his whistle while I was still buying it so I had to sprint back and only just made it back on the train in time, which was pretty scary because I stuck out like a sore thumb in Makhachkala station and if the train had left without me I would have been in big trouble...'

'I met a couple this morning,' I interrupted him. 'Ali and Samir. They were gay, but they couldn't even tell their parents because they were terrified of what might happen to them if people found out.'

Steve took a few moments to absorb this seemingly incongruous comment, mulling it over before forming a link to his next train of thought which was not quite the one I had hoped for. 'That's the problem with these repressive societies,' he said. 'Look at what's happening in Egypt. It's actually getting worse. I've been keeping up on the news while you've been in Dagestan. The UK has evacuated all of its citizens from Egypt. I'm beginning to wonder if we should keep it on our route, or if we should play it safe and skip it altogether...'

I closed my eyes and let him talk. My time would be better spent sleeping. Steve could debate with himself about the merits of missing Egypt for as long as he liked, but he would never convince me. I had come too far now. Nothing was going to stop me getting that record.

CHAPTER 10

MOTHERLAND

Distance remaining: 8,060 miles
Time to record: 74 days

———————

The road to Iran seemed to be one long flat; the headwind transformed into a tailwind, pushing us onwards; the road, built with oil money, was smooth, making our wheels sing with that particular high-pitched purr that can have a similar effect on the long-distance cyclist as dopamine. Our progress became so exceptional that it felt almost as if Iran was pulling us towards it, as if it exuded a magnetism or gravity, or both, which intensified our speeds and eradicated miles like they were metres. Iran grew closer with every revolution of the pedals and I was ecstatic. I was going home.

'We're nearly there!' I shouted at Steve when the border came into view. 'I can't wait!'

'I know,' Steve called back. 'You've only told me about fifteen times over the past twenty-four hours.'

'It's the only good thing about doing this journey in two legs. If we'd stuck to the original route, we wouldn't have gone to Iran.'

'The only good thing? How about the fact we don't have to go to Syria and cycle through the middle of a civil war? That, to me, is a good thing.'

At the border, I joined the queue for those with Iranian passports while Steve joined the other. His queue was long and moved with a tortuous sluggishness, while mine flowed forward with only the shortest pauses as each of my fellow countrymen zipped through. I turned to Steve, already some way behind me, and gave a smug thumbs up.

When it came to my turn, in no time at all, the guard took my passport, flicked through its pages and then looked up at me. 'Is this your only passport?' he asked in Farsi.

'No,' I admitted. 'I also have another, a British passport.'

'May I see it, please?'

I handed it over to him and, without even opening it, he left his booth and walked into a separate room, clutching both my passports in his hand. Five minutes passed without him returning. I could feel the disapproving stares of those behind me in the queue, and grew suddenly self-conscious about the Lycra shorts and T-shirt I had not bothered to change out of. My bare arms and legs were an emblem of disrespect here, and when I heard muttering behind me – loud enough to hear but quiet enough to remain unintelligible – I presumed that it was rancorous, and presumed that it was directed at me. Beside me, Steve had graduated to the front of his queue and, as he slipped through without incident, he directed his thumbs up at me with flamboyant relish.

A police officer appeared and asked me to follow him. We walked into a small, low-lit room with two chairs and a table and, on top of the table, my two passports. He gestured for me to sit, sat down himself, produced a form that appeared to be composed of at least a dozen pages, and then proceeded to quiz me for the next 45 minutes – firing question after question at me with such rapidity that it left me dizzy, and often repeating the same question at 10 minute intervals in an attempt to catch me out. 'Where were you born? What is your current home address? What was your address before that? When did you leave Iran? Why did you leave Iran? Why do you live in the UK? What is your current home address? Who is your employer? What is his address? When did you leave Iran? Who was your previous employer? What is his address? Who was your employer before that? What is his address? Why do you live in the UK? Where do you live in the UK? Who is your employer? Why are you travelling in Iran? Why are you travelling by bicycle? Where will you stay? What is your current home address?'

When the maddening barrage of inquiries finally came to a close, the police officer seemed satisfied and stamped both my passports. 'Please accept my apologies,' he said. 'This is routine for anyone with a Persian–British dual nationality.'

'You can't trust those Brits,' I joked.

The officer did not smile. 'No, you cannot. Britain has interfered with Iranian affairs far too many times for us to ever trust them again. I would not like to have to live in Britain like you do.'

'I don't *have* to live there,' I replied. 'I like it. I get on all right with them.'

'I can tell that,' he said, his eyes travelling down below my neck. 'I would recommend that, before you leave here, you put some trousers on.'

I looked down at myself. Aside from my bare legs, I was also filthy. Salt deposits had crusted around my shorts, my jersey, which I'd worn without changing for the past few days exuded a potent and offensive smell, and my skin was grubby and unwashed. 'No problem,' I said, finding a pair of trousers in my bag and removing my shoes so that I might put them on. An intense odour, the kind so thick and overwhelming you feel like you could bite into it, spread from my opened shoes to fill the room, and the officer, balking at the smell, informed me that he would give me some privacy and bolted out of the door.

Freshly changed, I made my way out of the office and towards the building's exit. Steve lurked about the doorway.

'I thought you'd be outside getting ready to set off,' I said.

'I took a quick look, then came back in. Thought I'd be better off if you were with me.'

The meaning of his words became clear the moment we stepped outside the building. A throng of hawkers amassed around us, insisting we buy Iranian rials from them. When I replied in Farsi that we did not need any, my evident Iranian heritage gave them pause for a moment or two, but no longer, for they were soon back to demanding we change our dollars or euros or pounds or whatever we had with them, for they would take anything, and they would give a good price, the best price, better than anywhere else in the country, or perhaps we needed a taxi ride to Talesh or Bandar-e Anzali or, better yet, Tehran, and once we were there they knew of the best hotels to stay, very cheap but very luxurious, and they could take us right to the door so that we wouldn't need to worry about a thing, or perhaps we simply needed a helping hand with our bags to the bus, because it was a long distance, far too long to cope without any help. We tried to push our way through, but this only succeeded in making the hawkers clamour with even more vigour, kettling us and pushing their faces close to ours as they shouted their offers and deals with hoarse urgency. Hands began to reach out, taking hold of handlebars or attempting to unzip panniers, not to steal, but to carry them to the nearest bus or taxi so that we would be forced to offer money to get our belongings back.

There seemed to be no way out. I realised with dismay that I would have to part with some money if we were ever going to be allowed on our way, and was about to pull my wallet from my trousers pocket when a booming voice halted me, and many of the hawkers.

'Leave these two alone! They are my guests! Leave them alone!'

A bob of neat, black hair appeared to my left. Two arms materialised below it, extending like monkey tails to wrap themselves around my and Steve's arms, and then we were pulled forward and into the narrow channel that the hair and the arms had somehow cleaved through the crowd. Beyond it, free from the hawkers, the arms finally released us, and we looked up to see exactly whose face it was that existed between them and that bob of hair. The face grinned at us – white teeth; pink gums; black stubble.

It had to be Kamyar.

I had not met Kamyar before. Originally, my friend Arash had agreed to film this portion of the journey, but when he was no longer able to, he had commissioned Kamyar – a local cameraman – to film us. I had little to do with the organisation of it all. I knew not what to expect of Kamyar, and I worried that, should our personalities clash, his constant presence might sour my time in Iran.

As it happened, I liked him instantly and I also liked his wife, Afrooz, who had agreed to drive Kamyar while he filmed Steve and me on this portion of our journey between the border and Shiraz. Both were affable and charming, with huge, infectious smiles that seemed out of proportion to their petite frames. They had recently married and had decided to treat this trip as a kind of working honeymoon. At a small restaurant not far from the border, we bonded quickly over lunch, swapping stories of our shared hometown Tehran, and devouring bowls of *baghali ghatogh* and *mirza ghasemi*, my favourite Iranian vegetable dishes.

By the time we stood up to leave, it occurred to me that the three of us had spoken only in Farsi for the entire meal and had excluded Steve from our rambling conversation.

'Sorry about that,' I said to him. 'I was getting to know them.'

'Don't worry about it,' he replied with a grin. 'I was totally occupied just by watching you. I've never seen anyone talk so much and eat so much at the same time before.'

While Afrooz drove and Kamyar filmed from the window, we cycled into and through north-western Iran. It was pleasant to have company again: the knowledge of a support car close at hand offered comfort, a reprieve from the myriad worries with which a journey can bombard the lonesome traveller. Even Steve did not seem to mind the continual filming.

Yet it was more pleasant simply to be in Iran. This was another watershed, of course. Azerbaijan had been in one way Asian and in another European, it had been both and it had been neither, an antechamber from one distinct continent to another rather than a formal part of either; but this, Iran, was purely and categorically Asian. I had left Europe: of the three continents I needed to cross to secure that record, the first box was now ticked. And, of all the places to enter the second continent, Asia, what better than my mother country, my true homeland: Iran.

Everything around me existed in a sheen of familiarity, and it all seemed so natural, so intimately *conventional*, that it made me giggle. I could read every road sign. I could name the body of water to my left and the range of mountains to my right. The smell of rice that wafted over from the fields beside the road was not exotic but wonderfully domestic. The bank of mist that descended from the mountains like white velvet could have been the same bank of mist that descended from the mountains like white velvet when I was a child. Even the portentous rain that began to sluice over us was somehow recognisable, as if Iran had its own unique style of rainfall, and so too were the reckless cars that screeched around us and aquaplaned down the dual carriageway. I knew this land, knew it elementally, and I cherished every inch of it.

Best of all, I knew the road. It was upon this very road that my first adventures – as a child, as an adolescent and as a young man – had taken place. Long before Steve and I set off from Norway, long before Madagascar even, I had cycled this road with my father, with my friends and with no one but myself. I recalled one instance in particular, cycling this road north from Rasht to the Azerbaijani border with two of my friends, and then bearing east to tackle and summit Mount Sabalan. We slept outside and ate whatever we could forage, and climbed the mountain with bare hands, joking to each other that we had turned feral, that if we kept it up we would mutate into wolves, and that such a transformation would suit us just fine, for we loved the outdoors and had rarely if at all thought about our homes since leaving them. Our bicycles were old and rusting contraptions with seized brake pads and crumbling chain links; our bags were torn rucksacks which rain could saturate in minutes; and when we charged into the sea to swim at every opportunity, we left it all in a heap on the sand – no chains, no padlocks, no security whatsoever, only trust.

I contemplated how I had changed since then, and how I had not. My bike, my panniers and my equipment were all so expensive that the younger me would have smirked and scoffed at such decadent accoutrements. But he would have approved of the journey. He would have approved of everything about it. Here I was: 39 years old; 3,000 miles into an 11,000-mile bike ride; no job, no property, no car, no savings, no assets, no idea when or from where the next pay cheque might come; as far removed from my comfort zone as I had ever been before – and I had never felt so alive.

———————

Iran had obliterated all negativity – or, that is, it almost had. A single worry nagged at me here and there, beckoning up at me as I crested the peaks of joy Iran had built, inviting me down to the lower ground where it perched and waited for me. I ignored it when I could, but it was patient, and when we concluded our day in the town of Talesh, I decided to air it over dinner with Steve, Kamyar and Afrooz.

'I've been thinking,' I said hesitantly. 'Thinking about this flight out of Shiraz. Are we going to make it?'

Steve let out a sigh of relief. 'I'm so glad you said it first,' he exclaimed. 'I've been mulling it over all day. But I didn't want to be the one who brought it up. Reckoned you might think I was just fussing over time again.'

'What's the problem?' Kamyar asked.

'Well,' I said, 'we've lost a lot of time in Russia thanks to the punctures and the rain, and then between Azerbaijan and here. Meeting Steve outside Baku took a couple of hours extra, and the last two border crossings have taken way too long. Actually, we should be a lot further on than Talesh by now. I'd say we might even be a full day behind. That's one of the reasons we've dropped Tehran from our itinerary. We just won't have the time to get in and out again.'

Steve nodded in agreement. 'I was working it all out in my head while we were riding today. Basically, Shiraz is about eight-hundred miles away and we've got six days to get there. So that's one-hundred-and-thirty-four miles each day. At the very least.'

'But that's possible, isn't it?' Afrooz asked. 'Isn't that pretty much what you were doing each day back in Norway and Finland?'

'It was,' Steve said, 'but that was right at the start. We were full of energy then, and full of spare fat when our energy ran low.'

'It's true,' I said. 'I've lost ten kilograms since then. And the exhaustion is cumulative. Every day I feel more tired.'

'We were already feeling worn down by the time we reached Russia,' Steve added. 'You can see from our tracker that we were doing fewer and fewer miles each day.'

'But you've got something you didn't have in Russia,' Afrooz said with a glint in her eye. 'You've got us. Don't forget that, for the next six days, all you have to do is eat, sleep and cycle. We'll do all the rest – we'll organise the hotels and campsites, we'll find the restaurants and order your food in advance so that it's waiting for you as soon as you arrive, we'll stay in contact with Base Camp each day, we'll do all the filming. All you have to do is just keep moving.'

'That's a good point,' Steve said, visibly cheered. 'One of the reasons we took so long in Russia was because we'd cycle all day and then spend half the night looking for a place to sleep, so we wouldn't get to bed until three or four in the morning, and we'd end up sleeping late the next day to compensate. If we get into a good routine of sleeping well, leaving early and then cycling for a solid twelve hours each day, I reckon we can do it.'

'You're forgetting one thing,' I said, sorry to have to dampen Steve's rising spirits. 'The mountains. This isn't going to be a lovely flat road like Finland. We're going to have to cross both the Alborz and the Zagros mountain ranges, as well as a bunch of lower peaks in between. There are some serious uphills ahead of us and they're going to slow us right down. Trust me, I know them well. One-hundred-and-thirty-four miles a day is going to be tough.'

'Tough but not impossible,' Steve said. 'And we'll make up for the uphills by racing down the downhills. No brakes allowed.' He grinned, and his positivity was infectious. That was Steve's great strength and perhaps the most valuable thing he brought to the team. When it came to blasting through miles, there was no one I knew who could equal him and his will and determination at moments like this were hugely motivational. *Maybe he's right*, I thought. *Maybe we can do it. Eight-hundred miles in six days.*

'Even if you missed the flight,' Kamyar suggested, 'surely you could just get on the next one. You'd only lose a couple of hours, and you could probably make that back over the next two months in Africa.'

If it were a straight shot down from Cairo to Cape Town, Kamyar would have been right. But the problem was the Sudan border. To get there from Egypt, we needed to cross Lake Nasser by boat. When we had been planning the journey, we had wondered if GWR would accept this, but since there is no way to cross the border by land, they had agreed. We had discovered, however, that there is only one boat per week that crosses the lake. And so all the planning we made, all the times and expected daily distances from Nordkapp to Shiraz, and then the flight from Shiraz to Cairo, all of it had been coordinated exactly so that we could make that one specific boat across Lake Nasser. If we missed it, there was no way we would be able to claw back seven days through Africa, especially since the roads and conditions would be ten times worse than they had been previously. We would be lucky to make 100 miles a day, let alone our 120-mile target. I explained as much to Kamyar. 'So, you see,' I said, 'we *have* to make that boat. And to make that boat we *have* to make this flight. It's the absolute latest one we can get to make it to the boat on time. The next flight isn't until the following day, it takes twice as long and by the time we'd arrive in Cairo it'd be far too late. If we miss this flight, it's game over.'

'So we've got no choice, then,' Steve said. 'One-hundred-and-thirty-four miles every day for the next six days.'

'Tough but not impossible,' I said, already exhausted by the mere prospect of it.

'Tough but not impossible,' Steve repeated, grinning across the table at me and rubbing his hands together with masochistic delight.

So we followed Afrooz's advice: we did nothing but eat, sleep and cycle. It seemed almost a shame to be sailing through Iran at such speed – I would have adored the opportunity to stop here and there and reacquaint myself with this magnificent country which I had forgotten I had missed so much – but the ache to make the flight (fuelled by the greater ache behind it: to make the record) superseded all else. True to their word, Kamyar and Afrooz made it all so much easier for us: waking before we did to buy and then make us breakfast; driving ahead to arrange rest stops and meal breaks, and then returning to encourage us on with the promise that the next was only a few miles away; and organising hotels so that all we had to do at the close of each day was stretch, strip and collapse into our beds.

The road from Talesh opened into a wide and smooth dual carriageway lined at sporadic intervals with colourful stalls selling local handmade rugs, immense balls of cotton, and thousands of plump and glossy olives. We navigated some 60 miles south from Talesh in the morning alone, stopping in Fuman for a celebratory lunch.

'See?' Steve said. 'We're nailing it. That's almost half of our daily quota already.'

'We did well,' I agreed, 'but we haven't reached the mountains yet.'

It was not long before we did. The road banked away from the coast and we followed it up and into the foothills of the Alborz mountain range: our first serious climb of the journey. Gradients rose at an astonishing rate and we fell into our own private rhythms. There was no talking, there was barely any thinking, as consciousness realigned itself, settling around basic motor functions, directing all energy towards movement and respiration. I became little more than two legs and a heart.

Gradually, the road began to level off and, with it, the ability to observe and to comment returned. We had left the coast behind and, it seemed, had left behind the colour green, too. The patches of vegetation that clung tenaciously to the otherwise bare rock faces had browned beneath the sun, and a rugged sable dominated the landscape. The undulations of this ethereal moonscape spread in every direction to disappear into valleys or rise into higher peaks or drop back down to the Caspian, and I was bewitched by it all. I had been here before, of course, more times than I could count, but it felt like I was seeing it all for the first time. I was not alone in my awe: cars stood stationary at the side of the motorway, and families had poured out to perch on rugs, drink tea, chop watermelons and devour sandwiches. Sadly, we had not the time to join them.

So instead we pedalled on, ever higher, ever slower, sweating our way through the tiny town of Rudbar where the men and women who strolled the streets waved at us and their children ran behind our rear wheels, shrieking with laughter and pointing at our Lycra-clad bottoms as they bobbed up and down. Some miles later, the town of Manjil, colloquially known as 'the windy city of Iran', lived up to its name and reputation. The famous wind that blows through Manjil towards the Qazvin plateau is funnelled through the small cleft in the Alborz mountains where the town sits, and it was this that gave us an extra lift just when we needed it, buffeting us with such force towards the town that, when I let my concentration lapse to gaze out at the sun sparkling off the Sefid Rud (the 'white river') below, a fresh gust caught me by surprise and sent me tumbling from my bike to land heavily on the tarmac.

'Are you okay?' Kamyar shouted to me as Afrooz screeched the car to a halt. I stumbled gracelessly to my feet and checked myself. Aside from a sore shoulder, there appeared to be no damage.

'He's fine!' Steve shouted over the wind as he cycled past us. 'He can have a good cry about it *after* we hit one-hundred-and-thirty-four miles!' His motivation may have been on the harsher side at times, but it worked. I climbed back on to my bike and resumed.

In fact, by the time we stopped that evening in the town of Lowshan, not far from Manjil, we had not managed the full 134 miles, but were eminently pleased with the 122 miles we had covered. This was, after all, the most strenuous day with the longest and steepest uphills we had endured so far.

The following day would now require a hefty 146 miles, but Afrooz had checked the map and informed us that there were only 40 miles of climbing left. Beyond that were hours and perhaps even days of creamy flats and breakneck downhills, and we were buoyed up by such a fresh and strong sense of confidence and self-belief that we were positive we could make it.

And we did. Indeed, we did even more. The town of Saveh was exactly 150 miles away, and we reached it by 9.30 p.m. the following evening. We had never cycled an equivalent distance in one day before. And it was barely night-time. The flight to Egypt was in reach. The record had never felt so attainable.

I should have been ecstatic. I should have been dizzy with elation. I should have whooped and pranced about and high-fived every single passer-by. But instead I was tense and apprehensive, raw-nerved like I was just about to step out on to a stage. Steve, Kamyar and Afrooz disappeared into the hotel we had booked for the night, leaving me out on the street alone. I took four deep breaths and then followed them inside. I needed to shower and to change. For I was meeting my mother for dinner that night.

'You look thin.'

I held my breath. Mum's first words were always the most important: the weathervane suggesting which direction our conversation would take. These three words – the classic physical assessment – delivered in a neutral monotone as we hugged, did not bode well. I awaited their successors with silent patience.

'It suits you.'

My breath escaped in a sigh, a pantomime of audible relief.

'You look good too, Mum,' I said, and she smiled at the compliment.

We entered the pizzeria and sat ourselves at a table for five. Steve, Kamyar and Afrooz were already seated, and I introduced each of them in turn to my mother.

'So what was Reza like as a kid?' Steve asked.

'This one,' she said, 'was a nightmare. A trouble-maker. A thorn in my side for twenty years.'

'Sounds familiar,' Steve replied, grinning at me and evidently enjoying himself.

'Always getting into trouble,' she continued. 'Always. Couldn't sit still. Wouldn't listen to his teachers. Wouldn't listen to me. Never studied. Just wanted to be outside all the time – playing basketball, or riding his bike.'

'So nothing's changed then,' Steve laughed.

'Precisely, Steven!' she cried. 'Precisely! Nothing's changed – nothing! Look at him now, gallivanting around the world, not a penny to his name. What he needs is to get his bum in one place and chill for a while.'

Steve laughed louder still and I do not think I had ever seen him so happy throughout the entire journey.

'At least gallivanting around the world has made me lose weight,' I offered.

'That's true,' Mum replied. 'You were getting too fat. Far too fat. It made you unattractive. But you don't have to cycle halfway around the planet to lose weight. Just go to a gym! That's all your brother does – twice during the week and then once at the weekend – and he's in the best shape of his life.'

I groaned and feigned extra interest in the menu, for I knew what was coming next. It would be, without doubt, a lengthy monologue that extolled the virtues of my brother, the apple of our mother's eye. I attempted a conversational coup. 'Which pizza do you want, Mum?'

'Mushroom. What I always have. Your brother would know that.'

The coup had failed.

'If you met Reza's brother, you'd never guess they were related.' She had turned to direct her lecture at Steve – without doubt, the most willing and gleeful listener at the table. 'He has such a calm and steady life. A wife, two children, a house, a great job with Apple. I do wish Reza would be more like him.'

'Why can't you be more like your brother, Reza?' Steve challenged me with a cheeky glint in his eye. I decided to fill his cycling shorts with mosquitoes later.

'Or just like any of us!' Mum continued. 'That's the problem – I don't know where he gets this from. It's not from his father, and it's certainly not from me. As far as I know, there has never been another Pakravan who, at forty years old, was unemployed and homeless.'

'I'm thirty-nine,' I said, and instantly regretted it, for it brought on one of the withering stares for which my mother is so famous (and, in some circles, so feared).

The arrival of the pizzas brought some respite from the conversation and, as if to bolster my rapidly dwindling sense of self-worth, Kamyar and Afrooz began to explain how excited they were to be part of the team.

'The funny thing is,' Afrooz said, 'when Kamyar came home and told me he'd been offered a job to do some filming for Reza, I already knew who Reza was! A couple of my friends at work were following him on his website as he got closer to Iran, and they had showed it to me the day before.'

'The same thing happened when I told my cousin,' Kamyar said. '*You're filming for those Kapp to Cape guys?* He couldn't believe it. He kept calling Reza and Steve celebrities. *Kamyar's going up in the world – he's filming celebrities these days!*'

It was noble of them to try, but I could see from her dispassionate gaze that Mum was barely listening. My mother is a very difficult woman to impress. I learned that a long time ago. Now it was time for Kamyar and Afrooz to learn it. They fell back to quietly munching on their pizzas when they saw they had elicited no reaction from her.

'It's nice to see you,' she said later as we walked arm-in-arm through the night-time streets of Saveh to where she had parked her car. 'I would like to see you more often.'

'Me too,' I said. 'But it's difficult. I live so far away. And, despite what you might think, I am incredibly busy with all the things I do.'

'I know, I know,' she shushed me. 'I could say a million things about you, but the one thing I could never say is that you're lazy. You're one of the hardest-working men I've ever known.'

I let her words linger for a while. Praise from my mother was rare and when it came it carried more weight than any of her criticism. Her hectoring and haranguing was often just her going through the motions, reading from the same script she had compiled when I was a teenager, and it had become so traditional I barely took it in any more. I sometimes wondered if she even acknowledged the words as they came out of her mouth, or if she just said them because she had always said them and it was too late to stop saying them now for if she did we might not know what else to talk about. But praise, or any words that could be construed as approving or commending – those words were so singular and unexpected that they had the effect of a struck match in a dark room.

As we drew close to her car, she stopped and turned to look at me. 'Do you remember Edwin?' she asked.

'The kid I used to hang around with all the time? Sure I remember him. How long ago was that?'

'About twenty, twenty-five years…'

I chuckled at the memory of that smiling, blond boy. 'I wonder what happened to him,' I said. 'I lost contact with him after we moved.'

'I saw him the other day. He came rushing up to me. *Haydeh Joon!* Of course, I knew who he was straight away, and I was starting to tell him all about what you're up to these days when he interrupted me. He knew everything about your adventure. He was following you online. He said it was exactly what he'd always thought you'd do. Something like this. Something incredible.'

She produced a set of keys from her bag and unlocked the car door.

'I'm very proud of you, you know,' my mother said, cupping my face in both her hands and kissing me lightly on the cheek. 'Very, very proud.'

And then she climbed into the car, started the engine, winked at me as she closed the door and drove the 200 miles back to Tehran. That she had come so far to see me reinforced her final words, and I began the walk back to the hotel with a wide and childish smile.

CHAPTER 11

THE WORLD'S STILL TURNING

Distance remaining: 7,559 miles
Time to record: 70 days

———————

'The Karakoram Highway.'

'Not long enough.'

'The Silk Road.'

'Better.'

'The Mongol Rally.'

'Don't think they allow bicycles.'

'The Trans-Amazonian Highway.'

'Now *that* would be a trip.'

'The Tour de France.'

'I reckon we could actually do pretty well at that. We're basically completing the equivalent of a stage every day.'

'What we're doing now – it's the same distance as seven Tours de France.'

'Shall we do it next year?'

'No.'

'Absolutely not.'

'I'm never cycling again.'

'I'm going to throw my bike down a volcano.'

'I'm going to buy a motorbike.'

'I'm going to buy a four-by-four with a massive, filthy engine.'

'I'm going to buy a helicopter.'

Hitting our 134-mile target every day was punishing, but somehow we were doing it. We had committed to our saddles, were spending at least 10 hours and often many more each day atop them, regardless of the weather or road conditions or inclines and declines. Breaks were short and strictly maintained by Kamyar and Afrooz, who handed us our food the moment we pulled over and then watched us as we ate, tapping their watches and clicking their tongues if we took too long. There was barely even time for conversation, and at the end of each day we were so tired that all we had the strength to do was eat some more before retiring to our beds, so our only opportunities to talk came while we were cycling. And, as cycling had come to dictate almost every aspect of our days, so too did cycling come to dictate almost every aspect of our conversations. We debated new roads and routes, and fantasised our way across the world.

These fantasies, whether they were serious or intentionally ludicrous, not only helped us to pass the time as we pushed on through Iran, they also kept us away from more insidious topics. The debilitating paranoia Steve had felt as we neared Dagestan was beginning to return, this time with Egypt as its source. His reluctance to cycle through the next country on our route grew increasingly palpable, and whenever he brought it up in conversation I changed the subject by listing new and exciting future adventures or, if that did not work, I simply took my camera out and began to film, for this guaranteed to quieten him. I knew that neither of these approaches were genuine solutions to our problem, and that, in fact, we did need to talk about Egypt and not just leave it to bubble and fester in unspoken discord. By changing the subject, by shoving my camera in his face, I was delaying the inevitable – but the inevitable was an argument, and I wanted to prolong that as much as I could.

Iran helped, its mountainous landscapes our ethereal and gorgeous companion. With such dazzling and exquisite panoramas in abundance, it was easy to pass hours without uttering a word. Instead, we cycled, breathed and gazed. Among the endless mountains, small towns such as Salafchegan, Do Dehak, Delijan and Meymeh came and went, though we rarely stopped in them. Time was too important. We had to keep moving. By Isfahan, I began to long for civilisation and begged the team that we stop there for a long lunch.

I remembered Isfahan as lined with trees and peppered with elegant architecture and, despite the occasional rubble and noise of a building site where the new metro system was being installed, I was not disappointed. We coasted through the city towards the gargantuan Naqsh-e Jahan Square, a UNESCO World Heritage Site and rightly so. Its two mosques are some of the most beautiful I've ever known and the Ali Qapu Palace epitomises all that is majestic about Iran, all its handsome dignity, all its cultivated grace.

The square was quiet and, although I would have loved to sit in its gardens to feast on an al fresco picnic beneath the sun, absorbing the splendour of all around, there was nobody about selling food. We had arrived late in the afternoon and it was likely that most people were cooped up in their homes, passing the time with a long siesta until the temperature became bearable once more. The streets were quiet, too, and as we navigated up and down them in search of a restaurant, we were continually dismayed to find each and every one of them closed.

I waved to a passing cyclist and called out to him in Farsi. As he slowed to a stop, I wheeled myself towards him and introduced myself. His name was Hamed, and all that was discernible of his face below his flamboyant Afro and beneath his oversized glasses was a bulbous nose and huge, toothy grin. I asked if he knew of anywhere we might eat.

'Your only hope is the hotels,' Hamed said. 'All the restaurants are closed now, but you should be able to find something at a hotel, as long as it's a large one. There's one not too far from here. I'll show you. Follow me.'

He pushed down on his pedals and lurched into a sprint, powering off down the street, his Afro flowing backwards in the wind like the ears of a spaniel with its head out of a car window. It took us a few moments to catch up with him.

'Why so fast?' I panted as I drew level.

'I like to ride fast,' he grinned. 'Fast and far.'

'Yeah, me too,' I replied.

'Are you from Isfahan?'

'Tehran.'

'First time here?'

'No, I came here when I was younger. I have very fond memories of it.'

We came to a bridge over a dried-out riverbed. Hamed stopped and gestured for me to do the same. 'Then maybe you remember this,' he said, tying his hair back into a squirrel-like tail, perhaps to get a better view of that which he was pointing out. 'But you probably remember it very, very differently. This is the Zayanderud.'

It took me a few moments to register. I did remember the Zayanderud, the largest river on the central Iranian plateau, and I remembered it as huge and fast flowing. It seemed almost impossible to me that it could have dried up, like trying to imagine London without the Thames: the London Eye glaring at Big Ben over a no man's land of dried and cracking mud.

'It's been like this for years now,' Hamed said. 'There's not even a drought here. It's the dam – it cuts off the river and diverts it so that it doesn't flow through Isfahan any more. It's heartbreaking, right? Absolutely heartbreaking.'

The plight of the Zayanderud made Hamed reflective, more talkative and slower. We cycled side by side the rest of the way to the hotel and, after he asked what we were doing in Iran and I had explained our journey, he became simultaneously maudlin and animated.

'This is what I would love to do. An adventure. I want to take a big adventure. Something extreme, maybe a little bit crazy. Just like you have done. That's what I want for my life.'

'Well then, why don't you?' I asked. 'You said you like to ride fast and far. Go for it.'

'I have too much work and not enough time. My family owns a restaurant. It is my father's, but I am the one who runs it, who manages everything. My father is too old to cope with it and my brother is too lazy. Without me, the business would collapse.'

'I used to think the same thing. I had this big, important job in London. I thought that what I was doing was so crucial that if I stopped it could put my whole company in jeopardy. But look what's happened. Nothing. They carried on just fine without me. I left, and the world's still turning.'

Hamed thought about this, scratching gently at the skin beneath those enormous sunglasses. 'Perhaps they will be all right. Perhaps. But then I must also think about myself. Will *I* be all right? I have a comfortable life now. I have money, I eat well, I live in a nice house. I could have a big adventure, but what if all those things were gone when I came back? What will you do when you finish? Go home? Return to life as normal?'

'I don't know,' I admitted. 'I don't think so. I'm not sure it'd even be possible to return to life as normal. And I don't think I want to anyway. All that isn't important to me any more. I've changed the way I look at life. I was like you – I had money, nice things, pretty much whatever I wanted really – but I wasn't happy. Now, right now, doing this, riding this bike along the streets of Isfahan, talking to my new friend Hamed, with thousands of miles behind me and even more ahead, I'm happy. I'm happier than I've ever been. Even if I go back to the UK and end up working at McDonald's and living in a squat, it still would all have been worth it. For this. For this moment right now.'

We arrived at the hotel and although I invited Hamed to join us for lunch, he politely declined. Instead, he signed our evidence book, shook each of us by the hand and wished us well, and then swapped email addresses with me. I implored him to stay in touch and he promised that he would, before disappearing back into the leafy streets of Isfahan.

It pleases me to report that Hamed did stay in touch. Four months after our meeting, I received an email from him. He had finally mustered the courage to inform his family that he would be taking a year off from the restaurant to cycle to and then around Turkey. They had not been surprised in the least, and had merely asked him when he was planning to leave and why it had taken him so long to get his act together. His email came from Ankara where, almost halfway through his journey, he had chosen to rest for a few days in the Turkish capital. 'I can't believe I cycled here,' he wrote, 'all the way from home. The road has been wonderful. I've seen things I would never have imagined. And I'm so happy. So very, very happy.'

―――――――――

In order to meet our quota for the day, we still had to cover another 40 miles. Getting out of Isfahan meant climbing a series of long and gruelling hills, and so those miles took longer than we had hoped, but we bore on and eventually reached our goal late in the evening: the town of Shahreza. We followed Afrooz and Kamyar towards the accommodation they had nominated for the night: a small guesthouse next door to Shahreza's main mosque.

Outside the mosque, a large crowd had gathered, perhaps a thousand-strong. A loudspeaker boomed the trills of a prayer into the night sky and the men repeated it back in a call-and-response singsong. I recognised it as a religious ceremony, though I could not pinpoint which one. The men massed in a thick and soupy confluence of arms, beards and voices, entirely impenetrable by car and difficult to navigate through even by bike. Afrooz pulled up on its outskirts as Steve and I attempted to wend our way towards the mosque. Men began to grab at our panniers and handlebars, pointing at our bare legs and loudly denouncing us. I looked over at Steve. He was visibly petrified. Someone laid a meaty hand on his forearm. Someone else shoved me from behind.

'*Go away!*' Two burning eyes, inches from my face, stared me down as others took up the chant. '*Go away! Go away!*'

'We are looking for the guesthouse,' I said to no one and everyone, but my Farsi seemed to have the opposite effect to that which I had hoped. Rather than assuage them with my Iranian heritage, my words only seemed to incense them further.

'He can speak Farsi! Why can he speak Farsi?'

'He's a foreigner. Tricking us with our own language.'

'Go away!'

Going away seemed, indeed, to be our only option, and so we turned our bikes around and began to push ourselves out of the pack and back towards the car. But the ordeal was far from over. As we reached the limits of the crowd, six motorbikes appeared as if from nowhere, circling us with over-revved engines that popped and snarled as we desperately tried to push ourselves free.

'Fuck off!' one of the riders yelled and, although we obliged, breaking free from the crowd and cycling back the way we had come, the motorbikes followed, swinging towards us as we rode with alarming and threatening proximity. I felt the forceful nudge of a tyre against my back wheel, lurching me forward so that I narrowly missed the kick of another rider. Kamyar and Afrooz remained close in the car, but were forced to swerve away each time a rider veered towards them and beat a fist against a window or side panel.

There was fear. Real fear. Not the anticipation of fear that I had experienced in Dagestan, but present and actualised fear. It coursed through my veins, resounding in thudding heartbeats and twitching eyelids. Of all the places I had imagined this might happen, Iran – my own country – had been the lowest on my list. Something in me felt responsible for it all, and somewhere below the fear was the notion that this was somehow my fault, and that I needed to apologise to Steve for the rudeness of my countrymen.

If responsibility melded with my fear, pure anger melded with Steve's. Half a mile away from the crowd, with the motorcyclists still on their bullying offensive, he snapped. *'Right!'* he screamed, and I turned my head to look at him, his face a mask of tortured anguish, a caricature of a man pushed too far. 'You motherfuckers are *dead!*'

I watched in disbelief as he pointed his bicycle at the nearest motorcyclist and began to pedal full-pelt towards him, wailing a weird and rather terrifying battle howl. The rider, stunned at the sudden role-reversal, immediately fell into his new status as victim and sped away. Steve continued his one-man attack, ferociously pedalling at each of the riders with a mouthful of sour invectives until each of them dispersed, finally leaving us alone.

'Steve!' I called after the last had vanished. 'My hero!'

Steve came to a stop and planted his feet on the ground, panting like a wild dog. My own heart beat in time to his breathing. Feeling the adrenaline finally begin to dissipate, I moved towards him, arms outstretched, hoping to wrap him in a brotherly hug to express my gratitude and newfound awe, but the vitriol he had succumbed to had not dispersed with the riders.

'*Don't* talk to me,' he hissed. 'Let's just find a place to sleep, and let's do it *now.*'

Kamyar guided us through the streets of Shahreza to a rough and dingy guesthouse on its outskirts. There were 20 rooms at approximately £1 per night. Half of them were occupied and there was just one communal toilet for all. The bed sheets were stiff with yellow and brown stains. Cockroaches had the run of the place. Kamyar and Afrooz took one of the rooms for themselves, and Steve and I shared another. As we laid our sleeping bags over the filthy beds, I felt the adrenaline still lingering in my veins and knew it would take some time to fall asleep.

'That was not Iran,' I said. 'Whatever you remember of my country, please don't remember that first.'

'I know, I know,' Steve replied, sitting down atop his bed and facing me. 'Don't get me wrong, I've loved Iran. It's been some of the best cycling yet. But tonight…'

'It's partly our fault,' I interrupted. 'We were there in the middle of a religious ceremony in our Lycras. It was disrespectful of us. If we're more careful it shouldn't happen again.'

Steve stared at me. It was a stare filled with reproach and disdain. I knew we were in for a long night. I knew the argument I had been avoiding so carefully over the past few days was about to surface. 'Yes, Reza,' he said. 'Yes it *will* happen again. It *will* happen again whether we're careful or not. That's your problem, mate. You flounce through this journey like you've got a daisy-chain around your neck thinking everything's going to be all peace and love. But it's not. We were in real danger tonight – *real*. And we will be again. Maybe not here. But definitely later.'

'We're talking about Egypt, right?'

'Yes, we're talking about Egypt! What else is there to talk about?'

'All right, so I'll admit it's getting dangerous there, but I really don't think anything is going to happen to us. We'd be pretty unlucky if it did.'

'Unlucky? *Unlucky?* Was tonight us being *unlucky?* And that was Iran, somewhere we were supposed to be safe, the place that *you* come from! If that's what happened to us here, what do you think's going to happen in Egypt? This is what I've been talking about all along. It was the same for Dagestan. Yeah, we'd be pretty unlucky if anything happened to us, *but that doesn't mean it won't happen!*'

'Dagestan was fine. I didn't have a single problem there.'

'So you weren't unlucky. In fact, you weren't even just ordinary. You were *lucky*, mate. And if we're going to make it through Egypt without any problems we'll be pretty *lucky*, too. And I don't know about you, but I'm getting sick of relying on luck when it comes to my personal safety. I'm not going to be stupid any more. I need to consider my dad, my mum, my girlfriend. I'm not going to risk getting killed for a record I'm not even part of.'

'We'll be fine—'

'Stop saying that! How do you know? How do you know we'll be fine? We were supposed to be fine here in Iran, and look what happened to us! In Iran! In a country where they *aren't* evacuating foreigners, in a country where they *aren't* under some national state of emergency, in a country where there *aren't* riots and violence happening on every single street every single day.'

'You're exaggerating.'

'*AM I?*' Steve leapt to his feet and leered over me. 'I'm exaggerating? Forgive me, mate, if me being worried about my life seems to you like I'm *FUCKING EXAGGERATING!*' His stance had evolved into one of pure aggression and for a moment I thought he might hit me. Perhaps it was this, the tangible threat of violence, the way he was physically backing me into a corner, which reset my thought patterns and transformed my reactions from those that exhibited compliance to those that matched his rage. I rose slowly to my feet, balled my hands into fists and squared up to him.

'So you're sick of all this, right?' I whispered. 'Then how about you do us both a favour. Go home.'

Steve remained standing, though it was clear the fight had left him. 'I'm seriously thinking about it,' he replied.

'Well then, why not?' It was my turn to shout. 'This is an *expedition*. It's not some organised cycling excursion in the Alps. If you can't deal with a certain level of risk why did you even bother coming?'

He seemed to think about this for a while. 'It's not just a certain level of risk though, is it?' he finally said. His tone had subdued somewhat, though there was still an unmistakeable edge of animosity to it. 'Egypt is dangerous, mate – it's genuinely *dangerous*. And I don't know if I'm prepared to put myself through it. Why are we even bothering with it? Why don't we just skip it and fly straight to Khartoum rather than Cairo?'

'The record,' I said.

'Forget the record. I don't even qualify for it any more after skipping Dagestan.'

'You might not qualify for it, but I do. And I still want it.'

'Then you can have it. I'm not coming. I'll meet you in Khartoum. You can do Egypt alone. I'll join you for the rest of Africa.' He turned his back on me, spreading himself across his sleeping bag and closing his eyes, leaving me standing alone in the middle of the room, his rage now spent, but mine still sparking its way along my synapses.

'No, Steve,' I said, walking slowly across the room to turn out the light. 'You either cycle through Egypt with me, or you pack up and go back to London.'

––––––––––––

There was nothing left to say. I stood by my ultimatum and let Steve debate with himself. He had reached a crossroads. It was Egypt or it was nothing and only he could decide what the correct thing was to do. I offered no further opinions, and Steve never asked for them. And so we cycled eating through the miles like fire through dry wood. Afrooz drove and organised our food and accommodation without discussing any of it for fear it would only incite further arguments. Kamyar, sensing the lack of cinema-worthy dialogue between his protagonists, instead pointed his camera out of the other window and filmed Iran's passing landscapes.

We reached Shiraz in time for our flight. In fact, we even had time to spare and so, once we checked into the airport hotel, I left Steve in our room and wandered off without a word to explore the city alone. I felt downbeat and sick, and my internal discord was only compounded by the knowledge that I should have been elated at that moment. We had reached Shiraz. Leg One was complete. The start of Leg Two – the start of *Africa* – was only a plane ride away. And yet that argument with Steve was all that occupied my thoughts.

I am not a religious man. I do not believe in miracles. Yet I do believe in extraordinary coincidences, and I believe that their occurrences can be enhanced by travel. I do not know why, and I do not want to know, but it is a truth I happily abide by. And so, when Edwin – that childhood friend whom I had not thought of for 25 years until my mother mentioned his name in Saveh – appeared directly before me in the streets of Shiraz, I was overwhelmed, but I was not surprised. We found the nearest teahouse, and then we sat and we talked.

'Mum was talking about you only the other day,' I said.

'We met. It was so strange. That morning I had been following you on your website and seeing that you were getting close to Iran, and just moments before I saw your mother I was thinking how nice it would be to see you here in Iran.'

'I can't believe I'm seeing you now. Or, even weirder, I think I can believe it.'

'There's nothing weird about it. I read your blog and saw you were due in Shiraz today. I flew here especially to see you. I was just on my way to the airport to meet you before you took your flight to Cairo.'

'Why did we ever lose touch? Do you remember, I used to come round your apartment all the time.'

'Especially at Christmas.'

'Could you blame me?' For my family, Christmas was just another day. But I loved the lavish celebrations Edwin's Christian family would hold on 25 December and I always knew that if I turned up on that day I'd get invited in.

'You just wanted the Christmas dinner.'

'And the games. And the presents. Your mum used to get a little present for me, too. But, yeah, if I'm honest, I *loved* that dinner.'

Talk of dinner made me hungry and I suddenly remembered Steve, who must have been hungry too.

'Where's the other guy?' Edwin asked with what was becoming an oddly typical serendipity.

'Steve? He's back at our hotel.' I explained the argument to Edwin, and when he laughed it off I realised just how absurd the whole thing was.

'I'm staying in Shiraz with a friend of mine,' he said. 'He's called Raham. A local guy. He's got a sweet Land Cruiser. How about we grab him, pick up Steve and go get some dinner?'

When Edwin, Raham and I piled into the hotel room, high on the gaiety of friendship, we found Steve, sitting alone on his bed, and the smile on his face was so hopeful and innocent that I felt compelled to hug him there and then. We all bundled into Raham's Land Cruiser, Steve and I taking the back seat, and while we toured the city like teenagers on a night out in their first ever car, Steve turned to me.

'I spoke to my dad on the phone after you left,' he said.

'And what did he say?'

'He said I should do Egypt. He said if I didn't I would regret it.'

'And what did you say?'

'I agreed with him.'

'Look,' I said. 'I can understand why you're reluctant about it. You're right. Something could happen. I'm willing to accept the risk because I could still get the record. But I don't want you to feel like I'm forcing you into it, because I can't be responsible for both of us if something does happen.'

'This is my decision, Reza. You don't have to be responsible for me. I want to come.'

'To Egypt?'

'To Egypt, to Sudan, Ethiopia, Kenya, all of it, all the way to Cape Town.'

I laughed then, laughed so hard it caused Edwin and Raham to turn around from their seats in the front to check I was okay. I held my bottle of water up in the air. 'Here's to Leg Two!' I cried.

Steve held up his own bottle and smacked it lustily against mine. 'To Leg Two!'

We drove on, raucous and adrenaline-drunk, beneath the sparkling street lights of a sleepy Shiraz.

PART THREE

LEG TWO

AFRICA

RIVER NILE

CAIRO
SAMALUT
EGYPT   LUXOR
LAKE NASSER   ASWAN
WADI HALFA
DONGOLA   DELGO
               KHARTOUM
SUDAN
METEMA   GONDAR
               GOHATSION
ADDIS ABABA
               ETHIOPIA

               MOYALE
               MERILLE
NAIROBI   MOUNT KENYA
               KITENGELA
               KENYA
TANZANIA   KILIMANJARO
DODOMA   IRINGA

CHINSALI
ZAMBIA
LIVINGSTONE/VICTORIA FALLS   LUSAKA
                             KASANE
KALAHARI DESERT
               BOTSWANA
                             MAHALAPYE
GABARONE   MAFEKING
STELLA
               SOUTH AFRICA
LAINGSBURG   BEAUFORT WEST
               WORCESTER
CAPE TOWN

CHAPTER 12

UP IN THE AIR

Distance remaining: 7,067 miles
Time to record: 65 days

———————

Kamyar and Afrooz accompanied us to the airport and, when we said our farewells, I was surprised by how much it saddencd me. They had been wonderful company and I knew I would miss them. But, below that, there was another layer to the sadness. I had felt the same way when Francesca, Paula and Peiman turned the van around at the Finnish border a month before, leaving us alone. Once more, we would be without support, and we would be without it in one of the most dangerous countries of the entire journey.

Egypt had never been far from the news since its role in the Arab Spring of 2011. With President Mubarak ousted and the Muslim Brotherhood-endorsed Mohamed Morsi taking power in 2012, the 15 months between that and our arrival in Egypt had been fraught with protests and violent clashes between those who supported Morsi and those who did not. When the Egyptian military removed Morsi in a *coup d'état* just two months earlier, more protests and more violence erupted as members of the Muslim Brotherhood battled against the military. Hundreds were killed on the streets; thousands were incarcerated and sentenced to life imprisonment or execution in a series of mass trials. Discord and dissent ballooned, and protests, demonstrations, street brawls, gunfire and homemade bombs were becoming ever more commonplace across Cairo.

The first plane did not take us directly there, but to the capital of Qatar, Doha, where we had to wait for an hour before boarding the connecting flight to Egypt. It was enough time to grab a coffee and latch on to the airport's free wi-fi to browse news websites, and I immediately regretted it. Each headline kicked my pulse up an extra notch and the caffeine only intensified it.

'Minister of Interior assassination attempt'

'Violent clashes in pro-Morsi neighbourhood'

'Tear gas and gunfire in Kerdasah'

'Police stations torched, 11 security officers killed'

'Two unexploded bombs found on tracks near Ramses Station'

'Pro-Morsi sit-ins dispersed, over 1,000 dead'

It was too much to take in, and so I closed my web browser and opened up my email account. It did little to help. Inside were a few dozen unread emails from friends and family, half of them with the word 'Egypt' in the subject line. The words 'dangerous', 'security' and 'avoid' were just as common. I smiled over at Steve, who had bought a cheeseburger and was munching away on it, said I was going to have a nose around the duty-free shops and tried to walk off my burgeoning trepidation. I thought of Dagestan, of how it had all been fine in the end, but then I remembered that I had endured that portion of the journey alone. Having Steve with me through Egypt might be added protection, but it was also added responsibility and the thought of him getting injured after all I had done to encourage him to join me there left me feeling sick.

On the plane to Cairo, still queasy with fear, I avoided making eye contact with Steve who, for all his recalcitrance through Iran, now seemed utterly devoid of anxiety about Egypt. I did not want him to see me like this, imagining as I did that my panic flowed from my pores in visible streams. Perhaps it was visible, for after we had taken off, he asked me if I was feeling all right. 'You're looking pale,' he added.

'It's the lack of sleep, it's killing me,' I said. 'And it feels odd not to be cycling. Flying is too fast. I'm not used to it. I prefer seeing the world at the speed of a bicycle.'

Steve nodded. 'Most flying is too fast, but this flight isn't fast enough.'

'How do you mean?' I asked. The conversation was helping, nudging my apprehension aside. I was grateful for it.

'Guinness World Records,' he said, and I suddenly understood exactly what he was getting at. Our transit from the end of Leg One to the start of Leg Two – namely, this flight – took us laterally but not longitudinally. By flying from Shiraz to Cairo we were losing 24 hours of time, yet we were gaining nothing in space. Indeed, we were losing space too – Cairo being located at a latitude approximately 80 miles north of Shiraz. We should have been given at least a day's grace by GWR to accommodate this flight and those 80 miles, but it had never been an option. They had stood fast by their 100-day rule, as arbitrary as that rule was in the first place. The unfairness of it all was an issue Steve and I had complained about to anyone who would listen before the journey, and we continued to complain about it to each other on the flight all the way to Cairo. It proved a marvellous distraction.

'Be cautious,' the security officer told us as the porter disappeared into the airport's thick crowds, on the hunt for our bikes which had not arrived with the rest of our luggage. 'This is a very bad time for Egypt. A very bad time for Cairo. There is a lot of danger here.'

'For foreigners?' I asked.

'For everyone. It is better for you to stay inside, especially at night.'

The porter reappeared with our bikes and then stood beside us expectantly as we checked them over for damage.

'You should give him a tip,' the security officer said. 'Welcome to Egypt.'

Francesca had booked us a hotel on the outskirts of the city. Though we were both eager to get back on our bikes, we had no idea what the situation on the ground was like and knew it would be best to assess it from the relative safety of a taxi first. Squeezing our bikes and panniers and then ourselves into the back of a cab, we set off for the hotel.

At first, we thought the driver had made a mistake. The hotel we pulled up outside was monstrously gargantuan, gilded, ornate and gauchely luxurious. A uniformed concierge opened the taxi's door for us, and then signalled for three others to carry our bikes and bags inside. We followed in a daze, tiptoeing across the gleaming marble floor to arrive at the reception desk: a fortress of mahogany and brass staffed by young women who answered phones and dealt with guests in a plethora of languages, smiling enticingly over every word. While we waited to be seen, I scanned the walls, taking in the various awards and plaques and certificates and endless references to the hotel's five-star rating, until I happened upon the price list. A single room, the cheapest possible accommodation here, was $400.

'Steve,' I said, grabbing him by the elbow and trying to lead him away, 'we're at the wrong hotel. We've got to be. We can't afford this. Francesca must have given us the wrong name. We should—'

'Mr Pakravan?'

I looked up to see the receptionist who had uttered my name. 'Yes?'

'I thought it must be you,' she said. 'Your friend who made the booking said to expect two men with bicycles. And she got one of our special deals for you. A twin room, one night, sixty dollars, including two free massages.'

The rate was astonishing and, as we stumbled towards our room, I felt a tremendous awe for Francesca. How on earth had she managed to secure such an exceptional deal? We had paid more than that for a drab and poky room in Finland, and here we were, in perhaps the most expensive and sophisticated hotel in Cairo, and somehow Francesca had managed to wangle us a room and massage for the equivalent of £20 each. There was only one reasonable conclusion to draw. Francesca had magical powers.

Later, sitting downstairs in the hotel spa, wrapped in starchy towels as we awaited our massages, we fell into conversation with an Australian couple and the reason behind our astounding deal became clear.

'All the hotels have put their prices down at the moment,' the man said. 'This whole country relies on tourism more than it'd like to admit. And there are no tourists coming here right now.'

'There seemed to be quite a few foreigners at reception when we were checking in,' I said.

'They were checking *out*. Everyone's leaving, more each day. You're the first non-Egyptians we've seen arrive for days.'

'And what about you?' Steve asked. 'Why haven't you left yet?'

'We've been looking forward to this trip all year,' the woman said. 'They won't scare us off. Not that we've had any trouble.'

'If you avoid the city centre you'll be fine,' the man added. 'So far we've been to the pyramids and Sharm El Sheikh and we haven't had any problems.'

'Most people are pleased to see us,' she said. 'They're worried that the tourists might never come back and they don't know what they'll do if that happens. I feel sorry for them really.'

If this conversation helped buoy up our spirits, the massages enlivened them. Explaining that we had cycled 4,000 miles in the past month, the massage therapists understood what needed to be done, and set to work on our hands and legs with painful but rejuvenating vigour. When we left the spa, we floated. All we needed was food and sleep, and we would be more than ready to tackle Leg Two. We resolved to get an early night and leave first thing in the morning. Regardless of our plans, this was our only option anyway: a curfew was in place across Cairo and we were bound to the hotel until it was lifted at 6 a.m. the following morning.

With the curfew ready to fall again at 7 p.m., we needed to push south as quickly as possible, out of Cairo Governorate and into Giza Governorate, where we could join the western bank of the Nile and follow it all the way to Lake Nasser. A ferry waited for us there and to get to it was another scramble against time. Only one ferry left each week and if we missed the one we had allocated we would never recover the lost days. It was clear that, despite the Australian couple's warnings and despite our own trepidation, the shortest and quickest route south passed directly through Cairo's city centre. There was nothing to do but launch into it.

Cairo was like a festival: an overheated and volatile festival, perhaps, with trace lines of malignance etched into its contours, but a festival nonetheless. To cycle along its streets and roads was an exercise in ducking and weaving that would have made Muhammad Ali proud. The traffic was a disorderly scrum of cars, motorbikes, cows, tuk-tuks, tanks, sheep, buses, pedestrians, donkeys with or without carts, minivans, camels, lorries and army jeeps, all beeping and honking and baying and farting thick clouds of pollution into the air, which mingled with the ever-present dust to hang like an asphyxiating mist over all of it. Largely paralysed by gridlock, so that we had to swing and manoeuvre our way between each vehicle and animal in zigzags and right angles, cars would lurch forward with sudden and unexpected jolts to fill any available space that appeared. If Steve and I happened to be in that space, it was up to us to remove ourselves from it in time. Twice I was too slow, and turned in shock to witness the bumper of an aged and battered car nudging my rear wheel out of the way.

Here and there, the road opened up into two or even three lanes, allowing the traffic to flow with greater ease. Yet this did little to diminish the chaos. Instead, it merely seemed to speed it up and we hugged the edge of the road at these times, re-familiarising ourselves with the same terror we had experienced on Russia's motorways. The vehicles that hurtled past us with alarming proximity bumped and careered across the tarmac, and some of the passengers pushed their torsos out through the open windows to wave and holler at us with Doppler effect shrieks. One car – a mud-streaked old estate – swung itself between me and Steve, its boot snapping open to reveal a washing machine, untethered and bouncing to and fro within the boot, and for a brief and terrifying moment I thought it might launch itself from the car and on to me.

Mostly, however, movement was slow if not non-existent, and wending our way through the city took most of the day. The one solace I could derive from the lack of speed was that it gave us the occasional opportunity to talk with those stuck on these roads with us. Many could speak English, and though most wanted to know who we were, where we came from and why we were in Cairo, some launched directly into their own political philosophies without provocation.

'When you have a bad authority, you must have a revolution,' one man explained to me as he leaned from his window and puffed on a cigarette. 'The revolution is not finished in Egypt. The Muslim Brotherhood must go, we must get rid of them. They do nothing for us. All Egyptians love the military. All Egyptians trust the army. We do not trust the Muslim Brotherhood. The revolution will end when they are all gone.'

Another, a motorcyclist with an enormous crack running the length of his helmet, which surely rendered it useless, held the opposite opinion. 'Removing Morsi was illegal. How can you remove a democratically elected president? It was against the law. Western powers did it. They did not trust Morsi because he was with the Muslim Brotherhood. They were scared of him. So now we are living in a dictatorship. I thought the West loved democracy? They only love their democracy, they do not love ours.'

Gradually, the city began to dissolve as we rode further south. The traffic lessened and space opened up on the road at the same rate as it receded beside it, where the glass, chrome and concrete of central Cairo gave way to overlapping corrugated iron, to the cardboard of the slums that spilled out from the roadside into the makeshift and labyrinthine shanty towns of south Cairo. Only the military presence stayed the same: a tank on every corner; convoys of kerb-crawling jeeps all over; soldiers as prolific as beggars; guns as ever-present as poverty.

As we passed Giza, the tips of the pyramids poked up from the horizon. With the thought of the ferry never far from my mind, I knew immediately that there was no time to visit them, to see them up close. Such knowledge left a sour taste, and suddenly the record seemed to me quite hollow and arbitrary. It was the same disheartening feeling I had experienced back in Volgograd. For a moment, I considered relinquishing the record and choosing instead to spend the day among the pyramids, but the moment was a brief one, and forgotten quickly. I was so focused and hooked on the idea of the record that I couldn't truly see anything else.

At Dahshur, with Cairo firmly behind us, we took a break. We had made it through unscathed and this called for celebration. We bought bottles of water from a local shop and, perhaps infected by our joy, the owner proudly offered us the gift of a pack of fresh dates. We sat outside and ate them slowly, watching the sunlight as it filtered through the palm leaves above us and then danced and sparkled off the placid waters of the Nile just metres away. It had been a long and gruelling day – already 3 p.m. and yet we had only covered 32 miles – but the relief of making it safely through Cairo, perhaps the most dangerous city we would have to encounter on the whole journey, outweighed any concerns over time or distance. We remained unharmed and for the moment that was all that mattered.

The peace did not last long. On the outskirts of Al Qababt, we found ourselves pedalling directly into the midst of a Muslim Brotherhood rally. Coaches and cars crowded the road, and people thronged about them, ages ranging from five to 85. The youngest scampered over the vehicles with the sure-footedness of cats, shrieking and hooting at the sheer excitement of being around so many people at once; the adults, on the other hand, ranged from sombre to angry – they debated fiercely with each other, spitting out their words with such force that it seemed they were fighting one another rather than the military. One symbol dominated – the Rabia, or R4BIA: the four-fingered salute, emblazoned across flags and posters and stickers everywhere, a black hand on a yellow background, the gesture of solidarity for those who supported the Muslim Brotherhood and opposed the overthrow of Morsi. The air was thick and pregnant, a thunderstorm of tension waiting to sound off in fury.

Soon, the demonstration grew impenetrable, and Steve and I had to stop and dismount, seeking out a path to push through. Few people paid attention to us, and when I asked participants how far forward the protest stretched, most ignored me.

'There is a lot of us,' one man finally answered me. He chewed on what looked like a splint of wood and although he spoke to me he did not look at me. His eyes were fixed on some remote point ahead of us, deep in the crowds. 'A lot of us and then a lot of military facing us. I think you can get through. But you do not want to be stuck between us and the military.'

More and more people were beginning to mass behind us, hemming us in, squashing us into the rabble. Twinges of claustrophobia trickled through my veins and, as the situation worsened, the fear of not being able to escape heightened into an all-consuming terror. We battled our way to where the crowd was thinnest, beside the road's central reservation. Looking ahead, I could see that the demonstration filled this side of the highway. On the other side, the traffic flowed freely, some cars slowing to toot their horns in solidarity, but none stopping.

'I've got an idea,' I said to Steve, and before he could ask what it was I implemented it. To hesitate would only have caused discussion and further time-wasting, and, besides, I did not particularly care what he thought of the idea. I had resolved to do it and he could follow me if he wanted. He did.

I hoisted my bike over the central reservation to get away from the crowd and waited for the next lull in the oncoming traffic on this side of the highway. Once I saw a break, I pedalled ferociously across the three lanes to the far side, narrowly missing a gleaming Mercedes whose driver was jabbering into his mobile phone and paying little attention to the road. At the far side, I hugged the wall and waited for Steve, who was making his own way across the lanes, sprinting towards me with a look of terror on his face.

'*That* was your idea?' he shouted at me as he pulled up.

'No,' I said. 'That was just the start of it. Now we have to cycle this way.' I pointed forward, into the oncoming traffic.

'This is ridiculous, mate,' Steve replied. 'I wouldn't like to cycle the wrong way down a road in the UK. But here? In Egypt? We've only been here a day and already I've seen that most of the drivers are suicidal. And there's not even a hard shoulder!'

'We'll stick to the slow lane and keep as close to the wall as possible. As soon as we pass the demonstration we'll cross back to the right side of the road.'

'We stuck to the slow lane and we kept as close to the wall as possible when we were going in the same direction as the traffic and I didn't feel safe *then*.'

I shrugged. 'It's a solution.'

Steve shook his head. 'It's a crazy solution. You first.'

The demonstration stretched for just over one mile. As we cautiously made our way along the slow lane, the cars that veered towards us seemed somehow to speed up once the drivers caught sight of the two foreigners cycling in their direction, and they passed with as little space to spare as possible. Nevertheless, none scowled or shook their fists at us as they flew by, but smiled and waved, as if grateful for the opportunity for a quick game of chicken. It was, after all, a game they could not lose. Our bikes were tough, but no match against even the front grill of a 25 mph Renault 4.

At last, the military's side of the demonstration petered out as the soldiers and army jeeps were replaced by civilian supporters and minivans. We took another wild swing across the three lanes of oncoming traffic, enduring the blaring horn of a lorry whose speed we had misjudged and which bore down upon us with a steadfast and terrifying conviction, and reached the central reservation just in time. The other side of the road – our side – was quiet, almost entirely devoid of traffic, for nothing could get through the demonstration, and the only cars here were those that had joined the road beyond the protest's fringe.

By the time the curfew fell at 7 p.m., we had cycled only 84 miles, making it to the town of Beni Suef. Our bodies still felt limber and lithe after the previous day's massages and we could have happily pushed on for another 40 or 50 miles, but the possibility of arrest was both unpleasant and highly plausible. We had seen police cars every few miles on the road south from Cairo, and doubtless their presence would only increase while the curfew was imposed. So we stopped, checked into a guesthouse, ate a meagre dinner and then fell asleep, to dream of head-on collisions.

―――――――――

When I think about the following day and about the things I did then, I still find it difficult to reconcile them with the person I know myself to be. I could perhaps attribute my actions to the heat, the dehydration, the pestering of the street children or the lack of food, but to do so would be to recite a litany of excuses, none of which would serve to justify. The truth is I just snapped and there's not much more I can say or offer as explanation.

It had, of course, been a tough day. We had cycled hard and yet had clocked less than 80 miles. Traffic had been dense, road conditions had been poor and whenever we slowed to less than 5 mph we were immediately surrounded by children – appearing, it seemed, directly from the earth – who slowed us further by grabbing at our bare legs and arms and threatening to poke sticks into our spokes, and trying to jump on to our backs, all the time pleading 'Money, money, money', the only English they knew. Although it was by now late September, the heat, peaking at 40°C, was near-insufferable and I could never seem to drink enough water. By the afternoon, my nerves were shattered, and Steve and I fell back into the old, familiar argument over filming, our exchanges almost verbatim facsimiles of previous conflicts, were it not for the wildcard Steve threw in: he was getting frustrated at having to stop so often to eat. So the argument about whether or not we filmed enough morphed into an argument about whether or not we ate enough: a different sentiment but largely the same phraseology, Steve's '*Less!*' versus my '*More!*'

By the time we reached the town of Samalut, I was so tightly wound I felt like I might seize up into catatonia. We stopped at a street food stall that sold fried liver in pitta bread and, while I went to buy a portion, Steve insisted he was not hungry – *making a point*, I thought – and stayed at the side of the road. When I returned, half-eaten pitta in hand, a tall and thin Egyptian man was hollering at Steve in Arabic and jabbing his finger in his chest. Steve was not replying, not even making eye contact with the man, but was instead attempting to push his bike away and through the small crowd of people that was beginning to build.

'Hey!' I called, principally to Steve, but also as a means to distract the man. 'What's going on?'

The man turned and began to stride towards me. Watching him as he approached, I could see from the corner of my eye that Steve was pedalling on to the road and away. It sounded as if he shouted something at me, but it was lost behind the chatterings of the small crowd, who had followed the man and begun to surround me. I folded the remnants of the pitta bread into my mouth and placed my foot on the pedal, ready to cycle after Steve, when the man grabbed my handlebars with one hand and, with the other, in a movement that was so deft I was almost astonished into submission, unzipped my front bag, reached in and plucked out my camera.

That was the moment when the wheels of reason stopped turning, when cognition took its final bow and stepped aside to let thoughtless reaction take over. Both my hands shot out to enfold his: my right pried his fingers back and my left palmed the camera and deposited it safely back in the bag. Yet, despite the recovery of my equipment, my right hand did not stop. It continued to bend the man's fingers back and back until there was a discernible snap. The man looked down at his broken finger in disbelief, looked back up at me and then lunged. We tumbled to the ground together, a mesh of flailing limbs and spinning wheels. I managed to extricate myself and stood back up, only to find him inches from me, shouting and cursing and buzzing about me like a wasp. He pushed me hard in the chest and I stumbled back, caught and steadied by members of the crowd. Others flowed in front of me, remonstrating with the man and attempting to calm him. For the briefest of moments, I could think clearly again and the thought I had was: *these people are on my side*. But then all dissolved to white noise once more as the man pushed the others aside and came back at me, the hand with the broken finger at his waist and the other clenched into a fist and raised high. I reached forward, locking one hand around his neck and the other around his jawline. And then I began to squeeze. And, now that I think about it, now that I am able to think and not just react, now that I can assess it all perhaps not with objectivity but at least with hindsight, it strikes me that I may well have continued squeezing, and I may well have done so with greater and greater pressure, and I may not have stopped at all were it not for the arrival of the police.

CHAPTER 13

THE GENERAL

Distance remaining: 6,905 miles
Time to record: 61 days

We were certain it was the end. Whether or not it could be construed as self-defence, the fact was that I had assaulted that man: I, a foreigner, had broken the finger of him, a local. And I felt terrible about it. I could not believe the circumstances that had pushed me to commit such violence against another human. It was not purposeful but instinctive – yet it was far more extreme than anything I was used to and I regretted it dearly. The police had us now and, though we weren't in handcuffs, we were in the back of the van, without doubt on our way to jail, and whether we spent two nights there or two years, we were never going to make the Lake Nasser ferry in time. I felt bad for Steve, who had not been a part of the fight, but had turned around and cycled back towards me when he heard the sirens and saw my bike being carried by the police officers into the van. The moment they noticed Steve, they ushered him inside, too.

At the police station, we were led into a small, windowless room. 'Wait here,' the officer intoned. 'The General will come soon.'

'The *General*?' Steve whispered as the officer left. 'Christ, Reza – what have you done to us?'

The General, when he arrived, was, to my surprise, exactly as I had pictured him: a giant of a man in a perfectly pressed uniform with epaulettes, brass buttons and a shoulder strap denoting his high rank; his moustache and eyebrows the luxuriant consistency of a shag rug; his eyes as dark and shining as his boots; his machismo bleeding from every pore. The officers who arrived with him seemed to wilt in his presence, and any notion of playing the rebel, which I might have earlier entertained, vanished. I was prepared to accept whatever penance he demanded.

'Had a bit of trouble in town, I hear,' he said in perfectly enunciated English.

'Someone tried to steal my camera,' I stammered.

'They'll do that,' he said with a smile. That smile seemed to transform the entire atmosphere in one fell swoop. It was one of the kindest smiles I had ever known.

'I was only trying to protect myself.'

'Of course you were, of course you were!' he cried. 'What, you didn't think we were going to arrest you, did you?'

'It crossed my mind.'

'No, no, absolutely not, we brought you here for your own safety. My boys said that you might have got into a bit of trouble.'

'Actually, most of the people were nice to me,' I said. 'They were trying to stop the man from attacking me.'

'I'm pleased to hear that. Us Egyptians are good people,' he said, chuckling again.

'So are we free to go?' Steve asked.

'Of course you are, of course you are!' he cried. 'But I wondered if maybe you might like some dinner first?'

Though we were eager to get back on the road, we were starving and the prospect of some dinner first sounded wonderful.

The restaurant reminded me of a Middle Eastern cafe I knew back in London – it had the same dim lights, the same Arabic music percolating out from speakers hidden within the carpeted walls, the same overweight men who stood in small groups, smoking cigarettes and playing with their balls. The General had brought two of the younger officers along with him and they could not believe their luck. As Steve and I sat on plastic chairs around a plastic table with the General, they darted between the pool table and the shisha pipes and the huge flat-screen television, only spending a few moments at each before the lure of the next grew too strong.

'It is after the curfew,' the General explained. 'They should be out patrolling now. That job is mostly boring and sometimes dangerous but never anything else. They are lucky to be here.'

He ordered for us, and when the falafels and baba ghanoush arrived, followed by plates of kofta and mahshi, we were glad, for they were delicious. As we ate, at the General's insistence, we divulged the details of our journey, concluding with our need to reach Lake Nasser in time.

'And what would happen if I just drove you to Lake Nasser myself?' he asked. 'Put you in the back of my car and put your bikes on the roof and took you all the way? I would guarantee to get you there on time.'

'That'd be very generous of you,' I replied. 'But we'd forfeit the record. We have to cycle every inch.'

'How would Guinness World Records know?' he asked. 'I wouldn't say anything.'

'They might find out by looking at our tracker and seeing how quickly we travelled from here to Lake Nasser. Or they might get suspicious when they see no one has signed our evidence book between the two places. Or they might request our video footage and work it out from that. Or they might not find out at all. It doesn't matter really. We would know we had cheated and it would make the whole thing pointless.'

'So you must pedal every inch,' he said.

'Every inch.'

He thought about something for a moment. 'And what about now?' he finally asked. 'This restaurant is about six kilometres south from Samalut, where you had your fight. Will you do an extra six kilometres somewhere else to compensate?'

'It doesn't work like that,' I replied. 'If you don't mind taking us back to the police station, we'll get our bikes and cycle back to Samalut, and then resume from there.'

'But that will take you another hour!' he cried, aghast at the thought.

'Not to mention it's after the curfew,' Steve said. '*And* we still need to find a place to sleep.'

This was all too much for the General to bear. He pushed his plate of half-finished mahshi aside and barked orders at the two officers, who sheepishly lowered their pool cues and came to his side at the table. 'Have you finished your food?' he asked us.

We nodded. While he had languorously savoured every mouthful of his dinner, we had wolfed ours down in a matter of minutes.

'Good. Then we will go now. We will collect your bikes and then drive you back to Samalut. I know a good hotel there. I will speak to the manager so he will not worry that you are out after the curfew. Then you can start from where you finished tomorrow morning.'

'Thank you,' I said. 'But I'm not sure about going back to Samalut tonight – what if that man is still there?'

'Oh, he will not be there. We took him away.'

'Did you arrest him?'

The General turned to look at me, his moustache quivering with surprise. 'Did we *arrest* him? Of course not, of course not! We took him to the hospital. You did break his finger, you know.'

'I feel awful about that,' I said, looking down at the floor guiltily.

'Well,' the General considered for a moment. 'He *was* a thief.'

When the curfew ended each morning, it was like someone had fired a starter's pistol. I watched from the hotel room window that looked out over Samalut as 7 a.m. struck. Within seconds, the silent streets, empty save for the occasional emaciated dog and the ubiquitous dust, became filled with cars, bicycles, motorbikes, donkeys, carts, men, women, children and chaos, all of it pushing outwards beneath a cacophony of blaring horns. There was nothing and then there was everything, and the juxtaposition of the two opposing states, wrought over a matter of seconds, was astonishing to behold.

We cycled out among it all as soon as we were ready. Our mileage had been low since stepping off the plane. We had been prepared for that, and had understood from the earliest days of planning that we would not be able to cover as many miles each day in Africa as we had in Europe and Asia. For a start, we had replaced our tyres with wider specimens in readiness for the substandard roads we would be encountering here; and we had increased the stock of supplies in our panniers, knowing that as we approached and then tackled the Sahara civilisation would dissipate and we would need to be more self-sufficient.

Nevertheless, we were still behind schedule and the issue of the Lake Nasser ferry was beginning to grow increasingly pressing, so we pushed on hard, following the Nile south as far as we could. Steve had become the inveterate pacemaker of the team when it came to moments like this, and I gladly let him take the lead, maintaining the same strenuous speed as him and stopping for a break only when he allowed. Steve was in his element – when it came to devouring miles and reclaiming lost time, he excelled and I was grateful that he had those particular qualities, for I could often lack them.

For example, under any other circumstances I would have pulled over the moment the police car cruising behind me turned on its sirens. But Steve, who must have been able to hear it, too, showed no signs of slowing and so neither did I. Perhaps the officers in the car did not mind so much, for they turned the siren off, though they continued to tailgate us for the next hour until we stopped for an afternoon snack.

'Is everything all right, officers?' I asked in English as they climbed
from the car and approached us. I had learned some Arabic for my Sahara
crossing and still remembered a few words, but I was loath to use them
now, hoping to instead play the innocent-foreigner card.

'Police station,' the taller of the two said, pointing ahead. 'Two miles.
You stop.' With that, they both turned on their heels and walked back to
their car.

Following their instructions, we stopped at the station 2 miles later,
where we were greeted by a young captain who looked barely out of his
20s and who wore civilian clothes. 'I want to introduce myself,' he said.
'My name is Tarek.'

'It's very nice to meet you,' I replied, bemused.

'And my two men in the car are called Ayman and Youssef.'

'Good stuff,' I said, wondering why he was telling us all this.

'They will escort you to Lake Nasser.'

'How do you know we're going to Lake Nasser?' Steve pitched in.

'You are going to catch the ferry. You must catch the ferry.'

'Yes, you're right,' Steve concurred, 'but how do you know all this?'

'Because the General in Samalut tell me. You must have police escort
to Lake Nasser. You must catch the ferry. We keep you safe in Egypt.'

So the General, who had wanted to drive us to Lake Nasser, had instead
offered this compromise. I considered politely rejecting the offer, but the
captain spoke in absolutes and imperatives and we did not, it seemed, have
a choice.

'Now it is late,' he said, looking at his watch. 'And this town is
dangerous. Many Muslim Brotherhood here. You must stay the night
here. In station.'

It was not that late: there were still 2 hours left until the curfew, and
we needed to make it at least to the next town by then. It took some time
to convince the captain that we were grateful for his offer but would not
be accepting it, and when we finally did convince him, it was on the
condition that we would stop at the next town and spend the night at a

place he knew. Ayman and Youssef would escort us there and would show us where to find the accommodation. As an added bonus, we discovered that, with our police escort, the curfew no longer mattered to us and if we crossed into it before reaching the next town we had no cause for concern.

'The General, eh?' Steve said, pulling up level with me as we cycled on, Ayman and Youssef tailing us with their siren wailing. 'We must have made quite an impression on him.'

'I wish we hadn't,' I replied.

'Don't you like the escort?'

'I don't know. I'm glad we can ignore the curfew now. We can start cycling more miles each day and make back some time. But don't you feel weird with them behind us like this all the time? Look at the way people are looking at us. Like we're different from them, like we think we're special. No one's going to talk to us now whenever we stop.'

'I like it,' Steve said. 'They make me feel safe. Sure, no one's going to talk to us now, but no one's going to attack us either, not when we've constantly got the police around.'

Reaching the next town, Ayman and Youssef led us down a dark alleyway towards an imposing iron gate which appeared through the thick dust. Two young men appeared to open the gate and wave at our police escort – who promptly drove away – and then said: 'Welcome to our church.' They introduced themselves as John and George, shook our hands, and helped us carry our bikes and equipment inside.

They were Coptic Orthodox Christians, and as we followed them through the leafy courtyard and past the ageing but beautifully maintained church they explained that we would be spending the night in the bishop's house: a spacious yet homely three-storey building at the rear of the enclosure, filled with chandeliers, antique sofas and wood carvings from all over the world. We met our host – Bishop Thomas – before John and George and one of the residential nuns took us to the dining room, where a handsome spread of omelettes, cheese, eggs, salad, pizza slices, bowls of rice and loaves of fresh bread was already laid out across the table.

'This is amazing,' I said as John pulled out a chair for me to sit. 'It's so kind of you. Thank you. Thank you so much.'

Neither John, George nor the nun replied to this, but they looked at each other and smiled warmly.

'I love your house,' Steve said to our companions. 'It's like a little oasis. We've seen so much chaos in Egypt, but this is the complete opposite. Calm.'

'We are very lucky to live here,' George said. 'We do our best to maintain it.'

'And this food is hitting the spot!' Steve said, tearing into a fresh slice of pizza. 'I'm starving!'

'There is more if you want it,' John said. 'But only vegetarian. It is Wednesday and we do not eat meat on Wednesdays.'

As it happened, we did want more, and it was brought to us with such pride and pleasure that we were overwhelmed by how fortunate we had been, ending up at this splendid house eating splendid food and talking with splendid people.

'Have you spoken with many Egyptians while you have been here?' John asked.

'Some,' I replied, sensing that, as was so often the case in Egypt, the conversation was about to turn political.

'And what have they told you? About our current state of affairs?'

'Lots of different things. Some have said they are glad Morsi is gone, others have said they still support him no matter what's happened.'

John shook his head sadly. 'It is a civil war,' he said. 'Have you met any members of the Muslim Brotherhood?'

'We've seen them on the streets and in the demonstrations, with their flags and their chants. There was a man in Cairo, we were stuck in traffic with him, who supported the Muslim Brotherhood. He said that Morsi had been democratically elected to be President, and that overthrowing him was therefore illegal.'

'I disagree,' John said. 'There are ninety million people in Egypt. Eight million of them are Christian. Almost ten per cent of the population. And yet Morsi's government was made only of Muslims and everything they did was only for Muslims. This is not democracy.'

'Morsi was a liar,' George said. 'I don't hate him, but I hated his management, his presidency, his government. They wanted to control everything. There was no freedom, especially for non-Muslims. I am happier with the military in charge.'

John and George were becoming worked up. We could see it in their faces and hear it in their voices. Suddenly, the nun, who had until then been largely quiet, joined in, delivering her words just as passionately as her two companions. 'Many Christians were attacked by the Muslim Brotherhood,' she said. 'And because Morsi was in power, no one did anything about it, so they attacked us even more. Some churches were burnt to the ground. Did you notice the huge gates we let you in through? We put them up because we were scared.'

'We're still scared,' John said. 'Christians are still attacked, but now if the attackers are caught they go to prison. This is because of the military. We are grateful for the military.'

When dinner was over, we were shown to where we would sleep. Steve was shown to a room with a lush double bed and en-suite bathroom. Then John led me further down the corridor, opening the door on to a large room smothered with lace and cushions, a shower and Western toilet gleaming out from the bathroom, and the air-conditioning unit whirring comfortingly over it all.

'This is a very special room,' John said to me. 'The last person to stay here was the Coptic Orthodox Pope. He found it very comfortable. I hope you will, too.'

It was a remarkable end to an altogether remarkable evening. I showered for an age, letting the searing hot water carve its way through the dirt that caked my skin and then directing it towards and over my aching muscles. Then, sprawled across the huge sofa wrapped in nothing but a soft towel, I updated my logbook and emailed Base Camp. And finally, with a whimper of exhausted delight, I crawled beneath the sheets and fell asleep in the Pope's bed.

———————

Though we were up early and energised by a hearty breakfast laid on by our generous hosts, we were unable to leave until the police escort arrived. By noon, they had still not appeared. I grew impatient, angry at the miles we could have covered, frustrated that instead we had just sat on the church's step for hours. John and George had been keeping us company, at least, and we had managed to kill a couple of minutes by asking them to sign our evidence book. Other than that, there had been little else to do but sit and wait. Eventually, I suggested that we leave without the escort.

'No,' piped up George. 'They will arrest you.'

'Why?' I asked. 'We're not causing any trouble, we're not dangerous. They're escorting us for *our* safety.'

'Yes, and they will arrest you for your safety,' he replied cryptically.

'Not to mention,' John said, 'that they asked us not to let you leave without them. If we do, we'll get into trouble, too.'

By the time the police arrived, at 1 p.m., half of the day was over and I had already had enough of them. This time, there were four officers in the car – none of them Ayman or Youssef – and we learned over the next few days that the officers replaced each other according to a rotating shift pattern. This, too, took time and we often had to wait for anything up to an hour and a half while the handovers took place. Our progress lost any element of consistency and we cycled late into each night in order to cover our daily requirement of miles, our only solace the newfound capacity to ignore the curfew.

My patience wore thinner and thinner. The escort began to transform from a safety measure into a hindrance and I found myself cursing the General under my breath as we cycled. At times, the officers pushed us on with what seemed like sadistic delight, denying us any opportunity to stop, even for water, as we rode through the withering heat, their excuse that these were dangerous parts and it was better to be thirsty than attacked. At other times, they decided they needed a break, and forced us to stop with them while they sat around in cafes, drinking coffee and smoking cigarettes, pleasures that could likewise have been enjoyed on the road in the car. And always, with such relentless determination that I feared I might have a seizure, they sounded their siren. It wailed and blared and cawed behind me from morning to night, boring its way through my eardrums and rebounding about my mind until there seemed to be nothing else in there but it and it alone. When I dreamed at night, people opened their mouths and, instead of words, the siren's wail poured out.

A few miles north of Luxor, I snapped. I needed a toilet break, but the police had insisted we were not allowed to stop until we reached the city and the guesthouse we were due to spend the night at. Though I fought the pressure in my bowels, it soon became clear that I would not last much longer, and so I stopped, dismounted my bike and began to walk purposefully towards the banks of the Nile.

'Hey!' came a voice from behind me. 'Stop!' One of the officers had leaped from the car and was running after me, calling above the siren which was, of course, still on. '*Stop!*' I ignored him and continued walking. When he reached me, he grabbed my left arm. 'Where are you going?' he demanded.

I looked him steadily in the eye and then, in the calmest and most matter-of-fact voice I could muster, said: 'I'm going for a shit. Would you like to watch?'

He let go of my arm and took two steps back, his cheeks reddening in an instant, though whether it was from shock or shame I could not tell. Without another word, he turned and walked back to the police car and, when I returned a few minutes later, he refused to make eye contact with me.

I looked over at Steve, sitting on his bike at the roadside, and wondered if he would approve of what I was about to do. Probably not. But I found that I did not particularly care. I marched over to the police car and stuck my head through the open window. We've had enough, I explained to the driver. We did not need the police escort. We would be fine alone. They were slowing us down. They were making us late. He argued back with me – the escort was not optional, it was mandatory and we simply had to put up with it – but I stood my ground, concluding the argument with my firm announcement that we would be leaving Luxor at 7 a.m. sharp the following morning, that we would spend the day cycling to Lake Nasser, that we would stop wherever we liked for however long we liked and that we would not stop if we did not feel inclined, and that if a police car wished to accompany us while we did all that they could, but if they did not we would do it all anyway.

Somehow, it worked. At 7 a.m. the next day, packed and ready to leave, we stepped out of the guesthouse door and into the morning sunshine that flooded Luxor's streets. There were no police in sight.

Our ferry was to leave from the port of Aswan, and that was 135 miles away. It was unlikely that we would cover the entire distance in a single day – especially now that, without the police escort, we had to adhere to the curfew again – but we intended to get as close as we possibly could before 7 p.m. The ferry itself was not due to depart until 4 p.m. the following afternoon, but we knew well enough that departure and arrival times in this part of the world were rarely fixed, and should be treated more like guidelines than facts. In order to be safe, we needed to get to Aswan as early as possible, preferably before midday tomorrow.

The going was good for the first 70 miles. The temperature had cooled slightly and a tailwind boosted us forwards. The traffic was the calmest we had seen in all Egypt, and the absence of a persistent siren at my back gave me indescribable pleasure. Our good speed was hampered somewhat by the persistence of speed bumps, the sheer volume of which I have not seen outside Egypt, but these were at least forgivable after the chaos of those roads in the north of the country.

If the speed bumps had been our frequent companion throughout Egypt, the Nile had been even more so. Life had always flourished around and outwards from the Nile – the country's main artery – and the road travelled alongside the river like a faithful sidekick as they both wended their way from Cairo to Lake Nasser. I loved this proximity, often imagining myself on the cool water rather than on this hot and dusty road, skirting the thin islands that sprouted up from the river and gave a home to the sycamore, mulberry and lotus trees. Indeed, so lost did I become in this reverie that, as we began to pass through one of the myriad small towns that extended out from the banks of the Nile, it took me some time to notice the damaged buildings, the fallen rubble and the heightened military presence: all the signs of a recent conflict.

Steve saw the car first – it lay in the middle of the road, upturned and on its roof, a burnt-out shell. Those people who walked past it gave it a wide berth. Metres beyond it, two long strips of tape had been stretched across the road, cordoning off the area. We stopped and looked through. Smoke filtered out from an alleyway between two buildings. As we looked closer, we realised it was not an alleyway at all, but the place where another building had once stood. It had been burnt to the ground.

'I don't like this,' Steve said. 'We should turn around and find another route.'

A group of men stepped over the tape and walked into the restricted area, followed by a gang of tiny children and then more men.

'No one's stopping,' I said. 'We shouldn't either. Come on.'

We lifted our bikes over the tape and began to cycle forwards. Passing the smoking remnants of the destroyed building, I looked at those on either side of it. Some were shops, others were homes, all were riddled with the tell-tale pockmarks of bullets. As we continued, I began to realise where the bullets had come from. Many of the men massed here on this street openly carried guns: pistols, shotguns, AK-47s.

Ahead, a tank idled on the side of the road while soldiers began to erect a roadblock from tuk-tuks and flimsy fencing. The civilians with their guns were not marching towards it as such, but they were clearly getting closer, skulking and sidling their way in a crab-like system of advancement, and occasionally one would shout something we could not understand, but which sparkled with identifiable anger. The atmosphere thickened and grew muggy, swelling with a glowering mood that was as discernible as a current through water. The air felt flammable and someone was about to strike a match.

'We should definitely turn around,' I heard Steve mutter.

'Okay,' I agreed. 'Just let me get some quick footage of all this.'

'Not now. Things are about to kick off.'

'Thirty seconds,' I pleaded, holding my GoPro out at arm's length and pressing record. 'Say something.'

Steve sighed deeply and then, perhaps aware that this was the only way to get me to move on, began to talk to the camera.

I must have watched that short piece of footage close to a thousand times by now. I know it intimately and can describe it in detail, frame by frame, from memory. As it begins, from left to right you can see a group of men gathered beneath a tree, then Steve, then the soldiers building their roadblock behind, then a white minivan turning left, then a boy in a red T-shirt sitting on a stationary motorbike and then me. Steve is saying: 'I can feel tension in the air. There's seems to be something, you know, like a roadblock. I'd rather get out of here, to be honest. This is the wrong place and I just don't want to be here at the wrong time.' He looks uncomfortable, tightening his helmet at the back of his head. Another young boy, this one in a beige and blue T-shirt and riding a bicycle, approaches us. He is smiling, looking like he wants to be filmed. I start delivering my piece to camera. 'It's the people without uniforms carrying guns, and that makes me very nervous.' At exactly the same time as I am saying this, a man without a uniform carrying a gun almost the length of his own leg approaches and pushes aside the boy on the bicycle. We see him appear behind my right shoulder, and then all we see is his hand as it covers the camera lens.

Though the footage stops there, my memory of what happened next – off-camera, unrecorded – is as vivid as any film. That looming hand did not just obscure the lens, it ripped the camera from my grasp. I began to protest, but was silenced by the gun, which the man raised and pointed at my face so casually that he almost seemed to be bored. I froze, unable to look away from the gun's barrel, which appeared to widen and deepen the longer I gazed into it. I wanted to look over at Steve, to check how he was, but there was no way I was ever going to take my eyes off the gun, not even to blink.

The man lowered the weapon and my heart rate slowed in direct proportion to its diminishing height. I looked over at Steve, who had also frozen, although his stare was directed down at his own feet. Turning back to the man, I could see that he had now thrust the GoPro towards my face and was waggling it from side to side, shouting something at me in Arabic.

'Delete!' he cried in English when it became clear that I could not understand. 'Now!'

I took the GoPro from him and, guessing that he had never seen one before, removed and pocketed the memory card, pressed a couple of buttons, pretending to delete everything and turned it back on. 'See?' I said to him, holding it up to his face. 'Deleted. No film.' He took the camera back and jabbed at each button in turn, looking satisfied that there was nothing on there to be found.

While all this was going on, ten other men had sauntered over to surround us. They also wore no uniforms but carried a gun each. I reasoned that they were not police nor soldiers, but were some sort of local militia, perhaps Muslim Brotherhood, although of this I could not be sure, for they did not sport the Rabia flags I had seen other Muslim Brotherhood members waving all the way down the Nile.

Whoever they were, it was clear that they neither trusted us nor wanted us there. As the GoPro was passed in turn from one to the next, they began to argue, and from my limited knowledge of Arabic I could just about make out that they were debating what to do with us. Some wanted to let us go; others wanted to take us somewhere, though where that was I could not ascertain.

'What's happening?' Steve whispered to me.

'They're deciding whether or not to let us go.'

'Do you think they will?'

'No,' I said, and when I saw Steve's shoulders slump and his face darken, I wished I had lied.

Even if I had, it would not have mattered. One of the men had taken out his mobile phone and was speaking into it with urgent vehemence. When the call ended, he pointed at four of the men and issued them instructions. Two manhandled our bikes from us and the other two clapped their hands on our arms and shoulders and began to lead us away. Around the corner, a panel van sat beside the kerb, and Steve was roughly pushed into its open back door first. He complied meekly, head down, resigned to his fate, whatever that might be. I, on the other hand, felt so angry at what was happening to us that I considered kicking out, striking and punching at these men with their hands on me, screaming and flailing like a trapped cat, doing whatever I could, no matter how violent, to get us out of there. But when I looked around me, I could see that there was no love, no compassion for us on these streets, neither from the men nor from the bystanders and passers-by, who stared at us not with animosity, but with indifference. Steve had the right idea, I realised, to struggle would be pointless, and so I followed his example and let them push me into the van, saying not a word in protest as they slammed the door shut and drove us away.

CHAPTER 14

'YOU ARE NEW'

Distance remaining: 6,614 miles
Time to record: 57 days

The back of the van was windowless, disconnected from the driver's cab by a thin panel and dark save for the shafts of light that streamed through the small, circular holes in the floor and walls. Were they bullet holes? I dared not wonder. Beyond the panel I could discern three separate voices, the driver and two passengers, who all rode up front; but back here – apart from myself, Steve and our bikes – it was empty. We perched on top of the wheel arches, gripping rivets in the walls behind us to keep us from toppling over each time the van swung around a corner or bumped over a pothole. Now and then, I looked over at Steve, but he never looked back at me, and when I once asked how he was he did not reply. I let us continue in silence.

I tried to listen closer to what the three men in the front cab were saying, for they never stopped talking, but it was impossible. My Arabic was too weak and what I could hear was only a muffled approximation of syllables. What I could recognise was tone. It was unremittingly serious, bordering on full-blown indignation, and was without doubt bitter. There was never any laughter. I imagined they resented us, having to drive us wherever they were driving us, having to deal with us and step up to action when all they wanted to do was strut the streets of their home town and gloatingly wield their guns. The thought of all this began to make *me* bitter, began to make *me* border on full-blown indignation, because they hadn't been forced into this, they could quite easily have let us pass and stayed where they were, lovingly massaging the shafts of their weapons, and we would have simply cycled on, with no trouble, just trying to get to a ferry on time. Somewhere in the back of my mind, I knew this was all just speculation, that I was only guessing they resented us, that I had less of an idea whether they actually did or not than I had of exactly where we were going. But because that was something I *really* did not want to think about, I let myself get swept away with my own speculation. The idea that they perceived themselves as victims when it was us, us stuck back here in this box that stank of petrol and veered and bounced on suspension that had rusted solid years ago; us who had committed no crimes and yet were being punished as if we had; us who were the real victims; and I wanted to stand up and slam my fist against the panel once, twice, three times or more, and yell any Arabic words that I could remember, and if I ran out of them I would move on to Farsi and English, where I had a whole arsenal waiting to be hurled; and the more I thought about it the more I realised I should do it, I *would* do it, and I wouldn't stop until they let us free or just shot us there and then, either way it would be better than this hellish uncertainty that had turned Steve catatonic and me into a seething ball of rage, driven to such irrationality and such stupidity that I was suddenly willing to fight guns with language…

The van stopped. I listened as the three men climbed out of the front and began to converse with another man, his voice far deeper than theirs: a familiar deepness, one I fancied I might even recognise. The side door slid open and sunlight rushed in, momentarily blinding me. No hands reached in to grab hold of our limbs and drag us out, and I was left to readjust to the bright and fresh air. Blinking furiously and extending my hand out from my forehead to shade my eyes, I looked out. And there – standing in the same uniform with the same epaulettes, the same brass buttons and the same shoulder strap, and wearing above it the same smile I remembered from Samalut – was the General.

———————

'Yes, they were local militia,' the General said, blowing smoke-rings so large they wafted around the rim of his cup of coffee. 'Some Muslim Brotherhood, some normal citizens. But really, they are just a group of fathers who want to protect their families. This happens in the smaller towns away from Cairo. People do not care so much about the politics, they just see the fighting, and so they decide to defend their homes themselves, defend them from anyone.'

'But we weren't causing any trouble,' I said. 'They didn't need to defend themselves against us.'

'You worried them with that camera,' he said, and I felt Steve's dark look bore its way into my cheek. 'Actually, you scared them. They thought you might be foreign journalists wanting to portray a bad image of Egypt.'

'Dressed like this?' I exclaimed, gesturing down at my skintight Lycra.

'How would they know what a foreign journalist looks like? These men have never left Egypt, most of them have never even left their own governorate. Maybe they saw you and just thought that was how all foreigners dressed. They think all Westerners are strange anyway, and you two aren't exactly dressed *normally*.'

I couldn't help but laugh at this and the General joined me. I noticed that Steve did not. Indeed, he had barely uttered a word since we had entered the police station.

'They called me because they couldn't think what to do with you,' the General continued. 'They wanted to let you go, but they were worried they would get into trouble with the authorities if they did. The minute they told me they had two foreign journalists who they had caught riding on bicycles, I knew it had to be you two, so I told them to bring you to me. You know, all this would never have happened if you had kept my escort.'

It was now too late to return to the town and continue from there, so the General agreed to let us spend the night in the police station, promising he would drive us back to the town the following morning. There was a condition, of course: that we join him again for dinner. Though it was a different restaurant, he ordered exactly the same – falafels with baba ghanoush, followed by kofta and mahshi. It was just as delicious.

By 11 a.m. the following day, we were back at the upturned car. The streets were still cordoned off, but this time nobody stopped us, for we had the General himself escorting us from behind in his police car. I looked at the people who watched us from doorways or beneath trees, searching for the men who had stopped and surrounded us not 24 hours earlier, but I recognised no one. Steve, cycling parallel to me, looked only straight ahead. He had still uttered barely a word to me: in the police station the previous night, once the General had shown us the cell where we would sleep and then left us, Steve had climbed on to his bed and turned in silence to face the wall.

With 5 hours before the ferry left and just under 70 miles still to go, we had little time for conversation anyway. Covering 14 miles each hour was not impossible – we had done it before – but nor was it easy. Making it to Aswan by 4 p.m. soon outweighed every other concern and became my primary focus. Perhaps Steve felt the same, for once the General had seen us to the limits of the town and then peeled off with a salutary honk of his horn, Steve took the lead and set such a brisk pace that we blasted through the miles in what felt like no time at all.

When we finally located the ferry terminal in the south of Aswan, it was with an overwhelming sense of relief. Against all the odds, we had made it. The record was still achievable. We bought our tickets, worked our way through passport control and customs, battled with the crowd who pushed and shoved each other as they surged towards the narrow entrance of the ferry, climbed aboard the boat, stumbled into our air-conditioned cabin and closed the door behind us. I fell on to my bed, feeling like I'd surfaced from the mania of the crowd. The air conditioning cooled the sweat that cloaked my skin. I could breathe again. Steve climbed on to the upper bunk bed, stretched his arms out before him and emitted a gargantuan sigh.

'You okay?' I asked him. 'I've been worried about you.'

'I'll be fine once this boat gets going,' he nodded. 'I just want to get out of Egypt. I'm done with this country.'

———————————

The ferry, an ageing steamer with a dented and rusting hull, was squalid, overcrowded and cacophonous. I loved it.

It was slow, too. We did not leave until 8 p.m. and would spend the next 18 hours travelling the 230 miles to Sudanese Wadi Halfa. Such an expanse of time without the need to cycle was liberating. I didn't know what to do with myself and I welcomed the uncertainty, the lack of a fixed timetable or quota. I could eat, sleep, listen to music, stretch my legs as and when I liked, and, with luck, talk to some of my fellow passengers. There was no internet access out here on the lake, so I could not even check my emails. It was heavenly.

Our cabin, first class, was a narrow room featuring a set of bunk beds, a wardrobe and an air-conditioning unit. It was hot out on the lake, suffocatingly so, and we were grateful we could afford the cabin. The second-class option was merely a space on the deck, where people huddled below makeshift canopies formed from bedsheets and towels strung between railings, their bare toes poking out and blistering in the fierce sunshine.

Our cabin had no private bathroom, and when we lurched into the corridors to hunt for a place to relieve ourselves, the communal lavatory we discovered was so filthy and rancid that we made a conscious decision to cut down our water intake so as to minimise any future visits. While Steve headed back to the cabin to sleep, I continued on, curious to explore, making my way through the hordes of people who filled every available space with their sacks and bags, their crates and food, machinery, air-conditioning units, fridges and various other household appliances and, in some cases, chickens. The noise and the sheer mass of bodies and objects was chaotic, a free-for-all that would have been overwhelming and even intimidating were it not for the comprehensive excitement that permeated the atmosphere, as if we were all one big family about to set off on holiday together.

I had read about this ferry back in London. It was a popular segment of the Cairo to Cape Town overland trail, and it was not unusual for Western travellers to happen upon other Western travellers in the corridors between the cabins, and then to congregate in the air-conditioned dining room. Yet with the recent troubles in Egypt, travellers had begun to avoid this part of the world, and I may well have been the only non-African on board. Not that it mattered, for I soon met Moneer on the deck as the sun slid behind the lake's banks: a young Sudanese student who was so friendly and interesting that I wished for no other company.

'This is how I pay for my studies,' he said, climbing up on to a lifeboat to find a comfortable perch. 'I bring goods from Egypt back to Sudan. If you know what to look for, you can make a very nice living.'

'What do you look for?' I asked.

He winked. 'Now why would I tell you that?'

I asked if he would sign our evidence book and then asked if I could film our conversation. He agreed to both. There was a refrigerator behind me and, as I rested my camera on top of it to capture us, Moneer signed the book and then explained that he was in his final year at Khartoum University, where he studied accountancy.

'My family find it very difficult to understand why I want to work with money. We are *Baggara*, see – it means "people of cow". Very strong people, very good people. Nomadic. My family live in a tent. It's a huge thing, you've probably never seen a tent so big. And we don't use money. We live from what we farm and by trading with other families, and we measure wealth by cows. Cows are like the currency, see. If you get married to a *Baggara* girl, you have to pay her family with cows. The taller she is, the more cows you need to give.'

'So is it a religious thing, like in India?' I asked. 'Do the *Baggara* think that cows are sacred?'

'No, nothing like that. They are more like a commodity. But we love them very much. *Baggara* never kill their cows, see. A family will only kill one of their cows if they get really desperate. But we love to drink their milk. When I was a child, I loved it so much. Milk is best when it's so fresh it's warm.'

Another Sudanese man, slightly older than Moneer, heard us talking in English and introduced himself. His name was Badr-aldin and, after discovering that Moneer was also Sudanese he fixed his attention on me.

'Are you American?' he asked.

'No,' I replied. 'I'm from Iran and I live in Britain.'

'Ah,' he sighed. 'No good. Iran, Britain, Sudan. No good.'

'I don't know,' I said. 'I quite like all three.'

'No!' he snapped. 'America is the *best*! I want to live in America. Miami. Los Angeles. You know the Rihanna song, "California King"? That's what I want to be. King of California!' He launched into a rendition of the song, singing slowly and without modesty. 'What work will you do when you get to the US?' I asked, hoping to halt his singing, for Moneer was beginning to snigger behind him and I knew he would set me off soon.

'I don't care,' Badr-aldin exclaimed. 'I do anything. It's not important what I do. Maybe work in CIA! I just want to be in America. Everyone in America is rich. I will be rich as well. I will make lots of money. It's my dream. I just need to get there.'

'I've been to America,' I told him. 'Life's not as easy there as you might think. Most people work round the clock. And there are a lot of poor people, a lot of homeless people.'

'Yes. The black people.' Behind him, Moneer stopped sniggering.

'No, lots of them are white,' I replied.

'I don't believe you!' And, for what it's worth, he really did not seem to. Before I could assure him it was indeed the truth, he started off again. 'I want to marry in America. Marry an American girl. But not a black girl. A white woman. White women are more understanding. Black women are not intelligent.'

That was the moment when Moneer jumped down from the lifeboat, said, 'Take care, my friend,' to me, said nothing to Badr-aldin, and then disappeared down below deck. I wanted to follow him, to re-engage him in conversation about Sudan and the *Baggara*, for it had been far more enlightening than this rapidly degenerating bigotry, but Badr-aldin had cornered me now, and there was no getting away from him.

'You can help me go to America,' he said. 'Please. You must help me.'

'How can I help you? I live in London.'

'You will help me. I know you will. Give me your phone number.'

I contemplated giving him a fake number, but I am glad I did not, for after entering it into his phone he then called me to check. When a ringtone sounded from my pocket, he was visibly relieved.

'You will help me,' he repeated. 'You will help me go to America. To find a wife. She can be fat. Thin. Tall. Short. I don't care.'

But not black, I thought.

'As long as I am in America I will be good. And you are a good man. You will help me go to America. I love you.'

It was all growing surreal, standing on this boat far out on an Egyptian lake while a Sudanese man took my phone number and professed his love for me. As if to complete the outlandishness of the scene, all of a sudden, a man appeared from beneath the lifeboat like a golem, blinking in the ferry's lamplight and then rushing towards me. 'Why do you film me?' he screamed. 'What is wrong with you?'

I looked back at my camera in surprise. I had forgotten it was there, still resting on top of the refrigerator and pointing at where Moneer had sat. The man made a lunge for it but I swatted him away.

'No permission!' he howled. 'Delete! No permission! Delete!'

Badr-aldin began to remonstrate with the man in Arabic, but he continued to snap and snarl at me over his shoulder like a maddened troglodyte, and I saw my opportunity to make my excuses and hurry back to the cabin.

———————

I stepped on to Sudanese soil with barely concealed joy. I had been here, in Wadi Halfa, before. Two years earlier, I had set the world record for the fastest crossing of the Sahara Desert by bicycle. It had taken me exactly 13 days, 5 hours, 50 minutes and 14 seconds, and had been undertaken for the benefit of SEED and – the driving force behind so much of what I do – those Malagasy children. I was able to raise £15,000 for them and it delights me as much to report that now as it did back in 2011.

The journey traversed the second-largest desert on the planet (after Antarctica), beginning in the Algerian town of El Goléa and ending in Sudan, where I joined the very road I was about to cycle now at Wadi Halfa, forging down along it until south of Dongola, where I veered off to complete the expedition in the middle of nowhere, not even a village, but merely a co-ordinate on the 18th parallel north. I remembered distinctly how I had fallen in love with Sudan back then: with the easy charm of its people; with the tranquillity and serenity of its eternal desert landscapes – and returning to the country for this new expedition did not disappoint.

If anything, this time my experience was superior. The tailwind – the same strong north-easterly wind that had propelled me through the desert two years ago – thrust us into an effortless and exhilarating 40 mph glide over the tarmac. The road, on the other hand, was unfamiliar, not the pitted and crumbling thoroughfare I had toiled and moiled along before, but new: Chinese-built, smooth and empty, a high-quality upgrade that sang beneath our wheels. That, the wind and the occasional click of a gear shift were the only noises to be heard. It could not have been more different to Egypt, where we had never cycled more than a few miles without enduring shouts or whistles or, worst of all, sirens.

'What do you think of Sudan?' I asked Steve as we rode.

'Stunning,' he said, white teeth grinning out from his browning face and thickening beard.

'It's so peaceful. Nothing like Egypt.'

'Don't remind me of Egypt.' A pause, and then: 'You know what I *really* love about Sudan?'

'What?' I asked.

'It's illegal to film here. So you won't be waving that camera in my face all the time.' He gave a spirited laugh and broke ahead.

I had forgotten about the filming. It was possible, of course, so long as I did it clandestinely, but, officially, in order to film or take photographs across Sudan, you first needed to acquire a permit from the government and I had no such thing.

The temperature soared: 40°C, then 42°C, then 45°C. By mid-afternoon it became impossible to ride and so we changed our strategy, breaking at 2 p.m. to take shelter in water stations or cafes, and then setting out again in the late afternoon once it had cooled, riding as long into the night as we could. We did not need to worry so much about accommodation: we simply unfurled our sleeping bags and slept outside, beneath an array of stars the likes of which only a person who has been to the desert can understand. If we felt decadent, we pulled into truck stops and rented outdoor stretchers to sleep on, dozing off amid the snores and farts and grunts of the dormant truck-drivers around us. Mostly, though, we spent the night wherever the odometer clocked up the final mile of our daily quota.

Our progress was sensational. Days and miles zipped by. I began to look forward more and more to our meal and siesta stops at roadside cafes. They all conformed to a similar design: a wooden frame, a corrugated-iron roof, palm leaves woven together to constitute walls, plastic chairs and metal tables, a barrel of water at the entrance for washing hands, old refrigerators at the back, and all of it painted green – except, of course, for the ubiquitous goats which wandered happily among the furniture. Delicious coffee was brought without being requested, and the menu only ever consisted of ful: a mash of fava beans, onions, oil and lime served with bread, Sudan's national dish.

In all our time in Sudan, not once were we asked for money, not once were we shouted or hooted at, not once were we surrounded and bundled into the back of a van. With the possible exception of Badr-aldin back on the ferry, the Sudanese were polite and friendly, and each helpful act or magnanimous gesture we experienced was always enacted without any thought of reciprocation or personal gain. In Delgo, a man called Ahmed asked if there was any way he might assist us and, when we told him we were looking for a place to get some dinner, he guided us to a cafe where joints of meat hung beside the entrance, said something to the man whose job it was to cut the meat while pointing at one of the joints, and then ushered us towards a table where he sat down with us. Coffee was immediately placed before us.

'These are different meats,' he said, referring to the joints hanging beside the entrance. 'You choose the one you want, you say how much, and then they barbecue it for you. But I ordered you goat, half a kilogram, because the other meat does not look so good today. I hope this is all right.'

'Thank you,' I said, fumbling to retrieve my wallet from my bag. 'How much will that cost?'

'Nothing,' he replied. 'I have already paid. You are new.'

'Please,' I insisted, 'you don't have to do that. We're happy to pay. We want to. You must let us.'

But he waved his hand and would not hear of it. 'You are new,' was the only opinion he held on the matter.

The goat was delicious and as we ate Ahmed told us about Delgo: a town built by, and for, gold. 'Men leave their families to come here and find gold. I left mine, too, but I do not look for gold myself. I work as a translator for a Chinese gold-mining company. Did you see the town as you came in?'

'I didn't take much notice of the town itself,' I admitted. 'I saw quite a few Chinese people here, but that's hardly a rarity in Africa these days.'

'It is all artificial here. The Chinese built it, built it out of nothing in the middle of the desert. It is not like any Sudanese town. Most of the buildings are empty. There are shops with nothing in them, houses with no one living there. It is like they built it this way because they thought this is what a town should look like.'

'Surely there's work here other than gold mining?' Steve asked. 'It's just, it's such a big place.'

Ahmed shook his head. 'Everybody here either mines gold, or serves those who mine gold. But these are still jobs, and that is important, so we do not mind.'

It was time for Ahmed to pray, and so he left us with smiles and handshakes and his final words, 'I wish you the best of luck. You are new.'

Cycling out through Delgo, it soon became clear what Ahmed had meant by the town's artificiality. At first glance, it seemed much like any other town, but the closer I looked the more I realised how odd it all was. The notion occurred to me that it was like a movie set. It had all the same trappings: the generic shops, the blandly painted houses, the carefully swept streets, and yet it had that distinct air of emptiness, that lack of soul, that characterlessness that occupies a movie set in lieu of genuine residents. It was a brand new ghost town.

Further down the road, at the far more Sudanese settlement of Dongola, we ate ful and described Delgo to the British couple Noel and Ping – a retired Metropolitan policeman and his wife – who invited us to share their table. They were on a grand overland voyage around Africa, and would be driving to and then through Delgo soon.

'It's one of the strangest places I've ever seen,' I said.

'Sounds like some other places we've been to in Africa,' Noel said. 'Let me guess, people walking around with metal detectors on the outskirts? More Chinese than Africans?'

I nodded. 'Pretty much.'

'The Chinese are definitely making inroads into Africa,' Ping said. 'Literally.'

'Ahmed was nice, though,' Steve said.

'Ahmed was a star,' I agreed. 'He bought our meal for us. Wouldn't accept any money for it. He kept saying *you are new*.'

'We've heard that a lot, too,' Ping said. 'It's actually really nice when you understand that they use *new* synonymously with *guest*. They think that anyone new to Sudan is a guest and must be treated well.'

I liked Noel and Ping. They were kind and well-informed, and they had been to many of the countries we were due to pass through. I wanted to talk to them more, to ply them with questions, to extrapolate advice, but I had suddenly begun to find it difficult to concentrate. I went to take a gulp of tea but my hands were starting to shake and it was impossible to hold the cup steady. I must have spilled some, because Ping laughed and said something, but then when she looked up at me she stopped laughing and said something else, and I was struggling to latch on to the words, like I could recognise them but not quite understand them, and something was happening to my vision, because when I looked at Ping she swirled and swam and then so too did the table and then the walls and then the whole restaurant.

And that was when I fainted.

CHAPTER 15

NUBIAN DAYS

Distance remaining: 6,470 miles

Time to record: 54 days

Steve revived me with water and electrolytes. I was on the cafe floor, wedged where I had fallen between my chair and the table. The tiled surface beneath me felt impossibly hot, as if flames rose from it and licked at my skin, and I groaned in discomfort. 'The heat,' I whispered.

'We need to get him some place cool to rest and rehydrate,' I heard Steve say to Noel and Ping. 'It's exhaustion, poor nutrition, lack of sleep and now this heat, it's too much.'

I was hoisted to my feet, my arms draped over Steve and Noel's shoulders, and then half-carried and half-dragged to a guesthouse on the opposite side of the road to the cafe. Steve negotiated a room for us for a few hours and, as he bade farewell to Noel and Ping, I stumbled into the windowless cell and collapsed on to one of the stretchers, slipping into unconsciousness like a drunk.

The unmistakeable smell of fried fish woke me. It was 6 p.m. Steve stood above me, a plate of salty fish in one hand and a large bottle of water in the other. 'Eat this,' he said, holding out the fish. 'And then drink this.'

I took a mouthful: it was limp and wet, like an unpleasant handshake. 'Disgusting,' I mumbled.

'Eat it anyway. You're probably low on sodium. It'll make you feel better.'

Steve was right. Within half an hour – fed, rehydrated and with my sodium-levels restored – I felt well enough to climb back on to my bike. We had lost some hours to my episode, but no more than our usual siesta and I was ready to push on into the night.

I did not faint again in Sudan, but those next few days were a struggle. Steve felt it, too. We were cycling through the Nubian Desert, one of the hottest areas on earth, evidenced by the numerous camels that lay dead at the roadside, and as our wheels spun so too did we, through a carousel of dizziness, fatigue, nausea, dizziness, fatigue, nausea. I could never drink enough. I seemed to be imbibing gallons every day, and yet when I stopped to urinate all I could produce were a few drops of a thick and miry yellow liquid which hurt to pass. Another reaction to the heat, one I remembered from my Sahara adventure, was a complete lack of appetite. My stomach felt as if it had sealed itself off from the rest of me, stubbornly shutting down regardless of how my other organs might have felt. I had no inclination whatsoever to eat and the easy response was simply not to. But it was necessary, more so than ever, and I forced myself to consume salt and sugar in whatever form I could lay my hands on every few hours. More often than not, the only food was ful with mouldy bread. The dish was largely devoid of nutrition and, given that we were burning 6,000 calories every day, we began to rely heavily upon our fat reserves.

By the time we reached Khartoum, after a punishing 158 miles in one day, I felt like I could sleep for the next 24 hours. In fact, I was so exhausted I barely registered the fact that we were stopped at three separate checkpoints as we entered the capital; barely noticed how thoroughly they searched us and our bags and how comprehensively they checked our documents; barely saw the barbed wire fencing around the petrol stations and the armed guards who prowled behind it. What I did notice were the gunshots: three of them, not too close but not too distant, and then the smell of smoke, not the pleasant aroma of woodsmoke, but the acrid tang of burning plastics. The sounds and the smells were unmistakeable, and were as indicative of threat as an upturned car, as men with guns but no uniforms.

'I guess you wouldn't have known, you've been stuck out in the desert for the past few days, but Sudan is going to shit.'

We were sitting in the stone courtyard of an old Khartoum hotel, sipping water and enjoying the cool night air as it enveloped our aching muscles. My friend Midhat had come to meet us, as promised, and was filling us in on the demonstrations and riots that had taken place across the capital over the past few days.

'It's basically the fuel prices. The government has been subsidising fuel for a long time, but they say they can't afford to any more, and the price shot up overnight. So do you know what the demonstrators did? They set fire to a bunch of petrol stations! Man, how is that going to make fuel *cheaper?* So for a few days I couldn't fill my car up because my local petrol station was burnt down! And then do you know how the government responded? They turned off the internet! Such a weird punishment! I tell you, man, I love my country, but we can get *weird!*'

'Are we going to be all right here?' Steve asked.

'Oh yeah, sure, you'll be fine,' Midhat said with a cocky smile. 'You're with me.'

I first met Midhat during my Sahara expedition, at Wadi Halfa. I was sitting in a shop taking lunch when he approached me, introduced himself and shook my hand so hard it made my already aching fingers spasm. Then he sat down next to me and proceeded to monologue his way through a series of self-aggrandising stories. I immediately disliked him. Though he was proud of his Nubian heritage, he seemed prouder of his westernisation, and was quick to belittle those who could not speak

English as well as him and even quicker to anger. He oozed machismo, a typical alpha male, refused to ever admit he was wrong and had a deeply embedded competitive streak that even I found off-putting.

But then I got to know him a little better, discovering his capacity for acts of extraordinary kindness. When I explained that the Sudanese army were attempting to block my passage through the final portion of my journey, he left without a word and returned less than an hour later with written permission for me to continue. And then, insisting that it was both the right and the natural thing to do, he took me to his house to spend the night, where I was fed a sensational meal and introduced to his charming family.

We became good friends that evening and have remained so. He confessed a deep admiration for what I was doing, admitting that he loved cycling but that the sanctions imposed across Sudan meant that it was difficult to find any bikes other than the cheap, Chinese knock-offs that flooded the market. When I returned home after completing the Sahara crossing, I sent him, via an overlander, my old mountain bike as a gift to represent my gratitude. It was an ageing Specialized bike, fairly basic, but in Sudan it was the two-wheeled equivalent of a Ferrari. The letter he sent me in reply was so overwhelming in its appreciation that I have kept it to this day. It sits in my desk beside the photo he enclosed with the letter: an image of him riding it towards the camera with the immaculate glee of a puppy.

The moment I realised that Sudan would be a part of my latest adventure, the first person I thought to contact was Midhat, and so I did, asking if he might like to meet us and if there was any way he could assist us with the red tape we might come up against in Sudan. His reply stated that he would be more than happy to help: that he would gladly organise our visas, collect our passports from us in Khartoum to secure the necessary official tourist stamps, and even arrange things so our crossing from Sudan into Ethiopia would be trouble-free. In fact, he proposed, surely everything would be easier if he accompanied us. He had been itching to take his bike on a long-distance jaunt ever since I sent it to him, and if we would do him the honour he would be delighted to cycle with us all the way from Khartoum to Gondar in Ethiopia.

At first, I was sceptical and so was Steve. I knew that Midhat was strong, but it took a specific kind of strength to cycle over 100 miles every day in perpetuity, a level of masochistic endurance that I was not sure Midhat owned. He knew his country intimately and this would be a boon – especially here in Khartoum where, if the situation turned sour, he could navigate us out of the city through the back alleys and lanes only a local would know – but I also knew of his superiority complex, and it suggested a callowness I suspected would not weather so well on the road. In the end, I agreed that he could accompany us. I remained sceptical, but the simple fact was that I liked Midhat a lot and it was very difficult to say no to him.

The following morning, he met us at the hotel half an hour before he was due to, with our stamped passports, a wad of Sudanese pounds in his hands, and clad in the slightly tatty racing gear someone had loaned him and of which he was immensely proud. He took the lead through Khartoum, chaperoning us along what he assured us was the shortest route, and charming the police who frequently stopped us to check our papers, so that we were out of the city quicker than I had anticipated.

'Good work, Midhat!' I shouted as we joined the road south, arriving at the base of a steep uphill.

'My pleasure!' he shouted back. 'I'm cycling to Ethiopia! That's so weird, man, but I love it!' And with that he took off on a sprint up the hill, racing against the ageing trucks that struggled forwards in first gear, and then pointing and laughing at those drivers he succeeded in overtaking. Later, on flats or downhills, when those trucks caught up with us, the drivers blared their horns and swerved in as they passed Midhat, but they never frightened him. A little bicycle-riding David standing up to these juggernaut Goliaths, he would shake his fist at the side of the trucks as they passed and scream his favourite English insult: *'Fuck mother!'*

As we progressed, it became clear that Midhat had no problem keeping up with us. Indeed, he was so exuberant and buoyed up by the journey that he often pushed far ahead, shrinking to a pin-prick on the horizon and then vanishing behind it. When we caught up with him each time, he would be sitting in a cafe at the side of the road, drinking coffee and inviting us to join him. Often, we did not have the time, but when we did, the pure luxury of Sudanese coffee and the particular way it was served was always a delight.

I adore Sudanese coffee. Velvety and infused with cardamom and ground ginger, it is served black and piping hot and is always delicious. The coffee-maker, always a woman, sits behind a small wooden desk filled with her tools and ingredients. You must sit in front of her while she prepares the coffee, boiling water over charcoal, and then pouring this over the strainer filled with ground coffee and into a gourd-shaped pot, where it is mixed with the spices. Finally, little cups are filled with sugar and the coffee is poured over it, presented to you on a tray ready to drink. The result, and the experience itself, is sensational.

Sometimes, Midhat stopped not for coffee, but because he had a puncture.

'Just buy a spare inner tube!' I would accost him each time.

'Don't be silly, man,' he would reply. 'I'll fix it.'

Yet he never did fix it. He got others to do it for him. Perhaps he was a thrifty genius; perhaps he was a stubborn fool – either way, there was always someone who would give him a lift to the nearest town, someone there who would fix his tyre and someone else who would give him another lift to catch us up. I cannot count how many times he leapt from the back of a pick-up truck with his bike, bellowing his gratitude to the driver, and then rejoined us, only to stop a mile later with yet another puncture and yet another scream of, *'Fuck mother!'*

To buy anything new was anathema to him: he had the make-do-and-mend mentality of those who live in warzones or in extreme poverty or both. One afternoon, while we stopped in a village for lunch, his right shoe fell off – just disintegrated and slid from his foot to land as a series of fragmented patches on the tarmac.

'Weird!' he proclaimed, and then turned to me to ask to borrow my gaffer tape. It was no use. The shoe was beyond repair. While Steve and I ate, he wandered off into the village, one foot bare, returning half an hour later with a smile and two gigantic flip-flops hanging from his petite feet.

'You can't cycle in those,' I told him. 'You could cut your feet to shreds!'

But he just smiled at me and said: 'They were free.'

And then he did cycle in them. It didn't matter to him that they caught on the ground as he pedalled or that they dug into the skin between his toes so much that his feet bled – he cycled on blithely: racing trucks, jeering as he overtook them, swearing as they overtook him, enduring puncture after puncture and smiling all the way.

The sun set as we arrived in Abu-harira. We had done well that day – the temperature had dropped enough to allow us to cycle through the afternoon, and by dusk we had reached our daily target. Midhat suggested we stay the night in Abu-harira, a tiny village of which he was fond.

There was no electricity and no running water in the village, but Midhat entered one of the round mud-and-straw huts to reappear moments later with a large, clear container of water. 'It's clean,' he assured us, and we filled our bottles from it. A small man with a concave chest and distended belly took the empty container from us, returned it to the hut, and then led us to a shack with brightly painted walls and a thatched roof.

'This is the cafe,' Midhat said. 'They will not have much, but they will give us what they can.'

Three bowls of boiled milk were laid atop the table alongside a shrivelled loaf of bread. I watched Midhat tear a chunk from the loaf, dip it into his milk until it was saturated and then noisily suck the liquid from the bread. He could manage three dunks of the same piece before it dissolved into the milk. I copied, and was surprised by the taste.

'This is delicious!' I cried. 'It might be the best milk I've ever tasted.'

'Fresh from the cow, man,' Midhat replied, and I remembered Moneer from the Lake Nasser ferry, of his love of fresh milk.

'Is this a *Baggara* village?' I asked.

'No,' he said. 'They are in South Sudan. But it doesn't matter. We're all Sudanese. The only people who are different here are you two. You are new.'

'Ah,' I said. 'I know what that means. We're guests.'

'*Exactly*, man. You are guests. That's why you got the freshest milk. You see this guy here?' He gestured to the man who had recently walked into the cafe and was making himself comfortable while he awaited his food. 'They will give him milk and bread, too. But I bet you that it won't be as fresh as this. We look after our guests in Sudan.'

There was no door to the cafe, just an open aperture that looked out over the southern aspect of the village. The round huts grew fewer at this end, replaced by a seemingly endless collection of damaged tyres. Small children scampered among them, and when they caught sight of us they charged forwards and gathered outside the cafe, staring at us with huge eyes and gawping mouths. I finished my milk and bread, rose to my feet and tiptoed towards them like a cartoon villain. They shrieked with delight, scattering into the dust as I chased them, and then popped up moments later on the periphery of my vision like meerkats. A game was soon afoot, and though I was never quite sure of the rules, it seemed to involve them creeping up on me to poke my leg or my arm. Each time one succeeded, I would let out a mighty roar, they would dart back to their hiding places, and we would begin again.

While Steve and Midhat stayed in the cafe, I played with the children for the next half an hour, and I was enjoying myself so much that I could have played for longer. But then, at 8 p.m. on the dot, a thunderous engine noise sounded, and all the children disappeared off away from the cafe and into the heart of the settlement. I followed them. The village's generator had been turned on – as it was at this time every night, Midhat informed me – and an old television cranked into life to play an Indian soap opera. The children were already sitting on the ground before it, self-organised by height so that everyone could see, and as I arrived the adults were beginning to appear from their huts, carrying mobile phones, which they plugged into the generator before settling behind the children to watch the television in rapt silence.

And then, at 10 p.m. on the dot, the generator was turned off, the television went blank, the mobile phones were unplugged and everyone – adults and children alike – quietly returned to their huts, leaving Steve, Midhat and me alone in the suddenly silent night. We slept out under the stars and, when we awoke the following morning, it was to birdsong and the warming rays of dawn. It was Day 50, and we were enlivened.

Breakfast was more milk and bread, which was just as sumptuous, at the cafe, and when I held out some Sudanese notes to the owner he raised his hand and said something in Arabic to Midhat. 'He does not want payment,' Midhat reported. 'You are new.'

That day was beautiful. A tailwind propelled us along good roads with few inclines, and when we stopped for a lunch of chicken shawarmas and mango juice, I called Steve over to my bike and pointed out the odometer to him. It was Day 50, and we had covered 5,500 miles. We were exactly halfway through the journey. And I was on target for the world record.

CHAPTER 16

BABOONS AND THIEVES

Distance remaining: 5,500 miles

Time to record: 50 days

———————————

As we passed the halfway mark, we began our crossing from Sudan to Ethiopia and the whole world around us seemed to change in the space of 100 yards. The temperature dropped dramatically and there was a distinct chill to the air. A *chill*! In central Africa! The dry, arid desert landscapes of Sudan had vanished and in their place was an abundance of chlorophyll. The Islamic world we had been cycling through since Dagestan was supplanted by Christianity – churches instead of mosques; Amharic instead of Arabic; crosses not crescents – and women, their shoulders bare, stared us in the eye as we passed. The sheer density of people all around was overwhelming after the peace of Sudan.

Even time changed. The 24-hour clock we had lived by appeared to be disregarded by many in Ethiopia. A 12-hour clock was preferred, with each 12-hour cycle alternating between the period from dawn until dusk and then the next from dusk until dawn. Each brand new day did not start at midnight in Ethiopia: it started when the sun rose. Thus, when it hit midday, the time was not read as 12.00 but 6.00, for the sun had been up for 6 hours. On top of this, just to confuse us even further, there were not 12 months in Ethiopia, but 13.

It wasn't just the geography, demography and clocks that changed as we entered Ethiopia. Midhat did, too. He seemed to shrink the moment we passed through customs, shedding his confidence and machismo, and leaving them behind in Sudan like an old skin. Here, in Ethiopia, he became unnaturally timid, humble even, and when he spoke it was with soft uncertainty and a tinge of vulnerability.

'We shouldn't night ride in Ethiopia,' he said. 'It's too dangerous. Ethiopians are thieves.'

His sentiments were hyperbolic and we paid them little heed – they were borne, we decided, not from empirical evidence but from the entrenched and baseless hostility man can often have for neighbours beyond the border. Nevertheless, it was getting late, we were tired from a long day, our mileage count was ahead of target and we agreed it would be good to stop in the border town of Metema.

We found a guesthouse and checked in for the night, and when the manager handed us our key he winked with such a pronounced lack of subtlety that we wondered if he was having a stroke. Our room was dimly lit by a single low wattage bulb, and red velvet covers had been draped over the three beds. There was one bedside table: a quick inspection of its drawer revealed it to contain one pack of cigarettes, one box of matches and 12 loose condoms. In the garden, a small shed served as the guesthouse's restaurant and as we ordered food the young man behind the counter said, 'You will have a great time in Ethiopia,' and then performed a mime involving an extended index finger and the scuba diving 'OK' hand signal which horny boys the world over would recognise. He asked if we would like beer and, although it was the first time we had seen alcohol served since Russia, we declined. As the evening progressed, the turnover of our fellow diners was swift. Few came for a meal, and some not even a drink, as they stayed for no longer than a minute or two. Most of the men wore T-shirts with American slogans emblazoned across them –

'Los Angeles Lakers', 'Scarface', 'University of Michigan' – donated from foreign clothes banks; most of the women wore tight, colourful dresses or thin tops, which hid little, and belt-sized skirts, which hid less. Although they arrived in their separate groups, they soon paired off, entering the guesthouse as couples and reappearing an hour or two later.

'Midhat,' I said. 'What kind of guesthouse is this?'

Midhat, disgusted, refused to reply.

Occasionally, one or two of the women looked over at our table and, if we made eye contact, they would grin and raise their eyebrows. One woman was astonishingly beautiful, and had a crucifix tattooed on her forehead. I stared at her for longer than I should, and she was just about to stand and walk over to our table when I realised what I was doing and quickly looked back to my plate of food, focusing on it for the next 5 minutes. When I looked up once more, she was deep in conversation with a man in a *Family Guy* T-shirt, and was fingering the cross that dangled from his neck.

A storm broke out, so excessive and vicious that we were all forced back into the guesthouse, where we watched in awe from the porch as sheets of water lashed down and transformed the road into a slurry of mud. It was the first rain we had seen since Iran. It was the heaviest rain I might ever have seen in my life. Forks of lightning began to strike all around us without intervals, exploding into splinters of dying sparks as they hit the ground. The electricity died and candles were lit and hurried off to the bedrooms. Six were placed in front of us on the porch, and we huddled around one.

'Look at this weather,' Midhat grumbled. 'You wouldn't get this in Sudan.'

'I've missed it,' I said. 'It's good to feel rain again.'

Midhat muttered something unintelligible and then said he needed to make a phone call, disappearing off to our room while Steve and I stayed on the porch to watch the storm. He returned 15 minutes later, the ghost of a smile on his lips.

'I've just spoken to my work,' he said, waving the phone in his right hand. 'There has been an emergency. I must return to Khartoum first thing tomorrow morning.'

'I thought you were accompanying us to Gondar,' Steve said.

'Man, you know I would love to, but it is impossible now. I must leave tomorrow.'

We were under no illusions. Midhat was one of those people who felt secure only within the borders of his own country. The cultural differences of Ethiopia made him uncomfortable and anxious. He was desperate to leave, to return to the domestic familiarity of Sudan. I would be sorry to see him go, for I liked his company and regarded him as a good friend. I wanted him to stay, but I no longer needed him to. He had guided us south from Khartoum through the rest of Sudan and had successfully got us across the border to Ethiopia. In a purely functional sense, he had served his purpose, though that did not make it any easier to say goodbye.

'I'll miss you,' I told him the next morning as he packed to leave. 'I've really enjoyed spending this time with you.'

'So have I,' he said. 'I wish I could cycle all the way to Cape Town with you. But I must get back to work, you know. They need me.'

'Any final advice?' Steve asked.

'Yes,' he replied, looking serious. 'You must be careful of everything here. Ethiopia is a weird and dangerous place. But there is one thing you must be especially careful about. The children in this country are very famous for throwing stones at foreigners.'

'I'm sure we'll be fine,' I said. 'Kids tend to be fascinated by us anyway.'

'No, you must listen,' he said. 'You must wear your helmet at all times.'

'Come on. Are you really serious? Kids are going to chuck stones at us?'

'Oh yes, man, I'm very serious,' Midhat said. 'They will throw stones at you. And they will throw them hard.'

Though I missed Sudan, it was a delight to be in Ethiopia. The road –
financed by foreign aid and the World Bank – was smooth and quiet, and
it coursed through lush countryside, the green of which I hadn't realised
I had missed so much until I saw it again. There were mountains too,
and though the demanding climbs stretched us to our limits as we rose to
elevations of 8,500 ft, we tackled them with a happy fortitude, thrilled to
be away from the desert's monotony and back in a world where peaks and
valleys existed. The previous night's rain had left behind a lingering mist
that mingled with our sweat and cooled our skin. We managed 81 miles,
far less than our average daily quota, but the ride itself was so refreshing
and invigorating that, when we stopped for the night in Aykel, we were
pleased with our day's progress.

We feasted on injera – the soft and spongy flatbread that forms the staple
of many East African diets – along with pasta and sauce, processing the
carbohydrates slowly and almost falling asleep at the table as we did so.
A booming voice revived us from our near-slumber. 'You like the injera?'
I looked up to see a giant Rastafarian towering over us, his dreadlocks
spilling from his shoulders and reaching down to our table like fingers.

'Delicious,' I said.

'Injera can sometimes settle heavily in the tummy,' he said. Hearing
such a Herculean man with such a grave voice utter the word 'tummy'
was incongruously amusing. 'The best way to follow it is with a drinking
yoghurt. Would you like to join me?'

We saw no reason not to, and so paid for our bill and pursued our new
mountainous friend across the road to a cafe, where he ordered a round of
yoghurts and introduced himself as Solomon. The yoghurt had no flavour
and yet somehow still managed to taste atrocious.

'You like the yoghurt?' Solomon asked.

'Delicious,' I lied.

'And do you like Ethiopia?'

'Well, we've only been here for two days, but it's made a good
impression so far.'

'This is a fine time to visit,' Solomon said. 'The Ethiopian people are very happy right now. We have a brand new president, Mulatu Teshome, and he is a very good man. Fair and not corrupt. I think he will be our best leader since Haile Selassie himself. And when you have a good leader, you have good people. Look at Egypt. Bad leader, bad people.'

I smiled at his words. Politics again. It seemed the preferred topic of conversation with everyone we met in Africa, and that it always came up so soon after our meeting had stopped surprising me. His mention of Egypt prompted me to tell him that we had been there a fortnight earlier, and prompted me to reveal some of the difficulties we had faced. 'It wasn't all bad, though. We met some wonderful people.'

'I couldn't wait to leave,' Steve said.

'I think you will have a different experience in Ethiopia,' Solomon said. 'I think you will like it here very much. You will like us Ethiopians.'

'And what about the children?' Steve asked.

'Excuse me?'

'We've been told that the children are notorious for throwing stones at foreigners.'

'Ah yes, this is true,' Solomon said with a laugh. 'They will do this. But you should not worry. It is very easy to stop them. There is a good trick. When you see them, wave at them and shout *Salam*, which is hello in Amharic. They will be so excited and will want to wave back, and they will put down their stones so that they can.'

Beyond Aykel, the road skewered its way through an assortment of small Ethiopian villages. They were overrun with children who ranged the land with liberty, yet none of them threw stones at us. Instead they chased us, shouting 'YOU YOU YOU!', clapping their hands and shrieking with delight if we stopped, clamouring around us to prod our tyres and stroke the hair on our bare arms. Producing my camera had a similar effect to telling a good joke – I had never seen so many teeth instantly appear as they grinned and smiled for their photo, gently nudging each other aside to ensure they had the best position in the frame. When we climbed back on to our bikes and began pedalling again, the older children ran alongside us, in bare feet and hardly breaking a sweat, accompanying us to the next village as if that was simply the polite thing to do when a couple of scruffy, bearded foreigners rode into town.

After a morning of downhill leisure, coasting through these villages with ease, we hit our next bank of mountains. The gradients rose sharply, and even in the lowest gear it took all of my strength to pedal onwards. Buses approached slowly with crunching gears and whining engines, and then belched thick plumes of black smoke into our faces as they passed. Even the pedestrians – the men who carried sticks over their shoulders with food tied in cloth and hung from the end; the women who lugged giant baskets of cow dung or containers of water; the ever-present children who ran alongside us in their torn clothes – all of them could keep pace with us and some, particularly the children, grew bored of our plodding progress and shot off ahead.

When a nation of people live under the yoke of tyranny, the visiting traveller can feel it in the air. There is a rigidity, or perhaps a frigidity, to the atmosphere, a tight-lipped tension that permeates all meetings and conversations. People stand straighter and look you in the eye less; they talk slower, cerebrally measuring and inspecting their words before delivering them. Other countries that we might describe as free – in essence, democratic countries – have a less definable tenor. Liberty is not as easy to spot as oppression, for it is often taken for granted by those who have it and is not so much deliberately disregarded as simply forgotten about. Yet there remain some countries around the world where it is flaunted. Ethiopia is one of these countries.

I cannot explain why. Perhaps it is because, under its former incarnation of Abyssinia, it was one of the few of the continent's countries to retain its independence during the Scramble for Africa; perhaps it is because, aside from a six-year period of Italian annexation, it has never had to bow to any other power; perhaps it is because, with lawless Somalia to the east and the fractured Sudans to the west, Ethiopians can observe the strife just beyond their borders and feel blessed to be distinct from it; perhaps it is because, with famine and war common tropes of the twentieth century, Ethiopians are enjoying the comparative improvements of their twenty-first. Or perhaps it is all of these things combined and more, or perhaps it is none. No matter, what I felt in Ethiopia was a kind of joyful freedom that I had not felt for some time. Almost all the cafes seemed to boast huge speaker systems, which were placed outside and facing towards the road, so that we cycled along to a mix of traditional and popular Ethiopian music. The coffee, grown locally, was delicious, served in a tiny china cup on a tray covered by a delicate leaf. There was colour everywhere, from the brightly painted huts to the garishly decorated trucks and lorries and taxis to the fauve rainbow of clothes sported by men, women and children alike. I smiled at every person I made eye contact with. No one failed to smile back.

Ethiopia was swiftly becoming my favourite country so far and it may well have stayed so were it not for the Highlands. As we passed Gondar and began our semi-circumnavigation of Lake Tana, the source of the Blue Nile, the road became a series of long and tortuous uphill grinds with only a handful of brief flats and downhills to punctuate them. The air grew colder and the fogs were gloomier and hung lower. It all reminded me distinctly of Scotland, a country I never before would have thought to equate with Ethiopia. Farmlands perpetuated, though we rarely saw any livestock, or indeed people. Which made that first stone, as it sailed silently through the air to rebound off my helmet with a thunderous crack, all the more surprising.

I braked sharply, Steve skidding to a halt beside me.

'Was that—' he began, before being interrupted by another stone, twice as large as the first, which whizzed past, barely missing his arm.

We looked over in the direction of the projectiles. There was nothing to be seen, no children anywhere. A third stone sailed high into the air from behind a hillock of rubble 40 yards away, aimed with such precision that I had to duck to avoid it.

'Hey!' I shouted. 'Stop that!'

This had an effect, though not the one I had intended. Twelve tiny heads popped up from behind the rubble, white teeth gleaming out from grubby faces. And then, 12 tiny arms launched a volley of stones at us with such force that we had no option but to kick ourselves off down the road and pedal ferociously. With fortune, we were on a flat, and so acceleration was easy and yet we still heard the thuds of raining stones behind us as we raced away.

'I forgot Solomon's trick,' I panted to Steve once we had rounded a corner and were well away from the missiles.

'I don't think it would have worked,' Steve replied. 'Little shits.'

Not 5 miles later, we found ourselves approaching another gang, this one unhidden, standing brazenly by the roadside with an assortment of rocks and pebbles clutched in their fists. They watched us approach and, as we neared, I raised my right hand to wave in long swooping arcs above my head, calling '*Salam!*' at the top of my voice. A stone hit me in the shin.

'For fuck's sake!' Steve shouted from behind me. And then, '*Ow!*' as a stone rebounded off his shoulder.

I aimed my bike at the pack of children and cycled faster, hoping to scare them away, but they stood their ground and doubled their efforts so that we were forced to the other side of the road, dodging and weaving through the rocky arsenal as it cascaded down upon us. Most missed their moving targets, but those that made contact did so with painful ferocity. As we passed the children, we could hear their laughter: not the squealing giggles of kids at play, but the jeers of a squad of bullies.

Another 10 miles passed. I felt exhausted and upset. There was a village on the horizon, and I suggested to Steve that we take a break and find some food.

'Not yet,' he said, shaking his head. 'Let's do another twenty miles before we stop.'

'But I'm starving,' I pleaded. 'Aren't you?'

'Not really,' he replied. 'We haven't done enough to deserve a break.'

His refusal made me even more irritated and I cycled ahead so that, when I stopped in the village, he would be sure to stop behind me. It worked, though he did not dismount his bicycle and looked away from me while I nosed about the village hoping to find a shop or cafe. I returned with two large pieces of bread and two packs of biscuits.

'I'm eating mine now,' I said. 'You can save yours for when you deserve it.'

He snorted testily as he placed his bread and biscuits inside his front bag. I was tired of his resistance and ate my food slowly, not so much to savour it, but more out of a desire to further antagonise him. After close to two months on the road together, Steve and I had come to know how to perfectly get under each other's skin, and my provocation was deliberate. An argument had been quietly building for the past few hours and I wanted it.

With perfect timing, 20 children appeared as one from the village, clamouring around us with stones clutched in their palms. They shouted 'YOU YOU YOU!' in chorus and began to supplement the refrain with demands for money. I stayed where I was, ignoring the children and watching Steve. *He can deal with this one*, I thought. The village's adults had begun to materialise from doorways and, rather than castigate the children, they instead seemed amused by their increasingly threatening behaviour. 'YOU YOU YOU!' the children chanted.

One of the larger boys gently crept up behind Steve and, with a jab that seemed to be exploratory rather than menacing, thrust the end of a long stick between his shoulder blades. Steve leaped from his bike with a yelp and, instead of yelling at the boy as I had expected, yelled at me.

'This is your fault!' he screamed. 'What are we even doing here? Why did we stop?' The boy with the stick jumped back and his fellows clamoured around him in fright.

'I was hungry,' I shrugged.

'You're always hungry!' Steve bellowed, now apoplectic with rage. 'Every few hours its *Steve, let's stop,* or *Steve, I want to do some filming,* or *Steve, I'm hungry.* I'm sick of it, mate!'

'And *I'm* sick of your constant naysaying!' I rejoined. 'I'm starving and want to eat something. What's wrong with that?'

'We haven't done enough miles.'

'We've never done enough miles according to you. And yet here we are, on target for the record. And *eating*.'

The argument did not last long, but it was loud and it was vicious. When a dark and pregnant silence fell between us, I suddenly noticed that the children had vanished, taking their stones and sticks with them. One of the adults, still standing in his doorway, was laughing and nodding over at us. 'You so angry! *Ra ra ra!*' he said, shaking his fist in the air and imitating our argument. 'You scare children!'

Steve sighed. 'So that's how you do it.'

———————

The roads worsened, and with them the weather. Often, we found ourselves sheltering from the otherwise impressive storms in cafes and roadside shops for hours when we should have been cycling. In part, it was a relief to stop for these enforced breaks, for the periods of cycling had become peppered with the ubiquitous gangs of children who lobbed their stones at us regardless of whether we tried to wave or argue or ignore them.

Steve's temper soured and when the food poisoning hit it worsened his mood tenfold. It was not surprising. Though we both suffered, Steve's nausea, stomach cramps, diarrhoea and vomiting were far worse than mine. Steve was, and remains to be, a stronger cyclist than me, yet over those days of illness he lost his fortitude. Inclines he could have powered up with relative ease at any other time now wiped his potency, and he walked up them with a downcast visage and his bike pushed before him. When we stopped for a break, he no longer harangued me but seemed quietly grateful. And when we ate during those breaks, it was never long before his body rejected the food in a series of noisy and painful evacuations.

For me, the food poisoning seemed to hit hardest at night, when the rain forced us to sleep in mildewed and mosquito-infested guesthouses.

I would wake every few hours, my stomach a tight and stabbing ball of gas, and when I fled to the toilets, feeling my way along the walls in the absence of electric light, the inevitable rancid stench was so sickening that I often had to use two squatters at once, one for each end. These squatters were little more than badly tiled holes in the ground with a channel of water running below, but the drainage was so ineffectual that heaps of rotting excrement had piled up, and while I heaved into the squatters, the only positive thought I could cling to was that the lack of light meant I could not see that to which I was adding.

Hygiene, or the lack of it, was constantly on my mind. Even the smallest interaction – such as someone handing us money in a shop – could be concerning. Banknotes were old and filthy, hands were rarely washed whether they were offering us our change or some food, and the transfer of dirt and germs was almost tangible. The skin on my hands felt like it might erupt into a rash just from the touch of a door handle.

During the day, we cycled on the perpetual brink of exhaustion. We stopped eating altogether. Even water became a challenge to keep down. Children continued to batter us with stones – one striking my helmet with such force that it nearly knocked me over – and we had not the strength to do anything but ride weakly past them. They saw how dispirited we were and they threw harder.

Finally, we reached the Blue Nile Gorge and freewheeled the long downhill that plummeted into the canyon. The relief of not having to pedal, of being able to stretch out my legs and swap effort for gravity, was matched only by the fine views of this Ethiopian beauty spot. A new, Japanese-built bridge – the Millennium Bridge – crossed the river at the base of the gorge and we stopped on its far side to take photographs of the panorama: the baked-red cliff faces; the thin goat tracks curving away from the black road; the Blue Nile itself, not quite the colour its name here promised, but sparkling vividly in the unfettered sunlight. We drank water and allowed ourselves a short rest. We needed it. For the only way out of the gorge was up.

The road to the capital Addis Ababa stretched out before us: a ghastly example of poor civil engineering. Rather than navigating the steep climb via a series of zigzags and hairpins, it instead simply pushed forward along a straight and punishing 20 per cent gradient. Trucks clogged the road, crawling towards the summit at less than 10 mph. We comforted ourselves with the thought that, once we had conquered the ascent it would be downhill all the way to Addis Ababa, and estimated that the top of the road, where it disappeared from view, was perhaps just half a mile away.

With a grim determination, we stepped back on to our bikes and began the climb. The slog was painful and energy-sapping, and all the while I reminded myself that the top was only a short distance away, less with every revolution of my pedals, nearing perceptibly above us. Yet, when we reached the top, it turned out to not be the top at all, but merely a bend in the road, from which another half-mile, straight, 20 per cent incline stretched, and then another after that, and then, once that was finished, a further 10 miles of winding mountainous roads, most of them uphill, before we would reach the nearest settlement: the small town of Gohatsion. There was no choice. We had to keep moving forward. Perhaps the only relief on this long and tortuous climb was the absence of stone-throwing children. Other roadside bandits took their place. Troops of baboons, their babies clinging to their undersides, swarmed down from the mountains in the afternoons to ransack the open-backed trucks, which, never able to move higher than first gear, climbed the hill at walking speed. Many of the trucks had barbed wire looped over their rears, and while this prevented the baboons from gaining entrance, they were no match for the human thieves who waited beside the road, opportunistic to the core, and limber enough to skirt the barbed wire and pilfer what they could. The drivers, unable to stop (for starting again on this gradient would have been near-impossible), ignored the banditry and remained in their cabs, focusing on the road and the road alone.

In this regard, we were fortunate, for we cycled past it all without ever once being robbed by either the baboons or the thieves. While we carried hundreds of pounds' worth of equipment in our panniers ripe for theft, we were ignored in favour of the trucks, which often transported food. This was, in essence, all that the bandits, regardless of their evolutionary status, wanted.

We were far less fortunate with our health. As the sun set and darkness began to drift in, still miles from Gohatsion, Steve collapsed. There was no warning. One moment, he was upright; the next, he was supine on the tarmac. I helped him to his feet and guided him to the roadside, then tried to flag down one of the passing trucks. He needed medical attention, that was clear, and if it meant hitching a ride to the next town and then cycling back to this spot the following day to resume our journey then so be it. But none of the trucks stopped for us.

'They won't stop,' Steve muttered, gasping for breath. 'The road's too steep. Even if they could, they'd probably still think we were thieves.'

'We have to get you some help.'

Steve shook his head. 'I'll be all right. It's the stomach cramps again. They overwhelmed me. But they're starting to settle a bit. I can't cycle, but I can push.'

Three hours had passed since we had left the Millennium Bridge and we were still nowhere near the top. We could see it ahead, the blinking light of a telecom tower, but it was impossible to ascertain exactly how far away it was. It took us another 4 hours to reach it. Steve pushed his bike almost all the way, growing steadily worse. The frequency of breaks increased as he stopped to vomit into the bushes. Soon, even this thin veil of etiquette dropped and he began to vomit directly on to the road, barely pausing to do so. I tried to encourage him on with supportive words, with offers to carry some of his kit, with reduced estimates of how much longer we had left. But he invariably ignored me, focusing only on the road ahead, always pushing. I had never seen him look so bad – his legs trembling perceptibly, his face drained of colour, his eyes heavy and bloodshot, his breathing laboured and his shoulders sagging – but I had also never seen him look so heroic. No matter how many times he was forced to stop, to double over with the pain of the stomach cramps or the violence of the vomiting, he always returned to his bike, and always started pushing it uphill again with a relentless fortitude. I could not help but wonder if my stamina would have held out as long as Steve's: pushing a heavy bike through cold darkness up a mountain for hours on end while my guts twisted and wrenched inside me. I doubted that it would. I suspected that I would have given up long before. I looked over at Steve – still pushing, always pushing – and felt a tremendous sense of awe for my teammate. While his fears about personal safety had often seemed too extreme to me in the past, there was no one I knew who could equal him in terms of sheer endurance.

Finally, after 7 hours of climbing, climbing, climbing, we arrived in Gohatsion. There, we accepted the first price the first guesthouse offered us for a twin room and collapsed on to our beds. The following morning, we were both so paralysed with pain and high temperatures that we knew an entire day's rest was necessary. Wrapping ourselves in our sleeping bags, we slept and drank water and ran to the toilet and passed the intervals between it all by attempting to decide upon the source of the food poisoning. It was impossible. There had been so many places on that road through the Ethiopian Highlands on the way to Addis Ababa where the meat was undercooked and the vegetables were washed in tap water and all of it was served by staff with filthy hands – there were so many places that to narrow the cause of our ailment down to one specific eatery was like trying to work out which piece of gravel had caused a puncture.

Not that it mattered. The food poisoning was here to stay and, in my case at least, it was soon to be eclipsed by something far, far worse.

CHAPTER 17

DERAILED

Distance remaining: 4,842 miles

Time to record: 43 days

──────────────

The stomach cramps persisted, but with the aid of some ibuprofen, Ethiopian medicine and a bowl of plain rice each from the cafe next door to the guesthouse we felt well enough to continue by noon the following day. Aware that we had lost a day and a half to our food poisoning – maybe more, for the illness had slowed our progress ever since we had contracted it – we were determined to make it to Addis Ababa by the end of the following day. And perhaps Ethiopia recognised our need and decided on some much-needed sympathy, for the two days passed without one single stone-throwing child and by the second sunset the convolutions of our stomachs had finally begun to recede. The relief was as overwhelming as its predecessor, pain, had once been. While my abdomen crunched with each revolution of the pedals, it did so not with the stabbing jolts of illness, but with the pleasing ache of muscles flexing.

It grew dark and began to rain, but we were not deterred. Wrapping up in our waterproofs, we pushed forward into the twilight, determined to reach the Ethiopian capital, even if it took us until midnight. The road was in poor condition, but there was enough flat tarmac left to ensure that we could make decent progress. I began to daydream and, to my surprise and delight, food took prominence: a carousel of hearty and delicious meals filling my thoughts. I was getting my appetite back. *What I could eat right now*, I thought, *is a proper Sunday roast. Beef and the works. Dripping in gravy; a pint of ale on the side.*

I checked my GPS. We were only 20 miles from Addis Ababa. Perhaps I would not find that particular meal, but I would find something and I would savour every moment of it. It felt wonderful to want to eat again. To celebrate, a pee was in order, and so I squeezed my brakes and slowed, turning around to tell Steve why I was stopping.

He was not there. The road behind dropped downwards for 100 yards before arcing around to the left and disappearing behind a clump of bushes. I considered making my way back to check on him. Despite GWR's demand that we stay no more than five bike lengths apart at all times, it was not unusual for us to drift apart from each other as a day progressed. It was never a cause for worry – we always regrouped again somewhere further along – but our recent illness and the fact that Steve had collapsed on the road two days before gave me some basis for concern. I decided to urinate and drink some water and, if he had not appeared by then, I would look for him.

He materialised from behind the bushes as I opened my bottle of water. He was pushing his bike alongside him and, even from that distance, I could see from the expression on his face that something was wrong. I hopped on to my saddle and coasted back down the hill towards him.

'What's up?' I asked.

'It's the derailleur hanger,' he said, pointing down at the rear end of his frame. 'It's broken. Just split in two and fell off as I was riding. I don't know how it happened.'

The derailleur is the device on a bicycle that changes the gears by shifting the chain between sprockets. Most bikes have two, one behind the pedals and one at the back, and the latter is held in place by a hanger.

This is a small and thin curve of punctured metal, shaped rather like a seahorse, and while it may look seemingly insignificant in comparison to the rest of the assemblage, it is an absolutely integral part of a bike, which rarely breaks. Without it, cycling is impossible.

We did not have a spare hanger to replace it and, after 20 minutes of failed and frustrating repair attempts with cable ties and gaffer tape, we understood that our attempts were fruitless and that we would not be cycling to Addis Ababa. We recorded our exact location and marked the co-ordinates on our GPS, and then waited at the side of the road with our thumbs stuck out. The few cars and lorries that stopped – rather than sounding their horns as they passed and veering into puddles in deliberate attempts to soak us – were populated by drivers who demanded exorbitant rates for taking us to the capital. The prospect of hitching a ride for free was alien here. Every vehicle was an impromptu taxi, and if one was going to transport us and our bikes on this cold, wet night, it was going to cost. After 2 hours of negotiations and refusals, a truck driver offered us the lowest quote yet – £20 sterling – and we grimly agreed, hoisting our bikes on to the back and climbing into the front cab, where the fan heater was cranked to its highest setting, boiling us into a soporific stupor, the rainwater clinging to our clothes fogging up the windscreen in minutes.

Arriving at our guesthouse for the night, we immediately sent an SOS to Base Camp and then began to search the web for forums and advice. Francesca emailed back to tell us it would be impossible to get a new hanger sent out in time. All the sites we checked and people we exchanged messages with confirmed what we had suspected: that to find such an unusual and particular piece of kit in Ethiopia would be nothing short of miraculous. We were offered only one hope and it was a slim one. An email we received provided some information on a bike shop in the centre of Addis Ababa. It was unlikely they would have the right kind of derailleur hanger, the writer explained, but it might be worth a try.

It was too late to venture out into the city. The bike shop would not be open at this hour and we had little inclination to visit the establishments that would. The guesthouse had a small restaurant attached where we bought tuna pasta and then ate it in our room. It was tepid and sloppy, a far cry from the exquisite roast dinner of my dreams, but it caused no discomfort as it settled into my stomach and for this I was grateful.

'How are you feeling?' I asked Steve.

'The food's going down well.'

'Mine too.'

'I'm not happy though. I can't believe that hanger. Such bad luck.'

We fell silent. There was plenty we could have said, and perhaps should have said, but it didn't feel right to verbalise it. We both knew what it was – giving it voice would only have served to heighten its reality and neither of us wanted that.

For the simple fact was that, if we could not get Steve's derailleur hanger fixed, I would have to go on ahead alone.

———————

By the next morning, as I navigated us through the streets of Addis Ababa while Steve plaintively pushed his broken bicycle behind me, it was a struggle to concentrate, and I often lost my bearings. For all our arguments, for all our cattiness and petulance and mutual antagonism, we made a good team, a *great* team, and we were far stronger together than apart. I was prepared to do all I could to keep Steve beside me on the rest of the way to Cape Town, but what if it just wasn't feasible? I could stay with him while we shipped a new hanger in from London, but that would take days, maybe even a week, and I did not have that long. Steve did have that long, of course: Steve had as long as he wanted. Ever since skipping Dagestan he had become ineligible for the record. But I had not. I could still make Cape Town in 100 days and I dearly wanted to. My only question was whether I wanted the record so much that I was prepared to leave Steve behind in pursuit of it. Although I pretended to myself not to admit it, I knew what the answer was.

Such thoughts whirled around my head as we walked, distracting me into wrong turns and dead ends. But the city itself, Addis Ababa, proved to be an equivalent distraction. It was filthy and it was chaotic. The pavements were crowded with a surging mass of people who pushed and shoved each other as they walked with such an absence of sensitivity that I was put in mind of London Bridge; and the roads were just as over-populated, swimming with motorbikes and hatchback cars and buses and bicycles and blue taxis that mounted kerbs to block our path while the drivers hooted their horns and asked us where we were going. Beggars pestered us for money we could not afford to spare, and then spat at our shoes as we walked past. Twice, I felt the unmistakeable sensation of fingers curling their way into my pockets, seeking my wallet or phone, and when I swung around and shouted 'Hidu!' ('*Go away!*' in Amharic) at the culprits, they scarpered off into the crowds. Two men in grey hoodies and dark sunglasses pounced on Steve's bike and attempted to swipe his front bag and panniers. When they realised the bags were attached and saw Steve's raised fist and menacing grimace, they disappeared with the same swiftness as their pickpocketing brethren.

Finally locating the bike shop, we stepped inside and our hearts sank. A blue-fronted unit with a leaning canopy and faded sign, it was a single, mouldy room: a row of cheap, low-end bicycles leaned up against one wall and a stack of children's pedal-cars against another. We could tell instantly that the shop would not have the part we required. We were about to turn and walk out in dismay when the owner stopped us with a hand on my arm. He was thin and gangly and sported a spry leather jacket. His eyes had lit up when we entered, and he was determined to help.

'Would you like to buy a bike?' he asked.

'I need to get my derailleur hanger fixed,' Steve replied.

'Please,' the man said. 'Wait one moment.'

He made a call on his mobile phone and then, when it was over, explained in sparse English that a friend of his was coming and that he might be able to fix the hanger. He led us into the tiny office at the rear of the shop – a desk, an ancient cash register, two chairs and a gas stove – and insisted we sit down while he made us coffee. He had no milk, and when we asked for some he rushed out, leaving the shop (and the cash register) with us to supervise, returning moments later with a carton with which he topped up our mugs. As he fussed about us, doing everything he could to ensure our comfort, I remembered those first few days in Ethiopia, which I had loved, and then the juxtaposition with the next few days, which I had loathed. What a strange country this was – at once delightful and infuriating. And therefore, I thought, perhaps not so strange after all.

The friend appeared an hour later and, buzzing from the cups of coffee our host had made sure remained bottomless, we explained our problem to him in slow and broken English. He took the hanger and held it up to the light from the open doorway to inspect it.

'This should be no problem at all,' he said with perfect erudition. 'I can't fix this, it's beyond repair, but I think I can make you a new one.'

He sent our host out to secure the tools and materials he needed, which were somehow located within minutes, and then, transforming the office desk into a makeshift worktop, he set about building a brand new derailleur hanger.

'So how do you like Ethiopia?' he asked, focusing on his craft as he spoke. He was a tiny man, clad in jeans and a red Specialized branded hoody, an expensive pair of sunglasses perched on his close-cropped hair.

'Sometimes I love it. Sometimes I…' I struggled to find words which would be apt yet inoffensive. 'Sometimes I don't.'

He laughed, tapping the metal before him into shape with an oversized hammer. 'You sound like an Ethiopian.'

I was mesmerised by his work, which was both rapid and meticulous. The hanger was moulded, shaped and drilled as we watched, and before we knew it the piece was complete, slightly distended in some places and slightly dented in others, but when he fitted it to Steve's bike it worked impeccably.

'How do you know how to do that?' Steve asked as he handed over the paltry remuneration the man had postulated. 'Do you specialise in derailleur hangers?'

'Never made one before in my life,' he said, offering half of the money to the bike-shop owner and then pocketing the rest. 'But if you want to be a cyclist in Ethiopia, you've got to know how to build a bike up from nothing. No replacement parts round here.'

———————

That Steve's bike was fixed, that we still had time left to catch a taxi out to where we had stopped the day before and cycle back into Addis Ababa, that we were in our guesthouse fed and watered and caught up with our logbook and communications by 8 p.m. – that all this had happened in the space of one day struck us as miraculous. We made some calculations before retiring to bed and worked out that, although we had lost yet another day, the record was still attainable. I fell asleep gratified.

Of course, to make up for it all, we had to push ourselves hard. And so we did exactly that. The Kenyan border was just under 500 miles away, and we ploughed towards it with steadfast determination, buoyed up by that particular euphoria you feel at the cessation of an illness or the successful overcoming of an obstacle. In our case, we felt both, and the miles glided beneath our wheels with ease. We rode late into the night without complaint and we rose early in the morning to start all over again without an ounce of fatigue. We were on form, beyond it even, so merry and enlivened that nothing could dampen our spirits. When we saw a cluster of children with their stones, we struck up pretend arguments, bellowing hollow imprecations at each other with such force that the children scattered before a single stone was launched. How nice it was to *pretend* to argue. Our genuine exchanges were only convivial.

'Back on the road!'

'In perfect health!'

'Smashing through the miles!'

The Highlands well and truly behind us, southern Ethiopia levelled out into an Eden of dreamy flats, which spun us through a picture-postcard vista of leaning trees and red earth. Brindled dogs, tails high and ears flapping in the light wind, ran alongside us from village to village, glad of the race. Tribesmen on splendidly adorned horses waved from the roadside and cheered us on, their tattered polo shirts and blue jeans adequate cover beneath the sky-wide haze. The churches, sometimes the only concrete structures in villages built otherwise from mud and straw, tolled their bells as we passed, as if both our arrivals and prompt departures necessitated celebration.

On the 64th day of our journey, we cycled for a punishing 11 hours, stopping only for toilet breaks and to buy food, which we ate as we rode. To spur me on, I set my iPod to a mix of Prodigy and Megadeth, and timed my pedal-pushes to the pounds of the kick drums. Finally, exhausted but ecstatic, we rolled up to Moyale, the border town that connects Ethiopia to Kenya, the ninth of the 13 countries we had to pass through.

It was too late to cross the border that night and so we checked into our last Ethiopian guesthouse. Like many of the others we had experienced, its rooms came with a sink and taps yet no running water, but this was countered by its excellent internet connection. I logged on. An email from Francesca directed me to our expedition fundraising page. A substantial donation had just arrived from an anonymous source, enough to build and equip a new classroom in Madagascar.

I wandered out into the guesthouse's courtyard to tell Steve the good news. He was deep in conversation with Johan, a solo Belgian traveller who had made his way through Ethiopia by bus and was keen to hit the Kenyan coast. They had pulled their canvas chairs up to the courtyard's centrepiece: a 3 ft high fountain that gushed out water and perhaps explained the lack of it in the rooms.

'Johan had the same problem with the kids,' Steve said by way of introduction. 'But he found his own trick.'

'It was simple,' Johan said. 'I travelled through Europe before here and I saved up all the soap from the hotels I stayed at. Whenever I saw the

Above: A militant with a gun coming towards us (Egypt)

Left: Signs of conflict – a roadblock in the danger zone (Egypt)

Below: In the church in Egypt – it was a lovely oasis

Above: Ful and mouldy bread was the only food you could get in the desert in Northern Sudan — we ate this day in and day out for breakfast, lunch and dinner

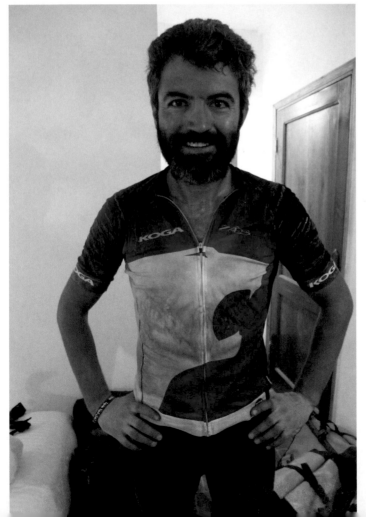

Left: Needing a wash and change of clothes after a week — you can see how much weight I lost (Coptic Pope-designated room in the church in Egypt)

Above: Blue Nile Gorge (Ethiopia)

Below: Sick and tired in Ethiopia

Above: Ethiopian Highlands

Right: The worst road in the world – Moyale to Marsabit (Kenya)

Below: Wilderness of Northern Kenya

Above: At the equator

Left: Tribesman running along with me (Kenya)

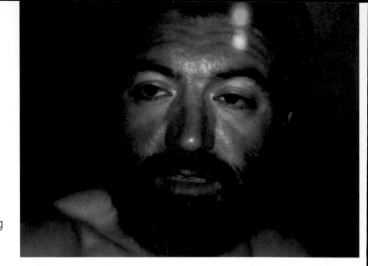

Right: *I am breaking down.
I thought, I am going to
pack up and go home* – I
had nothing left (Kenya)

Below: Suffering with
malaria and food poisoning
in my hospital bed in
Kitengela (Kenya)

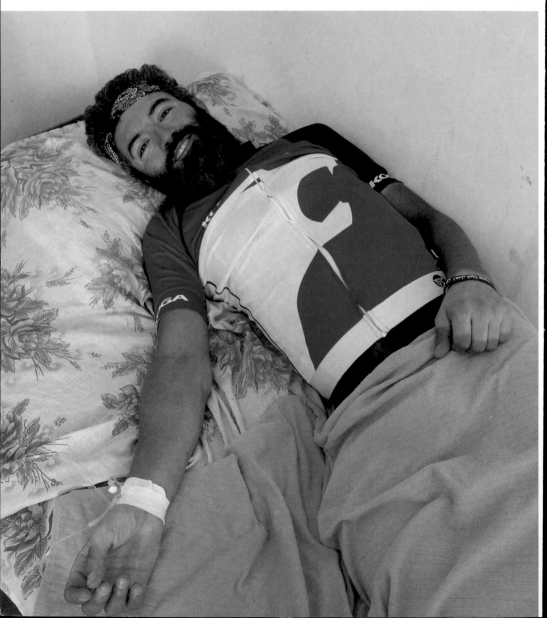

Left: An amazing local Maasai market (Tanzania)

Below left: Night riders (South Africa)

Below right: Steve in agony, pushing his bike up a hill in Tanzania

Botom: Victoria Falls — it was magical

Above: First sight of the Atlantic Ocean – struggling to express my feelings on camera (South Africa)

Right: Zulu dancers at the finish line (Cape Town)

Below: Marco and Francesca drove for hundreds of miles to come and see us – one of the happiest moments of my life (South Africa)

children, I offered them the soap. They put down their stones so they could take it. But I like your way, too.'

'Arguing seemed to work,' I said.

'I had no one to argue with. But maybe if I just argued with myself it would have had the same effect.'

We lazily sipped on our bottles of water and exchanged a few stories. Sometimes, when Johan was absorbed in one of his narratives, Steve and I would look at each other and grin. That grin was an acknowledgment of where we were, on the border with Kenya, a knowing nod to the fact that we had not only conquered illness and derailleur damage, but that we had also managed to make back some of the time we had lost to them. That was good. For we were about to face the worst road in the world.

CHAPTER 18

THE WORST ROAD IN THE WORLD

Distance remaining: 4,264 miles
Time to record: 36 days

The stretch of A-road between Moyale and the small town of Merille, which sits close to Kenya's epicentre, is arguably the *worst* in the world, although whether it qualifies as a *road* is another question altogether. It might be more apt to call it a route, a track, a trail or an artery, or simply just a line. At 250 miles long, there is no tarmac. Instead, the surface is composed of rough volcanic gravel rife with craters, potholes and variegated detritus as it wends its way through the inhospitable northern Kenyan desert. This is no place for life, and the scant smattering of villages along the route are home only to those too desperate and too poor to live anywhere else.

Steve and I had dedicated much of our research to this particular road: we had learned to dread it from afar for a long time. If we could have avoided it, we would have, but there was no other way. And now, finally, here it was. We were standing at its front door, ready to step over the threshold and commit, terrified of the outcome the moment we did. In order to traverse it, we needed to replace our regular 32 mm tyres with heavy-duty 50 mm specimens (which we had picked up from Kamyar in Iran) to account for the road's unpropitious surface; and we needed to carry more supplies than usual to account for the long stretches we would cross devoid of civilisation. This not only meant that our bikes would be heavier and far more challenging to keep upright as we cycled the rugged and uneven road, it also made us a likelier target for the thieves and bandits who lurked at its fringes, scouting for fresh opportunities.

'My friend, please forgive me for my rudeness, but you are crazy.'

Nahom, an Eritrean on his way to Kenya, sat with us as we waited for the border control to open. It was 11 a.m., but since this was a Muslim part of Ethiopia and Eid al-Fitr was being celebrated, the border remained closed until 2 p.m. There was little else to do but sit in the shade and talk. 'I'm only going along this road because I have to,' Nahom continued. 'If I could go back to Eritrea I would, if the Sudanese or the Ethiopians would let me stay I would. But Kenya is my last remaining option, so I have to use this road. Yet at least I will be on a bus. But you? You will be riding a bicycle? Crazy.'

'We've done the research,' I replied. 'We're ready for it.'

'Oh yes? How fast do you think you will travel?'

'We'll probably average about six or seven miles an hour.'

Nahom laughed derisively. 'That is very ambitious. Even if you don't get stopped.'

'We *are* worried about the bandits,' I admitted.

'Not just bandits. You should be careful of everyone on that road, my friend. There is a lot of regional conflict and tribal war in this part of Kenya. They will kill you just to make a point. You know there is a town down there called Badassa, right? Very appropriate! And you must also be careful of the Somalis, too. There are many in north Kenya. They kidnap. And then there's the Al-Shabaab also…'

I tuned out of Nahom's warnings and looked over at Steve. To my surprise, he did not exhibit the anxiety that customarily flowed from him before moments of potential danger. Instead, he was calm, listening to

Nahom with a wry smile and nodding his head. Perhaps he was still riding the high of post-illness, post-derailleur euphoria that had propelled us south from Addis Ababa. I hoped so, for mine had vanished when we had left the guesthouse that morning, replaced by trepidation and the churnings of a queasy stomach.

'... and it will be hot, my friend, insanely hot, so hot it's difficult to breathe,' Nahom continued, 'on this tough road with nasty, desert gravel and people with guns who will rob you, steal whatever you have and leave you for dead. I predict you won't make it to Merille. I think you will be out in that desert for seven days and seven nights.' His monologue ended there, hanging on that strangely ecclesiastical prophecy, which he did not explain despite my promptings. Then there was a silence: a brooding, heavy silence.

Steve was the one to break it. 'Still,' he said cheerfully. 'It's worth a go though, eh?'

Later that evening, as we set up our tent in the wild, Steve admitted that, despite his breezy disregard for Nahom's comments, he still nurtured misgivings about this portion of the journey. 'I'm just sick of people telling me how scared I should be,' he said. 'I've decided to make up my own mind about that. For a start, I'm keeping my knife *close*.'

By the time the border reopened and we were allowed through it was already mid-afternoon. The quality of the road was everything we had anticipated: a substandard pathway of rock and sand that jolted and jarred us along, our forearms cramping as we fought to maintain control of our handlebars. Afternoon soon morphed into dusk and, loath to cycle at night through these hinterlands, we found a sparse clump of low bushes that looked suitable for camping behind. We had cycled for 4 hours and had covered just 20 miles. This had not been helped by the fact that we were stopped at an army checkpoint for half an hour while they checked our documents and warned us of the dangers of the road ahead.

We waited for the sky to grow dark and then, once our presence was obscured by the lack of light, making sure one final time that nobody was around to see us, we jumped behind a bush and erected our tent using just one light between us. Our primary concern was not to draw attention to ourselves.

'I reckon Nahom was exaggerating about the bandits,' I said. 'I'm not so worried about them. I was more worried about Dagestan and Egypt. It's the road itself which concerns me.'

'Didn't you have to deal with roads like this in the Sahara?'

'Some. But none of them were as long as this. Two-hundred-and-fifty miles.'

'At an average of five miles an hour.'

'Did you see Nahom's face when I said we'd be averaging six or seven miles an hour? He wasn't having any of it!'

'He was right, though.'

We fired up our miniscule camping stove and cooked two of our boil-in-the-bag meals atop it. They contained a nameless curry with chicken and rice, and we ate directly from the bags, spooning the piping-hot contents into our mouths and chewing quickly. It was bland but satisfying, much like the rest of the meals we had in our ration packs: beef hotpot, chicken pasta, sausages and beans. Breakfast the following morning was equally uninspiring. We had woken early and so had the time to make porridge and then coffee on the stove – later, as we grew evermore exhausted, our breakfasts began to consist of whatever we had that did not need heating up: bread, jam, cheese, cakes and biscuits.

Making our own breakfast and dinner and sometimes also lunch would become a common template as we cycled the worst road in the world – with few settlements along it, we had to be as self-sufficient as possible. For food, this was not such a problem: our camping stove and ration packs were economically designed and took up little room within our panniers. Water, on the other hand, was not so easy to stock up on in preparation. Between us, we could carry a maximum of 9 litres in the larger bottles stored in our panniers and the smaller bottles attached to our bikes. In the sweltering heat of northern Kenya, 9 litres between two cyclists does not last long. We made sure to stop at every village to refill, as we did in Sololo on the second day, taking a break from our ration packs to eat a lunch of stale goat meat, stale rice and stale chapatis at the village's lone cafe. When we asked for water, the owner offered us a choice – we could buy new bottles from him or we could fill our own from his tap for free. We bought the bottles. I had begun to feel woozy again (I put it down to mild heatstroke and dehydration) and I did not want to risk another bout of sickness which the bacteria-riddled tap water would surely cause.

The most life we saw on the worst road in the world came not from the villages nor from the passing traffic – a maximum of one vehicle per hour – but from the military, which stopped us at each checkpoint and at each of the army jeeps badly parked at sporadic intervals along the roadside. The soldiers were often friendly and polite, they liked to explain to us how many miles to the next village and then the next village after that, but they were never succinct, and they held us up for far longer than necessary as they delivered their directions, which in actuality were always the one same direction. *'Next village, straight on.'*

If the soldiers slowed us down, they at least did so with warmth and kindness, and we found ourselves liking them. Everything else that slowed us down – the punctures; the falls, which left our knees and elbows wet with blood; the hellish road itself – everything else took another bite from our rapidly dwindling willpower. On the second day, after cycling for 12 hours, we were dismayed to learn that we had only covered 57 miles.

'We're falling behind,' I muttered, spooning pasta from a ration pack. 'There's no way we'll make the record at this rate.'

'We always knew our daily mileage would drop significantly here,' Steve said. 'We accounted for it by putting in the extra miles in Europe. You'll make the record, don't worry about it.'

'Still slower than I expected, though,' I said, finishing the pasta and lying back on the red earth. My bones were raw and I felt like I could have fallen asleep right there. 'Maybe Nahom was right. *You'll be in the desert for seven days and seven nights…'*

By the third day, I began to feel sick again. A dull headache settled behind my eyes, sending pulses of febrile nausea down through my nerves, and I developed an interminable thirst which, no matter how much I drank, I could never quench. A strong headwind rose, hot and raw, and my lips and nose began to blister under its relentless oppression. The volcanic gravel of the road transformed into a bed of fine and silty sand, as laborious to cycle as a beach. My front wheel buckled from yet another puncture, a plume of sand puffing out around it, and when I sunk to my knees to repair it I burned my hand on the wheel rim, scorched as it was beneath the torrid sun.

A shepherd materialised from the desert like a mirage, his flock grazing off in the distance. 'Brother, are you mad?' he cried. 'Why are you riding through this desert? You will be here for four days and four nights.'

'Why does everyone here speak like they're a character from the Bible?' I asked Steve as, puncture repaired, we pushed on.

'At least his prediction was more hopeful than Nahom's,' Steve replied with a grin. 'Being stuck out here for four days rather than seven is a pretty big improvement, in my opinion. Come on, I reckon we can make it to Marsabit by the end of the day.' And then he pulled ahead of me, setting a pace which, though it cannot have been faster than 4 mph, was still a struggle to keep up with in the claggy sand.

These were the times when I needed Steve more than ever, the times when my reserves of morale and stamina were low, and he always came through for me. It was never something we discussed, and I often wondered if he did it consciously, if he could see my wilting and waning and resolved to spur me on with a positive countenance and a burst of acceleration. I am a sucker for those two things: smile at me and I can't help but smile back; ramp up the speed and I'll be sure to race you. If Steve did know that this was how to motivate me, he always employed the strategies at just the right moment, exactly when I needed them, and obliquely enough so that I often did not even notice. Yet I also wondered if he was entirely unconscious of his carefully timed encouragements, if they came out naturally and symbiotically, not necessarily because I needed them, but because the *team* needed them. Either way, whether his actions were purposeful or automatic was unimportant. What mattered was that they worked.

It was by far the most gruelling day of the expedition thus far. The headwind intensified, lashing our faces with sand. Puncture after puncture came, and in the end we swapped our tyres back to our old, thinner road tyres. They were far more durable, but keeping balance became twice as difficult. Every judder of the bike sent shooting pains up my tensed arms, threatening to splinter my wrists, and, exacerbated by it all, my headache got worse, so painful that I could feel my heartbeat in my eyeballs. Then the final insult: the road began to ascend uphill. I checked my odometer. There were still 20 miles left to Marsabit. The sun had already set.

'I can't do it!' I shouted to Steve. 'I need to stop!'

Whether or not he heard me – and it was feasible that he did not, for the wind had gathered and gathered – he did not reply, but continued forward with the same methodical, determined strokes. How I wanted him to turn and reply so that I could engage him in an argument, one I would make last long enough to exhaust us and force us into erecting the tent there and then. But Steve didn't take the bait, he just kept moving, and that was the best thing he could have done, for I was compelled to follow.

Somewhere along the way, we stopped in a village without electric lights where the goat meat was stalc, the chapatis were mouldy and the tea was cold, but we devoured it anyway. Somewhere else, further on, we were stopped at a military checkpoint, where we were admonished for cycling at night. Al-Shabaab was operating in the area, we were told, but if we gave the soldiers a present they assured us they could protect us from the terrorists. We declined the offer and cycled on.

I fell into a muddled delirium, maintaining the slightest fragment of my focus on Steve's rear wheel and then allowing the rest of it to drift into chasms of self-doubt. Why was I doing this to myself? Why was I doing any of it? What kind of life was this? I lived in a tent, I had no friends, looked like shit, a loser, weak body, weak mind. Why was I even here? Why wasn't I back in London, with a job, with a home, with a life? I realised I was crying.

Alone, it would have taken me perhaps two more days to reach Marsabit. With Steve at the helm, we arrived by 11 p.m. I could barely string a sentence together. Steve found a guesthouse and booked us in, then went off to implore the owner for food while I waddled to the bathroom and then stood motionless, gazing at myself in the mirror. I was red, like a landed Martian or a painted warrior. Sand clung to my skin, hair and beard, and I stood there for a long time, staring at it all, staring at myself, not washing the sand away, and not even thinking that I should, but just staring, just standing and staring.

––––––––––––

'How long have you been here?' I asked, drowsily padding into the cafe to find Steve there already, pushing a plate of bread and eggs across the table towards me. He had almost finished his own.

'Half an hour?' he guessed. 'Thought I'd let you sleep in. How are you feeling?'

'A bit better.' I took a seat.

'Seventy-six miles yesterday,' Steve said with a smile. 'Not too bad at all.'

'I would have given up much earlier than that.' I speared a piece of bread with my fork. 'Thanks for pushing me on.'

'Don't mention it.' He swallowed the last of his food and rose to his feet. 'You'd do the same for me.'

He marched out of the cafe to pack his panniers while I stayed seated, forcing myself to eat the rest of my breakfast. We had another tough day ahead of us and I needed the protein. I thought about what Steve had said, his assumption that I could take on the same role he had played yesterday, that I would push him on when needed. And it left me wondering. Would I? *Had* I? I had nearly left him behind when his derailleur hanger broke. And when he had decided to skip Dagestan, I had let him and gone on alone. I had discussed and debated with him, tried to convince him with appeals either to rationality or emotion, but perhaps I had not done so enough.

Such thoughts played in my mind as we set off from Marsabit, but they were soon superseded by the road itself. We were cycling through the Marsabit National Park, home to nomadic tribes such as the Rendille, the Borana, the Turkana and the Samburu, who weave geometric patterns around these lands as they wander them with their herds of camels and cattle. I hoped to see them and, if not, to at least spot one of the numerous elephants and zebras that grazed their way through the nature reserve stretching down from Mount Marsabit. But I could not take my eyes off the road. The gentle gravel that constituted the surfaces of Marsabit town receded to sand back in the desert again, and the only way to get through it was to fixate all of my attention on the road and the road alone. We both fell to the ground with painful regularity, endured puncture after puncture, gasped in the dry, searing heat and depleted our energy reserves before it was even lunchtime.

'You know this morning, when I said you'd do the same for me?' Steve asked as we munched biscuits during a rest stop. 'I think I'm going to need that motivation now. I'm not feeling too good.'

'Dehydration?' I asked.

'No, I don't think so.'

'Food poisoning again?'

'Not that, either. I think I've pulled a muscle in my side. It hurts every time I breathe. Kind of feels almost like I've cracked a rib.'

As the afternoon wore on, Steve's ailment worsened. The unavoidable rocks and potholes along the road sent forks of pain through his torso, causing him to wince and inhale sharply every few seconds. When even the slightest uphill began, it was too much for him and he dismounted his bike to push. I did my best to rally him along: taking some of his load and squashing it into my bulging panniers; offering him my half of our remaining fruit; keeping the conversation light with puerile jokes and half-hearted encouragements – but I had begun to suffer, too, not from the same debilitating pain as Steve, but from the dark disquietude that had enveloped me the day before. I had barely enough energy to motivate myself, let alone Steve, and even though I knew he had done it for me and that I should be returning the favour, I was already too deep into my own enervation. We fell into a long silence, retreating from each other, and pushing onwards into the doldrums.

By the time the sun set we had covered only 40 miles. We both wanted to stop, but had run out of water an hour earlier. We had no choice but to keep moving until we found a supply, however far ahead that might be. Hours passed. The thirst became unbearable. I contemplated drinking my own urine. It was a disturbing thought, more so because it would not be long before it became a necessity.

The void of self-doubt returned, harassing me with a barrage of despair. I had started this expedition because I had wanted a change. I had wanted insecurity, uncertainty, risk, adrenaline, excitement. London had been too easy, life had been too easy, I had wanted more. And look where it had got me. I was in over my head, I had bitten off more than I could chew, I was not waving but drowning. I wasn't strong enough. The heat, the exhaustion, the poor nutrition, the dehydration, this *endless fucking road*, it was all too much, too much for me. Steve could usually drag me out of this kind of funk, but now he was done in, too. We could barely look after ourselves, let alone each other. We were fools, absolute fools to have thought we could do this. We should have been back in London, getting ready to go out on a Friday night after work. With friends and cold pints. Dinner I could actually enjoy, actually savour. Then home again, my own space, running water, a hot shower, a good bed. I had created a good life for myself in London and I had thrown it all away for this. So that I could be here, on the worst road in the world, ready to drink my own piss.

My front wheel hit a pool of soft sand and I was thrown to the ground, striking my coccyx against a sharp rock. I tried to pull myself to my feet, but it was too painful. This was the last straw. I rolled on to my side and, for the second time in 24 hours, burst into tears. Steve stopped beside me.

'That's it for me,' I wailed. 'Tomorrow I'm getting a truck to Nairobi, then I'm packing up and going back to London. I'm done.'

Steve didn't reply. He merely shook his head, disappointed, and then continued on. When 10 minutes passed without his return, I clambered to my feet and followed him. I was still crying.

Not long before midnight struck, we arrived in Laisamis: a cluster of ragged huts tucked behind a telecom tower. There was no electricity in the village, which bathed in the soft red glow emanating from the tower's aircraft warning light. All the shops were closed, but we stumbled upon a cafe where two men propped up the bar and glugged quietly from plastic bottles of beer. We ordered water, as much as we could get our hands on, and then the only food available: goat meat and chapatis. One of the men, a driver for the NGO based in the area, came and sat with us. His name was Dan.

'I passed you on the road this afternoon,' he said. 'You took your time.'

'What do you drive?' I asked.

'A minivan. Why?'

'I need to get to Nairobi tomorrow,' I said. 'Can you take me? I'll pay well.'

Steve placed his hand on my arm. 'Come on, Reza, you're not serious about—'

'I'm done, mate,' I interrupted him. 'Enough is enough. I'm done. I'm going home.'

CHAPTER 19

TRACK TO TARMAC

Distance remaining: 4,052 miles

Time to record: 32 days

Dan had a job booked in for the following day and would not be able to take me to Nairobi, but he was confident he could source another means of transport. We arranged to meet at 9 a.m. in the same cafe although, when I arrived, he was nowhere to be seen. I ordered breakfast – porridge and fried eggs – and waited for him.

Steve would not look at me. I asked him if he wanted to share my ride to Nairobi; he said he needed to think about it. I felt lousy. I had slept poorly through the night, kept awake by crises of confidence. I knew that to quit now would be a mistake, that the moment I set foot in London I would loathe myself, that cutting the expedition short would cause me deep and recurring regrets for the rest of my life. Yet, no matter how powerful the urge was to continue towards Cape Town, the moment I thought of the worst road in the world it vanished altogether. Approximately 100 miles of it remained and I knew I had not the strength to endure it.

'What if we rested here for a few days and then carried on?' Steve asked. 'We'd forfeit the record, but at least we could finish the journey.'

'No record, no point,' I grumbled.

'I gave up my chance at the record seven weeks ago. And I'm still going.'

'I wouldn't have bothered. I'd have just left Russia and gone home.'

Part of me wanted Steve to persist, to hassle and pressure and wheedle and nag me until I relented. If anyone could do it, Steve could and there was a chance it might work. But I had delivered my last remark with a snappish petulance and he had fallen silent as a result.

Dan was late. An hour had passed and he still had not arrived. The cafe stood slightly apart from the village, connected to it by a 300 m stretch of white sand. Then, beyond that, another pathway disappeared off into the heat haze, seemingly to nowhere. I had sat with my back to it to keep an eye out for Dan, but as I shifted my chair to keep within the receding shade and glanced behind me I saw a vast group of people, some 40 or 50 of them, emerging from the desert and walking towards the cafe. As tall and thin as supermodels, they were likewise as gorgeous, and were wrapped in swathes of cloth which, I realised, were pink for men and blue for women. All hair, regardless of gender, was short or shaved off entirely, and while the women adorned their heads with spectacular weaves of beads, flowers and coins, the men left theirs bare, save perhaps for the occasional tinge of red ochre. They gathered around the cafe, chatting gaily in a language I could not understand but which was beautiful nonetheless. They ignored me and Steve, who gazed at them, rapt, and instead struck up conversations with the locals who had wandered over from the village to see them. Dan was among them.

'Sorry I'm late,' he said. 'I scc you've met our friendly local Samburu.'

'Samburu?' I said. 'I thought they were Maasai.'

'Because they all look alike to you?'

'No, I didn't mean that, I—'

'I'm joking!' he interrupted, slapping me on the shoulder and then taking a seat next to me. 'The Samburu and the Maasai are distant relatives, but they'll be the first to tell you that they are completely different tribes.

They're nomadic by nature, but these lot tend to stick around here because of the well.'

'What well?'

'Where do you think this water you're drinking came from? The NGO I drive for builds wells, and schools. It's called World Vision. One of the biggest problems in this part of Kenya is that because the water is so scarce families can literally spend every day just walking from place to place in search of water. This means that they never settle, the kids never go to school, they grow up uneducated, and the cycle repeats itself. So we use solar energy to pump up water, we build a well so that a community can settle around it, and then we build a school for the children. It's how we break the cycle.'

Dan's words made me think of Madagascar, of SEED and of the Malagasy children I had devoted so much of my time to helping. The thoughts were neither sudden nor surprising – they had reappeared time and time again throughout the night, and they had only made me feel worse. By abandoning the journey I was turning my back on those children and betraying all those donors who had pledged money towards this expedition. And yet, every time I thought of them all, it was never long before an image of the worst road in the world materialised above their heads and then it all crumbled into blackness.

'It's what I do.' Made uncomfortable by the awkward silence that followed his description of wells and schools, Dan resumed talking. 'I help people. And that's why I'm here now, isn't it? To help you two gentlemen. You still want a ride to Nairobi?'

'Not me,' Steve said. I looked over at him. He was not looking at either me or Dan, but at the Samburu tribespeople, who continued to laugh and chat and mingle around us. 'I'm cycling to Cape Town.'

'Good on you!' Dan said, and then turned to me. 'How about you? I have a friend with a truck who can take you, but he won't be able to pick you up until tomorrow.'

'Come on, Reza,' Steve said, finally looking away from the Samburu and locking me into a stare. 'Don't chuck it all away now. Come with me.'

'I want to,' I said, feeling like I might be about to cry again. 'I really do. But it's the road. I can't take it any more. It's killing me. And there's still a hundred miles of it left. One hundred miles of that gravel and sand. It's impossible.'

'More like fourteen,' Dan said.

'What?'

'Laisamis is only fourteen miles from Merille. After that, it's tarmac. Trust me, I drive there three times a week.'

'But I don't get it,' I said. 'I thought the tarmac started in Isiolo, which should be another hundred miles from here.'

'It used to, but then they tarmacked the road all the way between Merille and Isiolo. It's good tarmac too, nice and fresh.'

I looked back to Steve, who was grinning at me triumphantly. 'Fourteen miles,' he said. 'We could be there by lunchtime.'

While 14 more miles did not seem quite so insurmountable as another 100, the prospect of trying to cycle it still left me with a distinct feeling of dread. 'I don't know...' I faltered.

'Let's at least try. If it turns out to be too much, we'll turn back. And I'll come to Nairobi with you. How about that?'

'And if you end up back here tonight,' Dan added, 'I'll drive you to Nairobi myself.'

Steve laughed and clapped his hands. 'There you go then!' he said. 'Dan's friend can't take you until tomorrow anyway, so we might as well try. Either we make it to Merille where the road gets better or we turn around and come back and then get driven to Nairobi tonight. It's a win-win situation!'

It did not feel like one to me, but the logic was at least strong enough to coerce my head into a nodding motion, up and down, up and down.

———————

Those 14 miles took us a full 4 hours to negotiate, and when we came to their eventual end and hit tarmac I wanted to get down on all fours and kiss the new road surface. I felt as if I had never seen anything so beautiful in all my life. We coasted its first mile, a slight decline, with barely a turn of the pedals and a warm cloak of bliss descended over me. We had made it to Merille. The worst road in the world was behind us.

'So do you want to turn back to Laisamis?' Steve grinned.

'Not a chance.'

'The next town's Archers Post. Think you can make it?'

'Definitely.'

'And then Nairobi?'

'Maybe.'

'And then Tanzania?'

'I'll get back to you on that.'

Every one of my muscles ached and the headache that had throbbed for the past few days continued to persist, but the sheer joy of being on tarmac began to outweigh it all and, before I knew it, cycling was spectacular again. I reached down and patted the side of my bike. While the worst road in the world had nearly destroyed me, my trusty Koga had endured it all without a hitch. It was a marvellous piece of Dutch engineering. Cape Town may still have been 4,000 miles away, but if my bike could survive what I had just put it through, then perhaps I could survive the rest. Thoughts of the record began to resurface, flickering somewhere just above my headache, and when we reached Archers Post that evening and settled down to a gargantuan portion of chicken and chips each, I felt an overwhelming urge to apologise to Steve and to thank him, too.

'I wouldn't have made that if it wasn't for you,' I said. 'There's no way.'

Steve smiled sheepishly and blushed, which made me blush in turn. An awkward but not unpleasant silence fell between us. While we were never slow to give voice to our emotions when they tended towards anger and frustration, expressing those more ameliorative feelings – care, warmth, amity – was more of a challenge. I wanted to tell him how much I treasured his companionship, that there was no one else I would rather be with at that moment, and that – why not? – I had come to love him like a brother. But the words stuck in my throat.

We were saved from our mounting embarrassment by a small boy who wandered over to our table and, with a wonderful cordiality, stuck out his hand for each of us to shake and said: 'Hello. How are yoooooooo?' We bought him a can of Coke and fussed over him as he guzzled it down and belched happily over the table. It was far easier to divert our sentiments through him than directly to each other and, while I was relieved that everything I wanted to say to Steve could be left unsaid, I wish now that I had said it anyway. Nevertheless, I hope that Steve knew, at that moment, the genuine affection I had for him.

I hope you still know it, Steve.

———————

Mount Kenya was no longer on the horizon. We were at its base. The climb was arduous and took us an entire afternoon, but the joy of having the worst well and truly behind us gave us the extra lift we needed, and we powered up the mountain with an intoxicated fortitude until we reached the road's peak, where we dismounted our bikes and took a moment to stand and stare and feel like kings. Far below us, a solitary elephant traipsed through the red earth; far above, a hawk eagle drifted across the cloudless sky.

'The second-highest mountain in Africa,' Steve said. 'How about we sack the expedition off and go climb Kilimanjaro?'

'Fuck that,' I said. 'I'm going to Cape Town.'

'Good. I'll race you.'

We plummeted back towards sea level, recklessly overtaking one another in defiant swoops, the setting sun firing the horizon into a symphony of cerise and magenta. Passing trucks blared their horns as we dipped and wove, and we chose to interpret them not as warnings but as salutations. The world may not have been ours, but this incandescent slice of Africa was and, as yet another landmark diminished behind us, I allowed myself the luxury of contemplating the record once more. It was still attainable. I could still make it. The hairs along my bare forearms prickled with excitement, and my feet pedalled faster and faster.

We arrived in Nanyuki by the late evening, thrilled and famished. A ramshackle yet vibrant restaurant, filled with teenagers who ignored us and instead checked each other out over super-sized milkshakes, served us our first salad in a month, which we followed with two mammoth pizzas. Feeling we should do as the locals did, we washed it all down with chocolate milkshakes.

'I've been thinking about the record today,' I admitted. 'Do you think it's still possible? We lost a lot of time on that road.'

Steve took a long draught of his milkshake, hoovering it up through the straw. 'We knew it was going to slow us down. But it was worse than we thought it'd be. We're about one-hundred-and-eighty miles behind schedule. We should have left Nairobi by now.'

'And how far are we from Nairobi?'

'About one-hundred-and-twenty miles. I reckon we can do it easily, though. It's supposed to be all downhill. And, you know, the worst is behind us now. From here, it's good roads all the way to Cape Town. If we get our heads down and really go for it, I reckon we can make it there by Day 100. We've pulled ourselves back from the brink before.'

Steve's assurance lent me confidence, even though the supposed downhill trajectory to Nairobi turned out to be a falsehood. The road peaked and dipped with such consistency that we felt we were back in Ethiopia again. There was, however, one major difference. At 8 a.m. on the 71st day of our journey, we arrived at the earth's equator. A yellow, black and red sign marked the pivotal moment, far smaller than we had believed it to be when we had gazed at online images of it back in London. I had, I remembered, imagined myself here, standing beneath the sign, and I had imagined myself as I was back then – healthy, clean-shaven, sassy. In reality, the photograph I have of the two of us with the sign reveals anything but those qualities. While Steve stands straight-backed and smiling, his arms folded across his chest and his stance rooted and confident, I am of an altogether different countenance. A ragged beard sits below sunglasses, worn to hide my bloodshot eyes. I seem drained of colour and drained of energy: my hands planted on my hips as if to keep my torso balanced on top of my bent and wilting legs. I am gaunt and angular, thinner than I have perhaps been since adolescence, and I am not smiling.

'We started at N70,' I said. 'This is ground zero.'

'And we finish at S33,' Steve replied.

'Being here makes it feel like we're only halfway.'

'I kind of wish we were. Another seventy days cycling could be fun.'

'Depends on the roads.'

'Depends on the food.'

It would have been pleasant to spend more time at the equator. It would have been pleasant to have spent more time at many of the places we had zipped through. But the prospect of the record was always there, ringing insistently like a bell, and I had heeded it for so long that to ignore it now felt unnatural, alien. Nairobi was still over 100 miles away and we had pledged to make it there by the close of the day.

It was not easy. Nothing on this journey ever was. The mutton stew lunch we bought from a petrol station sent my stomach into paroxysms of pain. An ageing estate car, weaving dangerously across the road as if the driver was drunk, clipped Steve's handlebar with its wing-mirror, almost sending him off the road and into the dusty earth. The motorway, which we joined late in the afternoon, was a tumult of wild and haphazard traffic, its hard shoulder littered with broken glass, perhaps a result of the collisions that the Kenyan drivers seemed to want to cause with each other, so perpetually terrifying were their manoeuvres across and around the motorway.

And then, on the outskirts of the capital, a motorbike holding one driver and two pillion passengers slowed to match our speed and drew level with Steve. Just a few metres behind, I watched as the driver leaned over to shout something. Steve stretched his neck forward in an attempt to hear what he was shouting, and as he did so the rear pillion passenger reached out and deftly plucked Steve's sunglasses from his face. Their prize secured, they shot off down the road.

I don't believe I have ever seen Steve cycle so fast as he did at that moment. The motorbike turned off the motorway, Steve behind him and me behind Steve, and we found ourselves being led into the heart of a Nairobi slum. People spilled out from their tumbledown shacks to watch as we raced past, but we were no match for the motorbike, which disappeared into a maze of lanes before we could catch it.

'*SHIT!*' Steve shouted as he skidded to a stop. Locals came forward to clamour around us.

'Forget the sunglasses,' I breathed. 'We should get out of here.' A thin gentleman with a bare, dirt-encrusted chest, sinewy arms and wild eyes began to poke at one of my panniers.

'The *bastards!*' Steve was ranting, oblivious to the burgeoning crowd. 'I fucking *love* those sunglasses.'

'Steve,' I implored. 'I really don't think we should be here.' Other men, all as thin and dirty and sinewy as the first, joined their compatriot to inspect my bags and jab at my spokes. 'I really think that—'

I was interrupted by the first man who had approached me. 'Do you have a problem?' he asked slowly.

'No,' I said, raising my hands up to shoulder height. 'No problem. We're leaving now.'

'I'm not leaving,' Steve snarled, turning on the man. 'Those bastards stole my sunglasses!'

'Steve, this isn't—' I began, but I was interrupted once more by the same man.

'Who stole your sunglasses?' he asked.

Steve described the three men on the motorbike and he must have done so with perfect clarity, for a ripple of laughter erupted across the crowd, and the man, once he had stopped chuckling himself, said: 'I know these men. They are local thieves. And they are, as you say, *bastards*.'

He began to bark in loud Swahili to two of the men beside him, who nodded at his words and then sprinted off into the slum's back alleys. Moments later they returned bearing Steve's sunglasses, which they offered to our interlocutor, who proudly presented them to Steve. 'Do they have damage?' he asked.

Steve inspected them. 'No, they're good,' he said. 'But where are the bastards who stole them? They need to come here and apologise to me right now.'

The man translated this into Swahili for the rest of the crowd, whose subsequent laughter resounded off the shanty town walls. 'Do not worry,' he said. 'We will give them punishment. You can go. We will give them punishment.'

'Come on, mate,' I said. 'It's sorted. Let's get to the centre.'

Placated, Steve agreed to follow me as we turned our bikes and pedalled back towards the road. A few metres away from the crowd, I turned my head to look back at the slum we were leaving. Most of those who had gathered around us were returning to their makeshift homes. A few stayed, the man we had spoken with at their centre, and as we rode on I continued to check behind me. He was always there, waving heartily, until we rounded a corner and could see him no more.

———————

Stepping into the Nairobi Safari Club Hotel felt like stepping into another world. The foyer alone was an overwhelming feast of extravagance with its thick red carpets, its grandiose architecture and its milling concierges in their pristine uniforms, and when we asked for the price of a room at the front desk, the $200 minimum seemed apt. Dismayed but not altogether surprised, we turned around and began to walk away. We had only entered because it was the first accommodation we had seen in Nairobi. We should have known that this vast tribute to colonial decadence would be beyond our means, stinking and filthy and deluged in sand as we were.

I still do not know why the receptionist called us back, and I do not know why she then offered us a room at the merest fraction of the price she had initially given us. Perhaps this hotel, like so much else of the tourist industry in Kenya, had suffered from the terrorist attacks and political fallout that the country had experienced over the past few years. Or perhaps she just took pity on us. Either way, the new price she offered was more than reasonable and we accepted it with gratitude.

It took some time to wrest myself away from that inimitable pleasure that a hot and powerful shower affords after a long and arduous journey, and when I finally did I found a note stating that Steve had already made his way down to the hotel's restaurant. I dried and dressed, and then chose the lift rather than the stairs to meet him there. He was already deep into a platter of fresh vegetables and fruit, and although I had cycled all day long, I had no appetite. My stomach was tight and I felt the onset of a fever. The few other occupied tables in the restaurant seemed to cater exclusively for Americans, who spoke and ate loudly, their expensive cameras swinging from the camouflage jackets that hung from their chairs. In the corner, a stout Kenyan tapped out a soft and inoffensive medley of Chris de Burgh, Frank Sinatra and Elton John covers on the hotel's grand piano, crooning Swahili-inflected approximations of the lyrics into a tatty microphone.

Back in the room, it took some effort to email Base Camp and complete the day's logbook entry. All I wanted was to sleep. When I was finally able to crawl between my bedsheets, they felt cool and starchy against my skin. I fell asleep to the sound of Steve talking to his father on the phone, his soft words a drowsy lullaby.

The same voice woke me in the morning. It took some time to recognise it as Steve's. The dream of an ornery elephant with its foot on my shoulder morphed into conscious realisation. There was no foot on my shoulder, only Steve's hand.

'Reza, are you all right?' he was murmuring. 'You look like shit.'

My eyes focused on a room that was spinning about me, with Steve at its centre. I leaped from the bed and sprinted to the en-suite bathroom, where

I heaved into the toilet with violent abandon for the next 10 minutes. My pulse was racing, my headache felt like it had burst free from my cranium to envelop my entire body, and I shivered with a feverish ferocity. It took all my effort to wrench myself from the toilet and back to the confines of our room where, unable to do anything else, I collapsed back into bed.

'Food poisoning,' I moaned. 'Again.'

'Stay there,' Steve said. It sounded like he was a mile away. 'I'll get the bikes packed up and then I'll bring up some breakfast for you.'

It took me half an hour to ingest the bowl of porridge he brought and as soon as it was finished I threw it all up into the toilet.

'You can't cycle today,' Steve intoned. 'You need to rest.'

'No,' I protested. 'I'll be all right. Honest. I just need a minute.'

'I did a quick recce outside before breakfast. There's a shopping mall next door with a clinic. It's open now. Let's at least get you there before we decide on anything. See what the doctor says.'

I reluctantly agreed, allowing Steve to guide me, shaking, to the clinic, where he sat with me for an hour and a half until I was called in. The doctor confirmed my suspicions. I had food poisoning again, so acute that he prescribed a course of medication and at least one full day of rest. We were still behind schedule, but the thought of taking to the road left me so dizzy that I had no choice but to retire back to our hotel room, where I collapsed into my bed and slept for the next 18 hours.

I awoke in bedsheets saturated with my sweat. The aches and the pains, which had become so familiar to me over the past week they were almost habitual, had not disappeared overnight. They were still there, flowing back and forth between my head and my stomach and stopping at each muscle along the way. Nevertheless, I felt slightly better and was well enough to keep a small breakfast down, following it with an equal weight of medicine.

'What's the target for today?' I asked. 'Another one-hundred-and-twenty miles?'

Steve looked at me with quiet disapproval. 'You know I think you should rest again.'

I shook my head. 'No. I can't afford another day off. We're too far behind. I'm not spending any more time in that room. I'd rather ride until I collapse.'

'Well, I'm up for it, but I didn't spend all of yesterday throwing up. If I had, I wouldn't be pushing myself today.'

'Of course you wouldn't, you don't qualify for the record any more, you can take as long as you want.' I immediately felt guilty. Steve disliked any mention of his failure to cycle through Dagestan. He quietened, paying extra attention to his cup of coffee. My remarks at least had the effect of halting his attempts to stop me riding, but I still wished I hadn't made them.

Packing my bags left me out of breath before I had even climbed on to my saddle. Out in the fierce sunlight, my temperature returned with a vengeance. The machinations of my legs as I pedalled awoke the sleeping beast that was my stomach, and it sprung back to life in a series of savage cramps and tempestuous jets of agony. *Ride through it*, I told myself, *ride through the pain*. To think it was easy; the actuality of it was near impossible. After 20 minutes, I begged painkillers from Steve, and they afforded some relief, but then the torment would return with even greater intensity, and soon no amount of painkillers, which I had begun to ingest in dangerous amounts, could quell it. Even water hurt as it flowed down my throat like lava. My stomach felt as if it was being stretched from the inside by sharp metal spikes, expanding at their points and threatening to burst at any moment. The throb of my headache was so nauseating and all-consuming that I could barely see. My muscles felt like they had been slow-cooked and were ready to slip from my bones. Less than 20 miles out of Nairobi, at the small town of Kitengela, the slight incline that led to its centre was too much to bear. I came off my bike with a yelp and then, leaving it in the road, stumbled into the soft grass of a nearby field, where I collapsed to the ground, curled up into a ball and succumbed to the pain.

'I'm getting help,' Steve said. 'Stay here.'

I could not reply and so, instead, I wept loudly.

Steve returned moments later with a tuk-tuk, which took us and our bikes to Kitengela's small and basic clinic. The receptionist barely looked at me, intoning only that I should wait until a doctor became available.

A wild and irrational voice began to shout, piercing through my all-encompassing pain. The voice was shrill, both angry and pleading at the same time, and it took me some moments to realise that it was my own, not in my head, but loud and real. *I need to see the doctor now! NOW! I'm in PAIN! Can't you see that? Can't you understand that? I'm in PAIN!*

A doctor appeared and led me to a bed, injecting me with a strong painkiller and then feeding two separate drips into my wrist. He took some blood and then left the room to test it.

He did not take long. I suspect he already knew what he was looking for. Malaria is rampant in East Africa, and when he informed me that I had contracted it, he did so with little surprise.

CHAPTER 20

JUNGLE FEVER

Distance remaining: 3,360 miles

Time to record: 28 days

I didn't know what to say. Everything we had been through, all the days and nights we had pushed ourselves, all the months of preparation, and now a single health problem had ruined the whole thing. The record was slipping out of my hands and there was nothing I could do to stop it.

Steve was tested soon after me and we were both relieved to discover that his results were negative. The doctor instructed me to remain in bed until the drip had finished, and so, understanding that another day was lost, Steve took the opportunity to find somewhere in Kitengela that would put us up for the night. Following the doctor's orders, I was to stay in the clinic, in bed, for the day. The doctor popped into the room from time to time to check up on me.

'What's your name?' I asked, bored and desperate for conversation, during one of his quick visits.

'Doctor Moses,' he replied.

'How long do you think it'll be before I can resume my journey?'

'Are you eager to leave so soon?' he said with a trace of friendly condescension. 'Fortunately for you, your malaria is not very advanced. We have caught it in its early stages. Your food poisoning, however, is severe and we must treat that, too.'

'So I've only just picked the malaria up?'

'You contracted it maybe ten days ago. For malaria, this is not such a long time. Most people start to feel ill two weeks or even a month after infection. I once treated a patient who had carried it for a whole year without feeling any symptoms.'

I cast my mind back ten days. We had been in Ethiopia then, ploughing our way towards the Kenyan border, our reserves of energy depleted by hostile children, a broken derailleur hanger and wretched bouts of food poisoning. It was almost predictable that, should I have caught malaria in any of the countries we had passed through, it was to be Ethiopia. That country had maddened and perplexed and frazzled and enfeebled me for close to a fortnight, and even when I thought we had finally left it far behind, it had still managed to secrete this little souvenir into my blood, a fitting tribute to Reza and Ethiopia's time together.

'How long should it take to treat?' I asked Doctor Moses.

'We will have to see how it all goes.'

'So if it goes well, I could be out of here tomorrow?'

The doctor laughed. 'Tomorrow is very ambitious. Your liver is in a bad state from the food poisoning. But maybe the day after. Or maybe the day after that. Or maybe later still. You must be able to feel it in your body, how much you need to rest.'

I explained to him my attempt at the world record and how, if I could not get back on the saddle soon, I might lose my chance of attaining it.

'A world record?' he gasped. 'That is wonderful! This is something I like about Europeans. They think and then they *implement*. Africans just think and think and think and don't do anything about it.'

'Surely there's plenty of Africans with world records.'

'Maybe, I don't know the statistics. But I have lived in Europe and I have lived in Africa, and this is what I believe. It is one of the ways in which Europeans and Africans are different.'

'Are there other ways?' I asked.

'Yes,' he replied, that same faintly perceptible condescension back again. 'We Africans respect the fact that malaria is a serious disease. If we can, we rest it off. We don't jump on to bicycles and ride to the other side of the world.'

His remark may have been understated, but it was true. Malaria is one of the world's most prolific killers, and nowhere more so than in Africa, where 80 per cent of all cases occur. According to the World Health Organization's annual Malaria Report for 2013 (the year of my journey), over half a million people died of malaria in Africa in that year alone, a distressing 437,000 of whom were children below the age of five. Other reports demonstrate how malaria impedes the economic development of African countries: with all the healthcare costs, the inability to work and the depreciatory impact on tourism that the disease engenders, it is said that Africa loses approximately $12 billion every year.

Lying in that Kitengela clinic bed, I knew none of this. Malaria had crossed my mind just long enough for me to buy some antimalarial tablets from a London pharmacy and then just long enough once more to remind me to begin taking them when we landed in Egypt. I continued taking them and, confident in their efficacy, I forgot about the disease entirely. It had simply never occurred to me that I might contract malaria. And so, instead of counting myself lucky that, although I had caught it, it had been identified in its early stages and was therefore treatable; instead of counting myself lucky that I would survive; instead of counting myself lucky that I was not on the brink of death as so many others less fortunate than me were and would continue to be for the foreseeable future – instead of all that, I looked away from Doctor Moses to face the wall, fell into a maudlin silence, and proceeded to feel very sorry for myself.

There was little else to do in that bed, little else save feel sorry for myself and think, thoughts sliding one by one through my consciousness like the drip into my wrist. Chief among them was the desire to get out of this bed, to get moving towards Tanzania. But I was stuck here, trapped by my malaria. The record was vanishing before me, and there was nothing I could do about it.

———————

I was discharged from the clinic in the early evening with another injection, a fistful of tablets and the imperative that I return the next day at 8 a.m. 'You will need more antibiotics, another injection and another drip every eight hours,' Doctor Moses intoned as he bid me farewell for the night. 'What I have given you will get you through tonight, but you must come back at eight o'clock, then four in the afternoon and then midnight.'

'Is there a doctor I should ask for?'

He laughed. 'No need. I will be here.'

And, sure enough, he was. Unable to move myself anywhere other than between our hotel and the clinic, I was to discover over my next few days in Kitengela that Doctor Moses was always present. 'I work forty-eight hours on and then take forty-eight hours off,' he once told me, but this was a clear lie, for I spent three days in and out of that clinic, and each time I entered, finding my own way to the same bed, he would appear within minutes, looking perky and unharrassed and not the least bit tired. I never saw any other doctors. The only other staff at the clinic were four nurses, and they and Doctor Moses somehow managed the entire institution between them: a ramshackle hodgepodge of accident and emergency, in-patient, children's and maternity wards. All around me, women gave birth, bodies crushed from motor accidents were wheeled in, children screamed and parents shouted, and Doctor Moses and his four nurses tended to each and every one of them with a relentless magnanimity. I felt like a burden to them all, but the malaria had made me submissive, and I lay in my bed with the drip in my wrist as the endless drama unfolded around me. Once, fresh from my bed and ready to leave and head back to the hotel, I felt the familiar rumblings of my bowels and rushed to the clinic's toilets. One of the nurses greeted me with a chirrupy '*Jambo!*' as I entered, and then turned back to her task. She was cleaning out the squatters.

By then, such unhygienic multitasking came as little surprise. When Doctor Moses pierced my skin with a needle and then took it out, the blood left behind was cleaned away with toilet paper doused in surgical spirit. Mosquitoes flapped about the bedside lamps, zipping towards any patches of bare skin if I lay immobile for long enough, and soon my arms and legs grew peppered with red and aggravating bites. The overall smell of the clinic was rancid and persistent, and even though I stayed there for hours at a time I never grew accustomed to it.

On the rare occasions that Doctor Moses could not administer my drip himself, he would delegate the task to one of the nurses, who would approach me with a nervousness that I quickly reciprocated. One, a girl who looked no older than 18, had to take several stabs at my arm before her shaking hand finally found the vein. She cleaned the excessive blood away with dry toilet paper and then stayed to swat the mosquitoes, which swooped in like sharks.

'Are you a qualified nurse?' I asked with some reluctance.

'Student,' she replied, following the haphazard arc of a mosquito towards its refuge on the wall, where she squashed it with her thumb.

'What year are you in?'

'This my first semester.' She wiped the wine-red stain of the burst mosquito on her apron, and then rushed off to attend to the latest incoming patient, who ranted and spat as he was carried into the clinic by his parents, blood soaking his clothes and dripping down to the floor. I watched as the nurse led him towards a bed and Doctor Moses administered a sedative.

'Car accident,' the good doctor told me later. 'As common as malaria. But we can cure malaria.'

'How on earth do you cope with all this?' I asked.

'Badly,' he said. 'We do our best, but we cope badly. We don't have enough equipment. We don't have enough medicine. We just don't have enough *resources*. So we must rely on our own skills and be creative to treat our patients.'

The next morning, I arrived for my 8 a.m. appointment. Doctor Moses, on the third of his consecutive 24-hour shifts, greeted me with his inexhaustible smile. 'And how are you feeling today, Mr Pakravan?' he beamed.

'Better, much better,' I said. 'I think I'm over the hump.'

'Good!' he proclaimed. 'I think this will be your last round of injections. You will not need to see me any more. Your malaria is now treated, but please, rest for a few more days. Ignore your bicycle. Your body is very weak now. Sleep well and eat well, and rest lots. That is my advice.'

The clinic was still its habitual pit of mayhem, and yet Doctor Moses found time to sit and prepare the bill, calculating the expenditures of medicines and labour administered to my disease, and arriving at a sum that seemed paltry in comparison to his unremitting care.

'Sleep well and eat well,' he repeated, making sure to shake my hand as I left. 'And rest lots.'

Steve had come to collect me from the clinic, and as we walked through the streets of Kitengela together I stumbled. He caught me by the arm.

'I told Doctor Moses I was feeling better,' I said as Steve pulled me back to my feet. 'I lied. I still feel like shit. But I had to get out of that clinic.'

While I slept in the hotel, Steve organised a taxi for us to the Nairobi Hospital, where I underwent another long series of examinations. When the results returned, they were a testimony to Doctor Moses' professional aptitude. I was clear of malaria. Feeling guilty for doubting him, I was nevertheless relieved to be away from that unsanitary Kitengela clinic. The Nairobi Hospital was ordered and aseptic, and their second opinion mollified me. My weakness, they assured me, was a malarial hangover, and as long as I heeded Doctor Moses' command to rest, I should be well enough to get back on the road within days.

'So that's it,' I said to Steve as we took dinner at our hotel's restaurant. He had guzzled his food while I picked at mine listlessly. 'The record's gone. I need to rest for a few days. There's no way we'll make it after that.'

'Hypothetically,' he postured, 'could you manage leaving tomorrow?'

'Why?'

'Because, hypothetically, if we did, we might still be able to make it.'

I sighed. 'I'm sorry. I can't. I'm finished.'

'No need to be sorry,' Steve said. 'If you can't do it, you can't do it. What you've done already is nothing to be ashamed of.'

I speared a chip, raised it to my eye line and stared hard at its burnt skin. Maybe, I thought, just maybe if I can eat this and then clear my plate after it, I could be all right. I could continue. I could complete the journey. I placed the chip into my mouth and chewed. It was tough and mealy, and when I finally swallowed it and looked down at my plate, I was dismayed to find that there were still two dozen left uneaten. I poked at one, wiped it into a pool of ketchup and then lifted it to my mouth. The sight of it, growing larger and larger as it neared my face, made me feel sick. I dropped it back on to my plate, the fork clattering off the ceramic to pirouette down to the carpet.

'I'm finished,' I repeated. 'It's over.'

We paid for our meals and climbed the stairs up to our floor. While I paid yet another visit to the bathroom on our corridor, Steve let himself into our room. He was already asleep by the time I returned and so, still battling stomach cramps, I laid myself across my bed and signed into the hotel's wi-fi on my mobile phone. A light drizzle began to fall outside, sounding off the room's single window. I opened my email account. Supportive and emotional messages from friends – among them, Francesca and Paula – abounded. They had been in touch with Steve; they knew about my malaria. Due to meet us in Cape Town on the 100th day of our journey, they had already booked their return flights and were unable to extend them. Even if I had chosen to continue the journey from Nairobi, we would not arrive in time to meet them in Cape Town. Their words were laced with a deep sadness, and that sadness was infectious, rising from the emails to envelop me.

One email remained. It was from Elena, the sister of one of my closest friends, Gianluca, who had lost his life to cancer the previous year. I clicked it open with a sorrowful abandon.

———————————

Gianluca had been so much more than a friend. He was a travelling companion, a housemate, a drinking buddy, a confidante, a sounding board, a role model and, to all intents and purposes, my brother. Originally from Rome, he had moved to London to study and then work as a physicist, in which he was highly regarded, and from the first moment I met him I found myself drawn to him, magnetised by his unaffected joviality, humility and compassion. We lived together in London for five years and I learned that, at the age of 20, he had been diagnosed with cancer and had been on a regular system of treatment ever since to keep it at bay.

Not long before my expedition, Gianluca found a new and promising job in the southern Italian city of Lecce. He was both nervous and exhilarated at the prospect of the move, especially since it meant a return to his homeland. When he asked me for my advice, whether I thought it was a good idea or a terrible mistake, I told him that, although I would miss him dearly, we both knew that taking the new job and moving to Italy was the right thing for him to do. He was grateful for my encouragement, yet it was the least I could do. Gianluca had been one of the first people I had told about Madagascar, about Annapurna, about the Sahara and about this very expedition. I valued his judgment and often asked him for it before members of my own family.

'Be completely honest with me,' I would say. 'Should I really do this?'

When asked the same question, many of my other friends replied with discouragement, disparagement or a sarcastic joke at my expense. But Gianluca always said 'yes'. 'Yes' was one of Gianluca's favourite words.

When the cancer returned after he had settled in Lecce, he fought it valiantly, transferring to Rome for the best treatment and care he could find, but this time it was not enough. I was able to visit him just before he died. He was so thin I could barely recognise him. I cried for days when I left Rome.

I felt similar tears resurface as I opened Elena's email. It was sweetly written, brief but filled with love. She had, she disclosed, been sorting through some of Gianluca's old things, and had come across his favourite jacket. Inside one of the pockets was a wad of banknotes: £300. Together, the family decided to donate the money to my school-building project. Gianluca had often spoken passionately to them about it and they agreed it was what he would have wanted. Elena had immediately deposited the donation and then written this email, feeling it was important that I should know of the contribution's genesis.

I was speechless. Gianluca – the man who had been integral to my adult life, a driving force behind so much of what I had achieved – was still there, as powerful a motivation as ever, the acts he had performed before his last days stretching forward into the future and somehow landing at precisely the times when they needed to. That this should happen now – that I should simply be reminded of him, reminded of his indefatigable faith in me, reminded of his indomitable warmth and generosity – that it should happen just minutes after my resolution to give up on the expedition altogether, was too much to compute and I felt my neck sag under the suddenly burdensome weight of my head.

Outside, the rain stopped, and replacing its patter against the window was the sound of Kitengela by night: soft voices; faint car horns; the yowls of two fighting cats; cicadas and katydids in the trees. I thought of Gianluca for a long time. Were he here now, his nudges would have been gentle but insistent. He had battled cancer for the best part of two decades. I had battled malaria for just the past few days. I imagined his voice. '*Come on, Rezino,*' it said. '*You can pull this off. Stay hopeful. Stay hopeful.*'

Perhaps I began to repeat the mantra out loud, for Steve stirred and opened his eyes. 'Did you say something?' he mumbled.

'You know earlier,' I whispered, 'when you said that, hypothetically, we might still make the record if we left tomorrow…'

'Yes?'

'Do you still think we could? Hypothetically?'

'If we covered one-hundred-and-forty miles every day, we could get to Cape Town in time.' He paused. 'Hypothetically.'

I told him about the email from Elena, and about the donation from Gianluca.

'What would Gianluca do in your situation?' he asked.

'He'd stay hopeful.'

CHAPTER 21

NUMBER TEN

Distance remaining: 3,360 miles

Time to record: 24 days

Tanzania was 80 miles away. According to our new stringent timetable we had to not just make that before the end of the day but exceed it by a further 60 miles. In early-morning darkness, we caught a taxi back to the spot where I had collapsed four days ago, mounted our bikes and set off.

The malaria-weakened delicacy of my body was immediately apparent. I was wired and eager to push on, but I had lost my rhythm and the cycling felt unnatural. My thighs began to ache after only a few strokes and my hands trembled over the grips, sending tiny yet perceptible tremors down through the frame. Sweat pooled in my armpits, soaking my Lycra top down to my ribs, and my gums began to tingle and then itch maddeningly. My stomach, the blight of my physicality for what seemed now to have been forever, squelched and rumbled with ominous disdain. It wanted me back in bed. *I* wanted me back in bed.

But as the sun rose to our left it began to spread a tangerine glow over a land of pure and incandescent beauty. The soil that drifted from the horizon-stretching scrubland to the edge of our road was no longer red but yellow, dotted with thin trees and low bushes, a rich desert that felt more Andalusian than African. Dik-diks, tiny and adorable antelopes, scattered from our path to cower in the shadows and watch us with keen distrust as we passed. Low hills riven by spiking goat tracks rose from the earth, dipping down again towards the swamplands of Amboseli, and behind it all, the ever-nearing mirage-like spectre of Kilimanjaro.

By midday, we drew close to our tenth country. We were making good time and although every facet of my being ached to rest, I drew succour from our progress and kept moving forward. At the town of Namanga, which straddled the Kenya–Tanzania border, we only stopped because the crossing demanded it, and decided to make the most of the opportunity by exchanging our shillings from Kenyan to Tanzanian and using the latter to buy lunch at a local restaurant. Maasai tribespeople in plastic sandals approached us with beads spread across their open palms, and when we told them we did not want to buy they loped away to try their luck elsewhere.

A young English cyclist in a cowboy hat, khaki shirt, khaki shorts and flimsy flip-flops spotted the bikes resting beside our table and rode over to greet us. His own bike was fully loaded with more bags, panniers and accoutrements than I have ever seen a single bike carry, all heaped atop tyres so thin and so bald it was a wonder they could stand the weight. Steve introduced us, stuck out his hand to shake and asked the young man his name. Ignoring the question, he instead asked Steve where we were going.

'Cape Town,' Steve replied, beginning to explain our expedition and the countries through which it had taken us. He was only able to get as far as Finland when the young man interrupted him.

'Yeah, I don't like Europe,' he drawled. 'I try to stay away from it as much as possible. But Africa, man, Africa's a *trip*. Took me a while to get out of Cape Town as I had free accommodation and the beer was cheap, too. Then I spent a few months in Botswana and Zambia, and by the time I made it to Malawi I needed a break. But, you know, Malawi is good, so

I decided to stay there for five months. The alcohol was cheap and I could have a good time every night. Then I got to Tanzania. Man, I had a hard time there. Nearly died. Check this out.' Lifting up his shirt, he revealed a spider bite, and began to proudly etch his finger over the veiny and septic lines that had spread out from the dark and inflamed welt on his stomach. 'It's hardcore, right? I like things best when they're tough. I'm going to Kenya next. See what's gonna happen there.'

'How long has it taken you to cycle from Cape Town to here?' Steve asked.

'About a year, I'd say. Something like that. When are you guys planning to get there?'

'In twenty-three and a half days,' Steve replied.

The young man was so affronted by this precise number that his feet were already beginning to rise to his pedals. 'Too fast, too fast for me,' he muttered, before pushing off and teetering away into Kenya.

We never did find out his name.

Fifteen miles later, stopping to buy supplies in a small town nestled in the shadow of Mount Longido, I turned to Steve and asked: 'Why do you think that guy wouldn't tell us his name?'

'He was probably far too cool for names,' he said, perusing the shelves of chocolate.

I left it at that, but the truth is I had been thinking about that nameless cyclist all the way from Namanga. While I had not warmed especially to his personality, there was nevertheless something resident in it – a rebelliousness, an independence, a semblance of the free-spirited – which I found myself jealous of. That latter quality, to be free-spirited, is one I am often accused of having. Before I left for this very expedition, my cousin had told me: 'It's nice to be free-spirited, but you need to think about your future.' I had laughed off the comment back then. But if I had had the temerity to answer my cousin truthfully, I would have told her that, actually, I was not free-spirited at all. I would have told her that I worry about the future all the time.

This expedition was a prime example. Here I was, not revelling in the wonders of this new country, Tanzania, to which I had never before been, but instead thinking – *worrying* – only of how quickly I could make my way through it. Despite what my family and friends may have thought, this journey was not in any way a testament to free-spiritedness, but a hell-for-leather race against the impending march of a future I somehow craved to contain within the pages of a book, the reels of a documentary, the notations of a GWR scribe. It was my life in microcosm. I had always attached myself to things, whether they were tangible like possessions or intangible like adventure or both simultaneously like money.

This journey had been a response to a future I had seen building before me and had suddenly wanted no part of. This journey, just like all the journeys I had undertaken over the previous four years, was a way of subverting that future, of moulding it into something of which I could be proud, something that would heighten not just my own existence but the existences of others.

And is that really such a bad thing? I thought as we cycled on towards Arusha. Everything in my life was planned, meticulously and methodically. Including this journey. But if, by the end of it all, by the end of me, if it had helped to create something *better*, whatever that possibly was or whatever that could possibly even mean, then surely it was all worth it?

I struggled on, both physically and emotionally. The malaria had left me fragile, and that young man's words and attitude had clearly taken their toll, too. Gianluca wafted back into my consciousness, a guiding spirit of nudges and encouragements to stay hopeful. I would, I *must* stay hopeful. I knew that. Yet I could not help but see a hollowness inside that record for which I had strived not just for the past 77 days but for a whole 2 years before that. I would do everything I could to make it to Cape Town by the 100th day, that was indisputable. But then, what after that? What came next?

Maybe, I surmised as I pedalled, staying hopeful, maybe I would do the whole thing again, but slowly and in reverse this time, forging my meandering way north, stopping where I liked and for however long I liked, just like that young man, nurturing not a determination for an arbitrary world record, but a hankering only for freedom of spirit.

Our target for that first day back on the road was Arusha, but we did not quite make it, falling short of our new 140-mile daily target by 18 miles. The last 35 of those miles were weathered on one single climb that scaled Mount Meru on the fringe of the Arusha National Park. Darkness had already settled by the time we began the ascent and with it came a headwind that whipped sand into our faces. The sky, covered by a thick bank of cloud, lent no light to the situation, and a chill set in, which, rather than a welcome relief, only left me weaker and more exhausted. I stopped. Steve turned his bike and came to me. I explained that I could go no further. He admitted he felt the same. But our options were bleak. With visibility limited by the pitch-black night, we scanned the roadside by torchlight for a viable spot to camp. There was only bare and uneven rock, impossible to pitch a tent on. We had no choice but to push on, every stroke of the pedal a Herculean effort.

And then, one of those miracles that the down-at-heel traveller can suddenly be presented with when it is most needed: a house, little more than a mud hut, appeared at the roadside, light flickering from its open window. We knocked at the door and, when it was answered by a young Maasai lady, we implored her for help with impromptu sign language, attempting to gesture our desperate need for food and a place to sleep. She smiled and beckoned us in. The hut was a single room with bare walls, a bare floor and a line of candles in the corner, which the lady's family – her husband and two infant boys – slept beside. At our arrival, the husband stirred back to life, and when he saw us he did not question or shout or grab us by the throats and forcibly expel us as I surely would have done should two bedraggled strangers have entered my home and disturbed my family at 10 p.m. No, instead he rose to his feet, smiled a lovely smile which matched his wife's, led us out to his car and then drove us 5 miles up the hill to the nearest village.

It was a small Maasai settlement, composed of a dozen or so huts built on to a meagre plateau on the shoulder of the mountain. In the centre of the plateau, two gigantic cauldrons of oil were suspended by a rickety system of scaffolding over a roaring fire. The women busied about this outdoor kitchen, throwing strips of fish into the cauldrons and chopping potatoes, while the men sat in small clusters away from the fire, sipping clear liquid that looked too viscous to be water. None of the villagers paid us much heed, and our host gestured for us to sit on a patch of ground while he approached the women. They placed two portions of food in plastic plates and handed them to our host, who brought them over and then sat beside us to watch us eat. I stared at the meal before me, hardly believing this was to be my repast in a tiny tribal village halfway up a Tanzanian mountain. It was fish and chips. And it had never tasted so delicious.

We tried to talk between mouthfuls to our host, tried to express our gratitude for this life-saving offering, but he shushed us and motioned that we should eat it all, smiling when we shut up and did so. Above us, the clouds parted to reveal an enormous moon, which lit up our surrounds with an incandescent glow. I gazed about me in wonder, at the women cooking and the men eating and drinking, all of them in complete calm acceptance of our anomalous presence, as if it was entirely natural to take in and feed two filthy cyclists. And perhaps it was natural, but for me it was a privilege, a truly magical privilege, one that I knew I would not forget for a long time. *How beautiful it is*, I thought, *to live in this world.*

Once we had finished our fish and chips, our friend took the empty plates from us, handed them to the women and then led us to his car to drive us back to his house. The two boys were still fast asleep beside the dying candles, their mother curled up behind them, and the man made it clear with the swings of his arms that we could bed down for the night wherever we chose. We threw the Therm-a-Rest on to the concrete floor and were asleep within seconds.

I was woken in the morning by the slam of a door and the sight of the two boys delightedly chasing a scrawny chicken around the room. The chicken hopped over my head in a manic display of feathers and wings, and when the younger of the boys followed it he tripped on my shoulder and tumbled over my chest, heaving himself back to his feet with a tiny hand clutching my nose for support. The mother appeared, grabbing the boy and laughingly pulling him to her bosom, and while I sat up and rubbed my nose the older boy piledrived into my back with a burst of snorts and giggles before being chased outside by his chiding mother.

We were left alone as we rose and packed, and when we emerged into the blinding light of the morning, the lady and the two boys were standing beside our bikes, all smiling. The car had gone, and I assumed the man had left for his day long before we had woken. We wanted to offer them something for their beautiful hospitality, but were unsure if giving money might lead to offence. On the other hand, who were we to presume on their behalf that they would be offended by our offer of money? In the end, I pulled some shillings from my pocket and held them out. The lady refused them, but no offence seemed to be taken. Searching our bags for anything we might be able to give them, we eventually alighted upon two blue biros and presented them to the boys. They squealed with delight as they grabbed them, and then ran off into the bushes behind the hut, proudly brandishing their pens before them as if they were made of gold.

'When we get home,' Steve said as we left the family in a furious bout of waves and cycled on side by side, 'and when someone asks me what the most incredible experience of the expedition was, I'm going to tell them about last night.'

'Same,' I replied. 'Although I don't know if I'll be able to do it justice. The whole thing was…' My words tailed off. I was right. I could not do it justice.

We passed the village 5 miles later, the smoke that curled from the dying fire the only sign of life present, and pushed on until we reached the peak and began the welcome descent towards Arusha. I still felt feeble and sluggish, but my torpidity had been assuaged by the wonderful hospitality of our Maasai hosts, and the night of good food and rest had refuelled my stamina.

'How much did we do yesterday?' I asked Steve.

'One-hundred-and-twenty-two miles.'

'So we've got to do one-hundred-and-fifty-eight miles today to catch up.'

'That's right.'

Yet by the time the sun began to set that evening we had only succeeded in covering 78 miles, less than half of our quota. Long hours of night-riding lay ahead of us, and we grimly pedalled on into the dusk, determined that if we could not make the full 158 we would at least cover the same mileage as the previous day and make back the mounting deficit later. Another climb slowed us somewhere around the 100th mile, and though it was shorter than the previous night's it was steeper and by its summit I was drained once more.

We stopped for a short rest. A pack of hyenas bayed from down in the valley, their howls echoing against the hills. From our vantage point, we could see a cluster of street lights huddled around a small town just a few miles away. We agreed to freewheel down towards it and break for supper.

It had become so commonplace upon this long, African road for a local to introduce himself, sit with us and engage us in conversation while we ate that it seemed only natural for it to happen again here. His name, or so he told us, was Double Man. 'Because I am big!' he exclaimed proudly. 'Double the size of normal man!' He had thick, matted hair, wore a vest that revealed his scarified upper arms, and spoke to us in a patchy and deliberate English, which seemed to suit his reedy voice.

'Why you in Tanzania?' he asked.

We explained our expedition to him. He appeared unimpressed.

'You want Bob Marley stuff?'

'No thank you.'

'Okay. You want place stay?'

'No,' I said. 'We need to keep riding for a few more hours. Then we're hoping to camp for the night. Do you know any good places to camp further down the road?'

'No campsites here.'

'It doesn't have to be a campsite. We don't mind wild camping. We've got everything we need. But local advice is always welcome. What do you reckon? Are there any beauty spots on the way to the next town which you'd recommend?'

'No, no, no, no, no,' Double Man intoned with a hefty solemnity. 'Do not wild camp here. You must go very far before safe. Maybe one hundred miles. You ride one hundred miles tonight?'

I looked over at Steve. We agreed it was far from likely.

'The animals very dangerous here. Hyenas and wild dogs the worst. You have food?'

'Yes.'

'They smell the food. They attack. While you sleep. Then you are the food. Better you stay here. In hotel.'

'Are there any hotels here?' I asked.

'My uncle own number one hotel! You want take?'

Steve and I acted out the parameters of a debate, but really there was no debate at all. Despite our poor mileage for the day, we both wanted to cycle no further that night, and we both knew it. We gave our assent to Double Man, who waited patiently while we finished our food and paid our bill before leading us to his uncle's hotel.

Double Man would not let us cycle alongside him. Instead, he insisted we ride behind while he marched through the town's streets. His pace was slow, almost meandering, and as we passed each open bar he would shout to the drinkers clustered at their tables, point back at us with his thumb and then laugh. Most of the drinkers, we noticed, ignored him.

After a long and painful rally through the streets, we finally made it to his uncle's number one hotel: a two-storey concrete construction that was little more than a room with another room built haphazardly atop it. The ground floor was a family home – Double Man's uncle's family – and we were led through it and then up a fire-escape stairwell to the accommodation. It was basic, little more than two beds laid at right angles, but we had grown used to that by now.

'You want?' Double Man asked.

We nodded and handed over the meagre amount of money he demanded.

'Thank you,' Double Man said, pocketing the cash and then shaking us each by the hand. He started towards the door and then, just before he closed it behind him, said almost as an afterthought: 'You want massage?'

Although we had not considered it before it was proposed, we agreed that a massage was *exactly* what we wanted. The ones in Egypt had been so rejuvenating and invigorating that another might be precisely what our bodies needed to get them ready for 140 miles, or more, the next day. Our IT bands (the ligament that runs down the outside of the thigh) in particular were causing us extreme discomfort, and massaging them ourselves as we had been doing only gave limited and temporary relief.

'Good,' Double Man said. 'I find girl. Wait twenty minutes. What kind massage you want?'

'Legs and feet,' Steve said.

'Shoulders, neck and back,' I said.

'Hands and fingers,' we both said.

'Full body massage,' Double Man confirmed. And then, with a salacious smile: 'Jiggy jiggy?'

Steve looked shocked and then giggled compulsively, understanding the colloquialism long before I did. 'Jiggy jiggy?' I faltered.

'Yes. You know. Jiggy jiggy.'

I looked over at Steve, hoping to wrest a translation from him, but he had clearly begun to enjoy my lack of comprehension and refused to illuminate me.

'What do you mean?' I asked.

Double Man sighed. 'I mean do you want to fuck?'

'No!' I cried, bellowing the interjection with such an explosion of surprise that Double Man bolted back behind the doorway while Steve's giggles morphed into full-blown laughter.

'Sorry,' Double Man said, all of a sudden a humble and scraping version of his former self. 'So sorry. You still want massage? No jiggy jiggy?'

'I think we'll be all right thanks, Double Man,' I said, regaining my composure. 'I think we'll just go to sleep.'

He left, closing the door behind him, and it wasn't until we had changed, switched off the light and climbed into bed that Steve finally said: 'Christ, Reza. What else did you think "jiggy jiggy" meant?'

His chiding laughter kept me from falling asleep. In the end, all I could do was laugh along with him.

Our laughter was not the only thing that kept me from sleep that night. The television in the family's room below us blared out a succession of Nollywood movies until dawn, and what respite I could succumb to was quickly fractured by the filmic sounds of gunshots and women screaming. I left the next morning with the jarred nerves of a hangover, but without the joyous memories of a good night out to justify it.

Yet despite all of it – despite the lack of sleep and the headache and all the remaining ailments of a body still on the mend from malaria – we made good progress that day. We had no love nor trust for Double Man any more, but his warnings to not wild camp nevertheless abided, and we eschewed a night in the tent for another night in another dingy and squalid guesthouse.

We had managed to claw some miles back from our deficit. We were still under our target and were now looking at an approximation of 150 miles per day to reach Cape Town on time, but Steve was hopeful and his confidence encouraged my own. We had crossed a large swathe of Tanzania and were well on our way to the Zambian border, where he assured me the roads would be as smooth and as easy down through

Zambia, Botswana and South Africa as they had been through Europe. This was a boon, for there were just 3 weeks left until that crucial deadline, and if we could match and even exceed the progress we had made during those first 3 weeks through Europe, then I still stood a chance of sailing into Cape Town on the 100th day and securing my world record. The fact that we were frail and shadowy versions of the selves we had been during those first 3 weeks; the fact that we had not back then been ravaged by food poisoning and civil terror and malnutrition and 80 days of pure cycling and, in my case, malaria; the fact that we had a far greater feat ahead of us than those first 3 weeks had ever demanded, as tough and challenging as they themselves had been: all these facts we chose to leave unsaid. Vocalising them would have been pointless. We both knew, deep down, that the record was growing more and more unattainable with every lost mile. And we both knew that, if we chose to remark upon it, it would only serve to heighten the exponential impossibility of what we had set out to do. It was far preferable to talk of good roads and good daily quotas. It was far preferable to not talk of a looming failure that we both felt in our bones.

Another morning passed, and we found ourselves at the end of it stopping for lunch at a Maasai open-air market on a roadside clearing. The market was huge and bustling, and we spent a few happy moments wandering among the stalls that spilled from minivan tailgates, or huddled beneath makeshift gazebos or just lay, uncovered, across the clearing's soil. Everything was for sale, from buckets to bananas, from spices to fuels, from bottled oils to homemade soaps, from vegetables to jerry cans to beads to rice to clay pots to potatoes to flip-flops. Both buyers and sellers alike greeted us with amiable nods and *jambo*s. A market-chef made thin tortillas by hand and then packed them with strips of fried chicken, and when we bit into the sandwiches hot grease burst from the meat and saturated our beards.

Feeling energised by the vitality of the market, we cycled on into an afternoon of 41°C heat. By 2 p.m., I began to nurture an odd sense of unease. At first, I could not quite grasp why. Although I still felt far from healthy, I was finding my rhythm once more and the going was no longer the punishing torture it had been for those first two days after leaving Kitengela. I was hot, achingly hot, but I had endured extremes of temperature for longer than I could now remember. No, the unease derived not from the internal but the external. There was something wrong with the view before me, yet I could not quite put my finger on it.

I voiced my feelings to Steve, who concurred with similar sentiments. It took us some time to realise, but when we finally did it came with a sudden clarity We were the only traffic moving south along the road. All else, from the juggernaut lorries with their payloads of goods and livestock to the diminutive children who carried jerry cans of water on their heads, were moving in the opposite direction to us. Our side of the road was empty save for ourselves. Nothing overtook us and we overtook nothing.

'If we're the only ones going this way,' Steve said, 'then I don't want to know what's ahead.'

When it came, it matched our worst fears. It was not man-eating lions, nor gangs of thieving baboons, nor gun-toting bandits, nor kidnapping terrorists. It was gravel. Gravel that was soft and sludgy and riven with crater-sized potholes and pointed, jarring rocks. We were back on the worst road in the world again.

In 3 hours we covered just 11 miles. We could have walked faster. We battled on, eyes glued at all times to the few feet of road ahead to discern which of the myriad hazards could send us crashing to the ground at any moment. Our vigilance was steadfast and yet, ultimately, ineffective, for we crashed to the ground repeatedly. As day turned to night, the obstacles seemed to become negatives of themselves in the shadows cast by our lights: rocks turned to craters and craters to rocks. We crashed to the ground more.

Battered and bruised, we reached the town of Dodoma late and stopped for the night. Thirty miles of tarmac lulled us into a false sense of security the following morning, but this was shattered once more when the gravel returned. Fortunately, it was easily navigable, and by the time we rounded the Mtera reservoir the tarmac returned and we managed to cross a further 70 miles to Migole by mid-afternoon. We stopped there to top up our supplies, neglected as they were. Our focus had only been on enduring the road, and we had forgotten to replenish our panniers with food and water back in Dodoma.

There was one shop in the village and its shelves were bare save for a healthy stock of bottled water. We bought as much as we could, filling our own bottles, drinking lustily from them and then refilling them. We asked the owner where we could buy some food. His shop, he explained, would not have another delivery until tomorrow, but if we rode on to the town of Iringa, where there were many shops, he was certain we could find food there.

'How far from here is that?' I asked.

'Oh, not so far,' he replied. 'Maybe only seventy miles.'

'And how's the road?' I asked. 'Tarmac or gravel?'

'Mostly gravel.'

We stepped back outside and rifled through our panniers. They contained four bananas, two bags of nuts and one packet of biscuits. If the road ahead had been paved by tarmac, and if a town lay at the end of it where we knew we could guarantee a hearty meal, another 70 miles on such meagre sustenance would have presented no problem. But the road ahead was gravel, Iringa's shops may not even be open by the time we arrived and we were famished already.

'What are we going to do?' I asked, not even to Steve, but to the sky.

Steve answered anyway. 'There's only one option. We try to make it to Iringa.'

We drank water, forced ourselves to piss and then drank some more. Then we returned to the shop, refilled our bottles and bought an extra

3 litres each: the maximum we could hold in our panniers. This would be our fuel over the next 70 miles and we needed as much as we could carry.

Although the condition of the road improved slightly – the uneven gravel morphing into a thick layer of dry dirt which had some semblance of smoothness – and though our miles-per-hour increased as a consequence, the temperature rose to 45°C and our world became a suffocating place. We rationed our food out for the next few hours as we rode, but the heat made us careless with our water supply and by the time we had covered 50 miles we were astonished to discover that we only had 1 litre left each. The bananas and nuts long gone, we divided the packet of biscuits between us and miserably munched a few each. This was a mistake, for they were dry and mealy and, instead of quenching our mounting starvation, they only served to make us feel all the more parched.

'Twenty miles to Iringa,' Steve said, climbing back on his bike. 'We can do this. We just have to be careful with the last of the water.'

'That's if it *is* actually twenty miles. Local knowledge is never an exact science in Africa.'

'Either way, we can't turn around. Migole is too far behind us. And it didn't even have food.'

'Past the point of no return.'

We cycled on for another hour, clocking 8 miles. I tried hard to ration my water intake, but in that heat and with my energy levels near zero I needed the fluid more than I ever had before. Within 2 more miles, my bottles were empty. It took me another mile to build up the courage, borne of nothing other than sheer desperation, to ask Steve if I could have some of his water.

'I was just about to ask you the same thing,' he replied sadly.

The record, I thought. *The fucking record.* I was no longer sick of it; I loathed it. Why was I putting myself through this? Why was I here, on this shitty road in the middle of this shitty Tanzanian desert, exhausted, ravenous and half-mad with thirst? If the hyenas came now, what possible defence could I exude? Would they even kill and eat me, or would they see me for what I had become, a wild-eyed lunatic deranged by the sun, and recognise in me a kindred spirit and welcome me into their pack?

What's the record for days spent living with a clan of hyenas? I thought. And then: *Oh shit...*

I had fallen again. My bike lay on top of me. Flecks of road-sand had found their way into my eyes. I considered rising to my feet, but realised I had no willpower whatsoever left within me. My vision was swallowed by a pure whiteness.

———————

I awoke to the sensation of Steve dragging me into the shade of a baobab tree. We stayed beneath it for the following half an hour, concentrating on nothing more than staying still and conserving energy. I was breathing heavily, sweat pouring down my spine. My throat was dry and my thoughts blurred and hazy. Suddenly, a Range Rover gleamed whitely on the road. Steve desperately ran towards it, flagged it down and I was placed on to its back seat. A bottle of water was pressed to my lips and I sucked at it as my skin prickled beneath the unmistakeable waft of air-conditioning. Rumbles overhead sounded like distant claps of thunder and I wondered if I was still half-asleep on the road, the air-conditioning wind, the water that moistened my open mouth thick raindrops. If it was, I welcomed it and I passed out once more, comfortable in its embrace.

As the Range Rover bounced us towards Iringa, my head began to clear, centralising on the bottle of water clutched in my hand and then spreading slowly outwards. It *was* a bottle of water, not rain. The rumbles, I realised, had not been thunder but the noise of our bikes being loaded on to the Range Rover's roof rack. Loud and laughing conversation spilled over from the front seats. I hoisted myself up on my elbows and looked ahead. Steve occupied the passenger seat and was in earnest conversation with a Tanzanian man who, when he saw my head pop up in his rear view mirror, turned around, grinned a splendid grin and introduced himself as Moji. Beyond him, through the grimy windscreen, I could make out the openings of a town.

'Where are we?' I mumbled, my tongue thick and dry.

'Just coming into Iringa,' Steve replied, turning around in his seat to face me. 'This is Moji. He said he'd take us to the hospital.'

'Thank you, Moji,' I replied. 'You're a life-saver.'

Moji laughed a deep and echoing chortle from behind the wheel. 'That remains to be seen.'

And so I found myself back in another hospital, back in another bed, back on another drip. Tests revealed that my malaria had not relapsed, but that I had heatstroke. Moji stayed with us, leaving only once to return less than 10 minutes later with armfuls of food and water, and then when I was discharged from the hospital he drove us to a decent hotel and negotiated a local price for us for an en-suite room with air conditioning. He was yet another small miracle on this long journey, another good person going out of his way to help us, fuelled only by genuine altruism.

'Good luck with your record,' he said as he bade us farewell and slipped out of our room and out of our lives.

The fucking record, I thought again, collapsing on to my bed and falling asleep within seconds. When I awoke, I was shocked to discover that it was 11 p.m. Steve sat on the edge of his own bed, the logbook on his lap.

'I've emailed Base Camp and completed today's entries,' he said. 'We're all sorted. How are you feeling?'

'Better. Well, you know, still tired and weak. But nothing compared with last time. I'll be fine to get back on the road tomorrow.'

Steve looked at me for a long time. 'About that,' he said. 'The record. I don't think—'

I cut him short. 'I know.'

'I've been working it out tonight. We've fallen too far behind. We can't—'

'I know,' I said again.

A silence fell. Because I did know. I knew and Steve knew. The record was impossible. And there wasn't much else left to say after that.

CHAPTER 22

JUST DOWN THE ROAD

Distance remaining: 2,808 miles

It was Day 82. To make Cape Town by Day 100 would have necessitated 148 miles per day. Even at our hardiest, even on the best roads in the world, that would have been near impossible. I woke early that morning and lay in bed with my eyes fixed on the ceiling for a long time. Somewhere among the angst and encroaching depression, I remembered one of my favourite books from childhood: *Around the World in Eighty Days* by Jules Verne. I remembered Phileas Fogg's final arrival back in London 5 minutes late. I remembered how he was certain he had lost his wager and how he had begun to resign himself to a future of poverty. I remembered how I had read and reread that book as a child, and how, when the twist came – that he had neglected to account for the fact that he had travelled east and gained a day and therefore was still eligible for his own world record – it had never failed to thrill me. I loved that twist, and I may have read that book over and over purely because of it. *That's what I need now*, I thought as I lay in that Iringa hotel bed. *A twist*. And I almost leaped up to check the time and date on my phone, before I remembered that I had not travelled east but south, and that I had not gained a whole day but a trivial 2 hours. There would be no twist.

Steve woke and we wandered out into Iringa together in search of breakfast. It felt strange to do so before we had readied our bikes. We had left them in the hotel room, our unpacked bags on the floor. A small cafe served us a mess of fried eggs that seeped into triangles of barely toasted bread. I picked at mine slowly with my fork, at once hungry and devoid of appetite.

'I'm really sorry, Reza,' Steve said after an awkward and protracted silence. 'The record should be yours. We just got very, very unlucky.'

'Fuck the record,' I snarled, pushing the plate of eggs away from me and taking a sip of coffee, which was tepid and tasteless. 'It was always a mistake. I think I knew it back at the Kenyan border. You remember that English cyclist we met?'

'The one who wouldn't tell us his name?'

'Remember how he said he'd taken a whole year just to get from Cape Town to Kenya? That made me jealous.'

'I didn't like him.'

'Me neither. But I admired him. He made me wish we'd taken our time a bit more. Not just rushed through everything. Not just rushed down the length of the planet! There's so much we could have seen and we ignored it all because of this fucking record.'

'You eating that?' Steve had finished his eggs and was eyeing up mine. I pushed the plate towards him and he tucked into it with thinly concealed relish.

'You know what annoys me the most?' I said as he ate. 'It's not even the record. It's the fact that I was so certain I could make it. So certain that I told everyone I would. And even that wouldn't be so bad. But there's all those people who had arranged to come and meet us in Cape Town on Day One Hundred. Francesca was going to be there, Paula, loads of the Base Camp crew. And then there's my other mates, and yours as well.'

'My girlfriend,' Steve muttered with a mouth full of eggs.

'Right! Exactly! Your girlfriend. All these people took time off from work, bought flights to South Africa, made arrangements for accommodation and everything else. And I've let them down. I've let them all down. I had to email each of them this morning. They're still flying to Cape Town, but their return flights leave before we'll get there. So they've wasted all that money and they've wasted all that time, just because I couldn't make the record.'

Steve finished my eggs and sat back in his chair, taking a long draught of coffee and then leaning back to belch into the air above him. 'So what do we do?' he asked. 'Chuck it all in?'

I felt despondent and angry. To have taken the two empty plates and smashed them against the nearest wall would have pleased me no end. But instead I looked up at Steve and saw within him someone who might be able to offer me invaluable advice. 'Why did you come and meet me in Azerbaijan?' I asked. 'After Dagestan. You knew then that you wouldn't be able to get the record. And yet you cycled all the way down here with me. Why?'

Steve took some time finishing his coffee. Then he placed the cup back on the table, looked me in the eye and spoke slowly, measuring out every word. 'Before Dagestan, all I wanted was the record. But then I had to make a tough choice. Knowing what I know now, I wish I had cycled through Dagestan with you. But I also know that if I had to go back and make the same choice again I would. The thought of Dagestan made me fear for my life. Genuinely. And when I got back to Volgograd I had this one night where I pretty much decided that that was it. I didn't qualify for the record any more, so what was the point? The funny thing is, as soon as I thought that I regretted it. I knew it would be easy enough to get myself back to London and go back to work as if none of this had ever happened. But I didn't want to. It's as simple as that. I didn't want to go back to London. I wanted to cycle to Cape Town. And so I decided I would. And you know what? This expedition has been so much more enjoyable once I knew that I wasn't doing it for the record, but just doing it because I *wanted* to.'

I was suddenly hungry again. I ordered another plate of eggs and, when it came, I tucked into it savagely. 'So what's your advice now?' I asked, fresh eggy breath enveloping my words.

'We've got the time and we've got the bikes,' Steve replied, a glint in his eye. 'Cape Town's just down the road. We've already cycled eight thousand miles. What's another three thousand?'

'And the record?'

'There's no way we'll make it. Honestly, I wish there was. But it's impossible.'

'And you reckon we should just keep going anyway? All the way to Cape Town?'

'Definitely,' Steve said. 'And trust me, it's so much better when you don't have to worry about that GWR bullshit.'

Steve was right. With the record an impossibility, there was no longer any point thinking about it. I left it back in that Iringa cafe, as empty as my plate of eggs, and as it diminished behind me I felt a tremendous burden lift from my shoulders. I switched my GoPro to record as we cycled on towards Zambia, perching it on my handlebars directed at my face and letting it film on constant. After the journey ended, I watched that particular piece of footage, and was struck by something that had been missing for a long time but which I only noticed once it returned again. It was my smile. It seemed to persist for hours, the same wide and goofy grin, and it was the first time I had seen it on myself, captured by the camera, for miles, for days, for countries.

Aside from the plethora of Tanzanian mosquitoes that ravaged my bare arms and legs, that day was a pleasant one, and by the time we arrived in Igawa and bedded down for the night in a cheap guesthouse, my head was clear and my determination to cycle on to Cape Town was firm. We woke early the next morning out of habit, and when we found a restaurant for a breakfast of dough balls, cakes and tea, we took our time, savouring the meal slowly. I swelled with a tremendous sense of liberty.

A tiny boy, no older than seven, approached our table. He was naked except for a thin and dirty pair of underpants, his emaciated frame a stark contrast to his protruding belly. He had no hair, not even eyebrows, and the shape of his skull was clear beneath his taut skin. Instead of begging from us, he stopped a few metres away from our table and stood silently, swaying slightly on feet encrusted with dried blood, and fixed his two gigantic eyes, reddened and cloudy, on mine. I reached into my bag and found a packet of jelly babies, which I pulled out, opened, and then held out to the boy. His face became so hopeful and desperate at the prospect of the jelly babies that I felt like I might cry. He wavered for a few moments, wanting the sweets but too timid to come any closer and take one, so I walked over, sat on the ground cross-legged beside him, produced two jelly babies from the packet, ate one myself and offered the other to him. He took it gingerly, placed it in his mouth and those eyes of his grew even larger as he chewed slowly. I offered him another. He took it from my hand with the same meekness and ate it with the same slow tenderness as the first.

I patted the ground next to me, he sat, and we ate jelly babies together until we had finished the packet. I tried to speak to him, but he only stared at me with uncomprehending wonder whenever I did, and so we resigned ourselves to the shared language of confectionery consumption. I showed him how to nibble off each leg and then each arm and then the head and finally the torso, and thereafter he ate every sweet in the same manner. He would focus on each jelly baby with immense concentration as he did so; once he had finished, he would stare at me again with those eyes that broke my heart. There was an uneven number of sweets in the packet, and when I fished out the last one and offered it to him while showing him the empty bag, he reached out his hand halfway and then withdrew it, placing it back in his lap. I tore the jelly baby in two and offered him half. A smile spread across his gaunt face and he accepted his half, nibbling away at it bit by bit until it was all gone.

We sat there for a long time together, watching the traffic pass on the road. Although we said not one word to each other, I enjoyed the boy's company immensely, and I think he liked mine, too. I could have sat there with him all day, not talking, just watching the lorries as they trundled along on their way to either Dar-es-Salaam or Lubumbashi, watching the people as they strode purposefully to and fro, watching the town come to life in the hustle and bustle of yet another Tanzanian morning. Had the record still been viable, I would have left the restaurant the moment I had finished my breakfast, ready to high-tail it along the next 100 miles, and I never would have met this boy. But the record was no longer a part of the journey and without it perhaps the journey itself could be richer. I certainly felt that way, as the morning blossomed around us, and as I sat there on the dusty ground with this tiny boy beside me, contented, and taking it all in.

A young woman appeared and the boy rose to his feet and scurried towards her, not looking back as she took him by the hand and led him off down the road. I returned to Steve, who had ordered and finished another breakfast. We bought some supplies, stuffed them into our panniers and set off.

Good roads, a strong tailwind and simple but delicious food made our progress to and then beyond the Zambian border straightforward and hassle-free. We arrived in Chinsali by the evening of the next day, happy and energised and not in the least bit exhausted.

'How many miles do you think we did today?' Steve asked as we dismounted our bikes at the front door of a guesthouse.

'I don't know,' I said. 'Ninety?'

'Try one-hundred-and-fifty,' Steve grinned.

'Seriously?' I asked, unbelieving. 'We've cycled one-hundred-and-fifty miles today?'

'Ironic, isn't it?' he replied. 'The moment we give up on the record, we make the best mileage of the whole journey. The tailwind and the amazing roads are partly to thank.'

'It's still too late, though,' I muttered, a tiny part of me hoping that Steve might disagree.

'Oh yeah,' he said, dissolving my hope in a second. 'It's still too late.'

We roared through Zambia over the next few days which – with its smooth tarmac, its greenly monotonous scenery, its lack of roadside civilisation and, more importantly, its lack of people to engage with – was like the Finland of Africa. Here and there, children in baggy Barcelona or Manchester United T-shirts played in sprawling clusters around the sporadic villages, but they were always more interested in each other than us. The adults who sat in the shade of their huts were much the same, occasionally offering a lazy salute if we waved to them first.

Trees diminished the deeper we progressed into Zambia, many of them decimated by the same unsustainable slash-and-burn techniques I had witnessed in Madagascar. The noticeable deforestation made me sad, but I knew I was in no place to judge. Had I have been a local from this part of Zambia, with few other sources of fuel around, deforestation would have been the last of my concerns. I would, instead, have thought only of how to cook and feed my family, and I would have gladly slashed and burned along with the rest of them.

As the trees thinned, markers of civilisation swelled. Small villages gave way to developing towns, many of them edged by thriving and colourful markets that bustled regardless of the time of day. Sellers perched on 20-litre jerry cans behind their stalls of fruits and vegetables, and everything – from bags of cement to bulbous families – was transported between the stalls and the markets and the towns themselves by staunch and ageing bicycles.

Each successive shop we stopped at contained more and more products which Steve recognised from his South African childhood. It became routine for him to lovingly pick up a carton of fruit juice or a packet of biscuits or a bar of chocolate, present the item to me and exclaim: 'I used to eat these all the time!' The familiarity of the foodstuffs turned him giddy and boyish, reminding me of my own excitement as we had drawn ever closer to Iran. It felt like a lifetime ago.

Though we saw little wildlife in Zambia, we were still reluctant to camp, and spent our nights in small guesthouses that offered comfortable beds, clean bathrooms and even, in some cases, free wi-fi. We used the latter to catch up on our emails, and were dismayed though not surprised to find that our social media accounts and blog had lost followers: a consequence, no doubt, of our announcement that we would not be making the record.

The guesthouses that had small restaurants attached were Steve's favourites. 'It's a one-stop shop!' he would exclaim with delight each time we settled into one for dinner. The waitresses would approach us and ask: 'You want coffee? Chipsy? Porridgy? Sandwichy?' I loved that. The unfamiliar affixes, delivered as a natural part of the Zambian–English dialect, rounded off otherwise hard words with a flowing, lilting beauty.

In one of these guesthouse restaurants, we met David: a Zambian-born man with British parents who had lived most of his life in Zambia, of which he had a deep and abiding love. He elucidated upon it at length in a smooth Home Counties accent and every word he uttered revealed his adoration for this diminutive African nation.

'I studied at business school in France,' he said. 'I had a good time there and I learned a lot, researching the impact of climate change on businesses, but I was always thinking of Zambia. As soon as I was finished I was on the next plane back. My friends there used to ask me why I didn't want to get a job somewhere in Europe and earn a bunch of money. I would tell them that I wasn't interested in money, that I just wanted to get back to Zambia. They didn't understand. I invited them to come and stay with me here. I thought that if I could show them how beautiful this place is they would change their opinions. But none of them ever came.'

'I know how that feels,' I retorted. 'Having friends who don't get why you make the choices you do.' For a moment, I considered embellishing, but I realised that I was more interested in hearing David's story than imparting my own. 'So have you been able to use your qualifications here?'

'I work a lot,' he said, 'putting together proposals for banks and businesses here on how to build environmental impact into what they do.'

'This seems like exactly the kind of place that would need that.'

'You would think so, wouldn't you? But it's not that simple, I'm afraid.' He revealed that the problem with his proposals was longevity. Getting a return on investment based on what he suggested would take about seven years, far too long for the people he was pitching to. 'That's the biggest problem Zambia faces,' he said, 'the short-sightedness of their leaders and captains of industry. They're only interested in making money now. It's why they're selling off all their natural resources to the Chinese.'

'We've seen lots of Chinese workers and projects all the way down through Africa.'

'Of course you have. They're everywhere. And why wouldn't they be? Corrupt African politicians are giving them everything they want because money's on offer. That's what it's all about. Money. I don't have any problem with the Chinese – they asked and they were allowed – what I have a problem with is the politicians who don't seem to give two shits about what effect all the Chinese mining will have on the people who actually live here. Their whole environment is being destroyed around them.'

I would have liked to have sat and talked with David for longer, but he needed to get home to take his children to school. After that, he would hole himself up in his study working on further proposals until it was time to pick up his children again. I admired David's tenacity, this lone man who, despite rejection after rejection, continued to formulate ways in which he could improve his country. Such relentless fortitude against the odds would have crushed many others, but David fought on regardless, his love of his homeland superseding all else.

'One more question before you go,' I said as he stood up to leave. 'We're hoping to make it to Lusaka tonight. Any advice on where to stay?'

'Avoid the hostels. They'll be full of kids saying "*Ooooh, I saw an elephant today, oooooh, life is so beautiful*".' He laughed at himself. 'I shouldn't say that. Tourism is one of the most sustainable industries here. At least it protects the parks and the animals. But, you know, all those wildlife dilettantes can get pretty annoying after a while.'

The going to Lusaka was easy, and then the going south from Lusaka was easy, too. I felt healthy, mine and Steve's relationship was high-spirited and jovial, and I was enjoying the cycling more than I had for perhaps the entire expedition. Zambia itself – with its good roads, food and people – helped, and we owed much gratitude to that tailwind which had not once abated since we crossed the border. And there was no denying that, without the record to worry about any longer, the journey had become far richer, immaculately pleasant. We no longer had the need to take photographs of each road sign or desperately find and then communicate to people that we wanted them to sign our logbook. Instead, we could cycle continuously for as long as we pleased and we could pause wherever we wanted. With that in mind, once we reached Livingstone, we decided to visit and stop for a while at Victoria Falls, just because we could.

Travel tends to rely on spontaneity far less than non-travellers might imagine. Whether you are forging your way deep into the uninhabitable spaces of the world or just backpacking around Thai beaches for a summer, there will always be a level of planning that precedes the journey, and that planning will be meticulous, whether or not the traveller likes to admit it. Nobody merely buys a ticket, lands in a distant country and then wanders away from the airport without a clue of where their first guesthouse or sight or watering hole will be. Much of the joy of travel comes from the planning, from the anticipation of what the new arrival might offer, from what can be seen and experienced and loved ahead. Sadly, the pleasures of this initial research can sometimes outweigh the reality of the places themselves: the painting was smaller than I'd imagined; the sea was colder than I'd been led to believe; the guesthouse and the beer and the street food were more expensive than the guide book said they'd be; the people weren't as friendly as everyone makes out and the views looked much better on those images I saw online.

Sometimes, though, you reach a place that exceeds everything your planning leads you to expect, and the reward of its sheer magnificence strikes with such force that the clichés 'breathtaking', 'mind-blowing', 'awe-inspiring' rise above their cliché status to become not banal and semantically void phrases but genuine and impervious actuality. That, for me, was Victoria

Falls. The waterfalls took my breath away, they blew my mind, they inspired awe, they were beautiful – and they were all these things and more because I had always wanted to visit them, ever since I was a boy, and had always imagined them to be as marvellous and as spectacular and as overwhelming as they, in reality, turned out to be. The first European eyes to observe them, after all, belonged to David Livingstone, one of history's great explorers, and one of my great heroes for as long as I can remember. He stumbled upon the falls in 1855 during a 4-year expedition along the Zambezi river, naming them after his Queen and writing of a spectacle that 'must have been gazed upon by angels in their flight', words I endlessly romanticised over while I lay awake in my boyhood bed through long Tehran nights, plotting out an adulthood that might one day lead me there, to that watery expanse of angels.

And, finally, there I was. At Victoria Falls. Another dream actualised. Tiptoeing as close as I could to the lip of an escarpment, I gripped the rock with my feet and leaned out as far as I dared. Across the gorge, a thousand cubic metres of water plummeted downwards each second, sending up a roar so profoundly violent that it seemed to contradict the gentle spray that caressed my bare legs and the perfect rainbow that arced over the myriad runnels in a delicate shimmer.

I felt a hand on my shoulder and turned to see Steve, who stood behind me grinning. 'Reza Pakravan, I presume.'

'Can we stay a little longer?' I pleaded.

'We can stay as long as we like.'

And so we did. An entire morning flashed by at the rate of the falls themselves, and when I finally agreed that perhaps we should start to resume our journey to Cape Town, it was with a reluctance that lasted long into the remaining miles.

Eventually, the reluctance was supplanted by gratitude. If we had still been chasing the record, it is likely we would have stopped at Victoria Falls for only a few minutes, and likelier still that we would have missed it altogether as we did the pyramids. How pleasant it was to be free of all that. How pleasant that we could enjoy these lands we were passing through, how pleasant that we could stop where we wanted for however long we wanted, how pleasant that we could *just ride* and how pleasant that the odometer and the watch no longer dictated our every move.

Further down the road, edging ever closer to Botswana, we stopped at a supermarket and, while Steve stocked up on supplies, I fell into conversation with a local who, enthralled by my bike, asked me question after question about each of the countries we had travelled through. I indulged each one and then, when I mentioned that we only had two countries left, Botswana and South Africa, he shook his head and whistled through his teeth.

'It would be better to avoid Botswana and to cycle through Zimbabwe instead,' he said.

'Why?'

'The north of Botswana is very dangerous, full of lions, elephants and other wildlife. I do not like to travel through it by car. I would certainly not travel through it by bicycle, out in the open.'

'I'd quite like to see some lions,' I said.

'Believe me, you would not.'

'I wouldn't like to see them, or I wouldn't see them?'

He laughed for a few seconds before resuming his solemn expression. 'Maybe both. Only three months ago, a Chinese man tried to hike through the north of Botswana. He was a bloody fool. My cousin was the one who found his bones.'

I related this conversation to Steve further down the road.

'It's true,' he said, 'Botswana has a lot of wild animals and it can be dangerous. And from the border there's about one-hundred-and-thirty miles of absolutely nothing except for one tiny lodge halfway through, which we'd need to reach before dark tonight. But, you know, Zimbabwe can be pretty dangerous, too. And it's not the animals you have to worry about there. I don't know about you, but I'd much rather we take our chances in Botswana.'

Bowing down to Steve's local knowledge, I agreed, and followed him towards the Zambezi river, where we exchanged our currency, boarded the ferry and crossed the water into Botswana.

CHAPTER 23

WILD

Distance remaining: 1,527 miles

We disembarked the ferry and stepped on to Botswanan soil. Before us lay the vast Kasane Forest Reserve, which we would have to negotiate our way through before alighting upon the only place to stay in the area: a small lodge over 60 miles away. A single road cut through the vast expanse of land and we pedalled furiously along it, desperate to make the lodge before nightfall. Camping, we knew, was not an option.

The Kasane Forest Reserve grew around us, bringing with it families of baboons, impala and elephants, who ignored us as we sped past. The road was good, and by the time late afternoon transformed into early evening we had covered 50 miles. Only ten more remained until the lodge. The air began to cool. More wildlife appeared – warthogs, ibis, zebras, antelopes – and I noticed an increasing alertness and agitation among them as the sun fell ever closer to the horizon. It would be night soon, and the night here contained true terrors: predatory packs of lions, hyenas and cheetahs, which came to life under the cover of darkness. Their breakfast-time impended, and the leaping kicks of the impala, the bellowing trumpets of the elephants and the toothy snarls of the baboons were warm-up rituals signalling the start of another long night of fight-or-flight reactions.

'How are you doing?' Steve asked, coasting back to cycle parallel with me. 'Scared yet?'

'Almost,' I replied as we passed a herd of elephants, the alpha-bull watching me with keen interest, its tusks longer than my arms and its legs quivering in readiness to charge. 'This is incredible, though. I've never seen anything like it, so many wild animals.'

'They'll get wilder soon. But we should be all right. We've just clocked fifty-five miles since the border – the lodge should be coming up any minute now.'

'I hope so,' I said, gesturing at the setting sun.

'I know. Let's stay cycling side by side. We're safer if we're close together.'

'Good thinking,' I said.

'Do you want us to hold hands again?'

I laughed. 'Maybe.'

It took less than half an hour for the sunset to transform the night into pitch blackness. A heavy bank of cloud rolled in with impeccable timing, obscuring any light that might have poured down from the stars and moon. I could see nothing around me other than the two thin jets of light that poured out from our bikes, could hear nothing other than the roll of tyres on tarmac and my own panting, could feel little other than the mounting pounds of my heart. I did not know whether or not to be grateful for the sensory deprivation. I could no longer see what might be lurking out there, waiting to pounce on us, I could only imagine it – and I did not know which, to see or to merely imagine, was worse.

The odometer clocked 65 miles. There had been no sign of the lodge. What if we had missed it? The nearest town was another 65 miles away. We would cycle it if we had to – there was no other choice – but the prospect of 65 more miles in this perpetual blackness pushed my anxiety close to the level of panic. Just one lion needed to spot us, that was all it would take. It could match our speed with little energy and take us down with less. I unzipped my front bag and scrabbled around for my knife, before remembering I had packed it deep inside my panniers. It was out of reach, although it would have been of little use against the claws and teeth of a lion. *At least*, I thought, *I'll have the last laugh. Whatever eats me will get my malaria.* And then: *Perhaps they'll smell it on me. Perhaps they'll understand that I'm tainted meat and leave me alone.* And then: *Can lions even get malaria?*

I may well have continued down that spiral of self-torture were it not for a sudden holler from Steve. 'This way!' He pulled off the dirt track and cycled between two open iron gates. I looked at them as I followed. There were no signs denoting the lodge.

'I'm not sure this is the place,' I shouted ahead, but Steve had already picked up speed and could not hear me. 'Steve!' I bellowed. 'Wait up! I think this is the wrong turning! I think—'

Any further words froze in my throat as an unmistakeable noise hit my ears. It was the sound of something running through grass, and it was right beside me. I pedalled harder, pushing myself forward as fast as the surface of the dirt track would allow me. To my horror, the sound did not fade, but intensified. It came from my left, a great thudding *ka-da-dun ka-da-dun ka-da-dun*, which could only have been an animal, and a large one. I dared not look. I sped forward as rapidly as I could. The animal kept pace with me. *Ka-da-dun ka-da-dun ka-da-dun.* I believe I began to emit a thin whimper, the kind of high-pitched whine that feels like it comes not from your throat but from somewhere deep behind your nose. In a sudden flash, the creature broke out in front of me, leaping across the road and just missing my wheel, its glassy black eyes glancing at me with the same terror that must have been encased in my own. It was an impala. It raced off into the wilderness and I calmed myself with the rationale that I had frightened him as I had whooshed past. The alternative – that he was running from something else, something other than me – was too much, at that point, to allow myself to contemplate.

The adrenaline slowly began to recede, supplanted finally by a cascading wave of relief as a cluster of electric lights came into view around the corner of a low hill. It was the lodge.

We rode in, welcomed by the reception staff who, not in the least put out by the fact that we had arrived here in the dark and by bicycle, offered us a pristine, air-conditioned hut for the night, and as much steak and fruit juice in the lodge's restaurant as we could stomach. It turned out that we could stomach rather a lot.

Botswana passed in a blur. As terrified of the wildlife as we continued to be, we never wild camped, but we did not need to, for after that race for accommodation on our first day the road opened up and we passed through numerous settlements where a room for the night was always ready and available.

There were likewise so many places to stop and eat that we rarely had to delve into our pannier supplies. In the small town of Mahalapye on the frontier of the Kalahari Desert, we found a cafe that served us a seemingly endless supply of tiny and delicious sandwiches. Bloated by so much bread, we ordered tea and then moved to a table outside, where we sat beneath a fraying parasol to sip and digest. It was a fine time. We were sated and happy, with Cape Town just 1,000 miles away and with no arbitrary record deadline to force us on towards it before we were ready, with the Kalahari Desert stretching out beyond us, and with the laughs and calls of laughing and calling Botswanans all around.

A car raced into the clearing beside the cafe, kicking up dust as it swerved to an awkward, diagonal halt between two resting lorries. Three young men and one young woman spilled from its doors, leaving them open so that the bass-rich house music that throbbed from the car's speakers could permeate the air. Two of the workers from our cafe rushed out to meet them, and together they danced frenetically across the dusty ground in bare feet. One of the men, tiring before the rest, left the group and, panting, approached the cafe. He wore shorts and a T-shirt and, over his hands, a pair of thick and shiny cycling gloves. When he spotted the bikes beside our table he rubbed his gloved hands together and marvelled at them in undisguised wonder.

'Are these yours?' he asked us.

We nodded.

'Then you are cyclists?'

We nodded again.

'*I* want to be a cyclist!' he cried, stepping towards our bikes and rotating his hands, still gloved, between fondling the tyres and caressing the frames.

'You look like a cyclist with those gloves,' I said.

He smiled proudly. 'Thank you. But I am not a cyclist yet.'

'So why wear the gloves?'

He winked mischievously. 'I want to start cycling so I thought it is better to have the gloves first.'

Progress was so spectacular through Botswana that we found ourselves nearing the South African border sooner than we had anticipated. We spent our last Botswanan night in the city of Gaborone. It was the end of Day 95.

'There's something I've been thinking about,' Steve said as we settled ourselves into the guesthouse we had chosen for the night. 'Something I've been thinking about a lot over the past few days, since we've been making such brilliant speed.'

'Go on.'

'I reckon that, if we keep to the same mileage we've been doing through Botswana, we can probably make Cape Town by Day One-Hundred-and-Two. Do you know what that means?'

'What?'

'Everyone who had booked to come and meet us in Cape Town had arranged to stay for at least a few days. So they'll still be there by the time we arrive. We'll only be two days late.'

It was all he needed to say. We contacted Base Camp immediately and were thrilled when Francesca replied within minutes. She would, she informed us with the authority I loved her for, urgently contact all those who had agreed to meet us in Cape Town on our behalf and inform them of our new arrival date. Only a few hours later, the emails began pouring in. Paula would be there. Steve's family and girlfriend would be there. And, of course, Francesca would be there. We climbed into our beds overjoyed.

'There's one other thing,' Steve said before he switched the light off. 'It might not be recognised by GWR, but I'm fairly certain that cycling from Nordkapp to Cape Town in one-hundred-and-two days will still be a record.'

Elation enveloped us as we crossed our last border. We had made it to South Africa, the final country. That we had arrived felt briefly implausible – had we really *cycled* here? – and while the prospect alone should have exhausted us, we were instead energised, so buoyed up by our achievement that we reached our nominated destination for the day, Mafeking, before it was dark.

It was the strangest city I had seen all the way down through Africa, not for any of its inherent qualities but by virtue of how it compared with every other African city thus far. Mafeking, and South Africa with it, was identifiably distinct from the rest of the continent, and I felt almost as if we had crossed one of our first borders rather than our last. Expensive cars shared the immaculate highway with us as we entered the city, and when we searched for a place to eat dinner, the first possible option was not a tiny roadside cafe with dusty floors and warped walls but a gargantuan, gleaming mall, complete with a food court the size of a Botswanan village. We loaded up on calories, gorging ourselves on thick burgers, fistfuls of fries and bucket-sized cups of Coke. Our bodies absorbed the vast quantities without reservation, leaving us eager to push on beyond Mafeking to Stella.

It did not take long for us to regret our decision. South of Mafeking, the city's veneer of affluence receded with each mile, giving way to grim townships composed of ailing corrugated-iron shacks, the inhabitants poor and malnourished, the children playing in dirty puddles. Lengths of barbed wire coiled along each side of the road, fencing off the townships but they fostered no perceptible sense of safety. Indeed, they only served to enhance our mounting fear. Behind the barbed wire, undercurrents of violence pulsed across the townships, signified by the occasional glimpse of a scar on a shirtless chest.

Darkness settled in, bringing with it a burst of rainfall. I pedalled forward to draw level with Steve. 'How far to Stella?' I asked.

'We've still got a while,' he replied.

'Maybe we should have stayed in Mafeking.'

Steve nodded. 'You want to turn back?'

'Not really. Is there any chance we can find somewhere to camp?'

'Out of the question,' Steve said resolutely. 'The only way to camp in South Africa is in people's gardens – if they offer it first. Otherwise it's not safe.'

'Because of the wild animals?'

'It's not them I'd be worried about.'

'So what should we do?'

'Hope we get to a town with a hotel soon. We don't want to be out here much longer.'

As Mafeking before them, the townships too began to diminish, supplanted by nothing other than arid and empty scrubland. Eerie and echoing howls floated on the humid air, and whether they were canine or human I could not decipher. Sweat began to gather on my forehead, dripping the filth of a long day's cycle into my eyes, which reacted in kind with hot tears. I could feel my thighs beginning to weaken, and the only scant comfort I could locate was the recollection that I had repacked my knife and placed it inside my front bag, a hand's reach away.

A band of lights appeared on the horizon and we stepped up our pace as we approached it. The beams came from a petrol station, and beside it sat a bar: a squat den with sooty walls and small windows. Three men stood outside smoking fat, weed-packed cheroots, and they eyed us suspiciously as we slowed to a halt at the bar's doorway.

'This isn't a good place to stop,' Steve whispered so that the three men could not hear him.

'They might have a room,' I whispered back to him. 'It's worth a look. Let's go in and ask.'

'I'll stay here and look after the bikes.'

I glanced over at the three smokers, who had not taken their eyes from us. 'Probably a good idea,' I said, and then entered the bar.

It was busy inside with barely a seat available, but there was no music and an uneasy quietness prevailed. Heads turned and rheumy eyes gazed at me as I walked through the door, glasses of frothy beer settling softly on the wooden tables. I felt the eyes follow me as I walked towards the bar and, though I listened out for it, I could hear little conversation going on around me. Each one of the customers was male, and they had the lean and exhausted look of farmers and labourers fresh from work, drinking away the day's toil slowly and consistently. I wondered how I must look to them, this Lycra-clad alien with grimy skin and a beard that made his head look disproportionate to the rest of his body. I hoped that my foreignness – in all senses of the word – would generate only an innocent curiosity and not spill over into its nastier brother: violence.

The bartender ignored me, the only man here to do so. All other eyes were still on me and the scrutiny was growing unbearable. I heard the unmistakeable scraping sound of chairs being pushed back from their tables and looked over my shoulder to see four men rise to their feet and saunter towards me. Three were black and one white. Avoiding eye contact with them and instead looking around the room with the greatest semblance of casualness I could muster, I realised that the white man was the only white man in the entire room.

'How is it?' he said, leaning against the bar beside me. I could tell straight away that he was ludicrously drunk. His legs swayed beneath him and his eyes did their best to focus on my chin.

'I'm good, thanks,' I said, choosing there and then not to ask for a room for the night. There was nowhere I would rather have stayed less. 'Me and my mate are on our way to Stella. Just stopping for a quick beer.'

The bartender heard me and began to open a can, placing it before me and then watching my wallet with especial interest as I fished it out of my pocket and found the requisite rand. I took a long gulp of the beer. It tasted sensational.

'Stella's all right. We work on a farm nearby,' the drunk man said, and his three friends nodded silently. 'It's shit, bru. Really fucking shit work. So we come here each night and get fucking plastered. Fun.'

I looked out of the window. Steve was standing on the other side of it, the three weed-smokers surrounding him. He looked terrified. I felt the same. I sank the can in four long gulps, stuck out my hand and said: 'Gotta go. Nice to meet you.' The drunk man ignored me, but his three friends shook my hand, and the action seemed to give me the authority I needed to walk out unharmed.

The weed-smokers had begun to inundate Steve with a volley of questions when I reappeared, and though he gamely replied to each one, his look of relief when I told him we could not stay here and had to press on was frank and discernible.

'What were they asking you?' I said as we pushed our bikes out through the car park.

'If I wanted to buy some weed,' he replied. 'And when I said no, why not. What was it like in there?'

'Like a Wild West movie. I had a beer.'

'You had a beer?'

'I had a *beer*.'

'What was it like?'

'Absolutely delicious.'

'The last time I had a beer was…'

'Back in St Petersburg. With Ivan and Katya.'

'Ivan and Katya,' Steve laughed, climbing on to his bike. 'What a night.'

I pulled myself on to my saddle, all ready to begin the search for the next town, when I was stopped before my feet could reach the pedals.

'*Hey, bru!*' came the shout from behind me. '*Wait up a fucking minute, will you?*'

I turned around. The drunk man was staggering towards me, his feet flopping haphazardly across the tarmac, his three friends behind him.

'Shit…' I whispered.

'Let's just go,' Steve said.

One of the friends peeled off from the group, retrieving a set of keys from his pocket and opening the door of an old and dirty pick-up truck.

'I don't think it'll do much good,' I said to Steve. 'They can catch up with us.'

The drunk man lumbered closer, his gait heavy and yeti-like. He drew level with me, his breath a rancid mixture of booze, tobacco and halitosis. 'How is it?' he slurred.

I wondered what would happen if I hit him – once, swiftly. He was too drunk to see it coming. But his three friends were not as intoxicated as him, and I could not help factoring into my mental calculations that they were huge.

'We're just about to head off to Stella,' I said.

'Now?' He waved a limp arm above him, gesturing perhaps at the sky. 'Too dark,' he said, 'too dark for all that. Listen, bru, I feel like I was rude to you back in the bar. I'm really sorry. So pissed. So fucking pissed. Are you looking for a place to stay?'

'No,' Steve said.

'You South African?' he shouted with such delight that it managed to refocus his eyes on ours rather than somewhere above our shoulders.

'Yes,' Steve said.

'Then I've *got* to put you up for the night! You're my fucking *bru*, bru! I'm Matt, by the way.'

'Listen, Matt,' I said, my voice polite. 'It's kind of you to offer, but we really need to get to Stella tonight.'

'*Pah*, Stella – that'll take you another four or five hours. And it's fucking late now. I live five minutes away. You can follow me on your bikes, I'll drive slow. What else are you going to do? We can fucking *party!*'

'Again, it's so kind of you,' I said, 'but we're exhausted, and we haven't got it in us to party tonight.'

'Have you got it in you to cycle all the way to Stella?'

I thought about it. 'Maybe not.'

'Then spend the night at mine! I've got a spare room. It's all yours if you want it. Honestly, I feel really bad for how I was back in the bar and I want to make it up to you. We'll probably party for a bit, but we won't disturb you. Doesn't that sound better than cycling all the way to fucking Stella?'

I could not escape the fact that it did, and neither could Steve, and so we thanked Matt for his hospitality and agreed to follow him to his house. He drove before us slowly, though this was perhaps less due to his promise and more due to his inebriation, which caused him to weave back and forth across the dark road, grinding gears and bellowing thick plumes of exhaust smoke into our faces. Here and there, an empty can of lager toppled out of one of the truck's windows.

We finally arrived, not 5 minutes later but 35, and before showing us the spare room Matt insisted on giving us a guided tour of the rest of his bungalow. It was a strange and sad mishmash of body-building equipment, enormous tubs of mass-weight-gain powder and unopened boxes. 'Shit, bru, I buy all this stuff,' he said as he bounced off the wall of one room into another and pointed at each box in turn. 'I've got this sick flat-screen, brand new PlayStation, couple of microwaves, electric guitars, all that, but I just never get round to unpacking it and setting it up. Too pissed all the time. See that one there? That's a brand new PC, proper full-on hard drive with I don't know how much memory. I bought it three months ago, but it's still in the box. I've just never managed to get my head around how to open the fucking thing.'

Once the tour was over, Matt left us in the spare room, only to appear at our doorway just as we had laid out and begun to settle on to our Therm-a-

Rest. He carried a box of 12 cans of lager in his hand, laid it at the foot of our makeshift bed, and then sat upon it, plucking out a can and breaking it open with his finger. 'You guys go to the gym much?' he asked.

'We don't really need to,' I replied with an exaggerated yawn. 'We get all the exercise we need from cycling.'

'I go to the gym a lot, bru,' he said, ignoring me. 'Most days I'm there and I'm working out hard. I start with a warm-up on the treadmill, and then it's all about the legs. You've got to start with the legs. Most people forget about them. But my philosophy is that if you build the legs everything else will follow...'

I think that Matt might then have monologued his way through his entire workout regime, although I can't be certain, for I fell asleep not long into it. All I do know is that I awoke some time later and he was still talking, not so much to us but to himself, and it was still about the most effective way to body-build. He had shifted himself to the very edge of his box seat, for most of the lager had been removed from it, and empty cans lay forlornly around his feet.

CHAPTER 24

THIS IS THE END,
BEAUTIFUL FRIEND

Distance remaining: 788 miles

———————

Our 6 a.m. alarm clock the following morning was a heavy metal track which pumped violently throughout the house and ripped us from our slumber. Matt stumbled into the room, hungover and bleary, shouted to us that he was off to work and then left the house to drive away in his pick-up. The heavy metal album continued to play at the same brash level.

Such an early start at least got us on the road quickly and we took advantage of the situation, stopping in the late afternoon at Vryburg for a chicken dinner and then pushing on to Kimberley, which we reached at 10 p.m. We had covered 152 miles: our best distance yet. If we kept this up, there was no question that we could make Cape Town by Day 102. We celebrated with a second dinner.

The next day followed much the same pattern – good roads and good food and a target-destination that we reached early enough to exceed – and, before we knew it, it was Day 99, and we were rolling towards Beaufort West. A strange and persistent sense of unease had begun to settle over me during those last 48 hours. I knew what it was – I knew *exactly* what it was – but I made the conscious decision to put it out of my mind, at least for the time being, for this day held a particular cause for joy. Francesca had landed in Cape Town that morning and was on her way to meet us.

We did not know where we would see her, only that she was planning to rent a car as soon as she landed in Cape Town and drive north along the N1 – the same road we were cycling along southbound – until our paths inevitably crossed. And, when they did, the loud honking that issued out from beneath her bonnet as she drew level with us was terrifying for only a fraction of a second, for I immediately recognised the hand that waved wildly from her open window. I waved back with all my might. A service station lay less than a mile away. We watched and then followed as she pulled ahead and turned into it.

There she was. Francesca. Leaning back against the door of her car, a warm smile on her lips. Seeing her was pure delight, and when we hugged I was wracked by a sensation of joy so overwhelming that I thought for a second I might burst into tears.

'Long time no see,' she said, leaning back from the hug to take my face in both her hands and look at me.

'Ninety-eight days,' I replied. 'Just a bit north of here.'

She giggled, but did not take her eyes from mine. 'You look so different. Like... like a... like a caveman.'

'Didn't I always?'

'No. The Reza I left at the Finnish border was a different Reza.'

'I agree with that.'

'We were all so worried about you when you got malaria. I know I shouldn't have, but I just kept thinking about Gianluca.'

'I've been thinking a lot about him, too. I probably would have given up back in Kenya if it wasn't for him, for his memory, for what he did.'

We hugged once more, a long and affectionate embrace. Finally, as if remembering something, she pulled herself back with a sniff. 'There's someone here to see you,' she said.

Hearing the car door open and then shut, I looked up from Francesca to see Marco, my closest friend, who had shared the same London flat as

Gianluca and me for half a decade. He walked towards us and, without a word, joined our hug. The three of us stood there together for a long time, our arms and necks and cheeks pressed close.

'We sorted out a room for the four of us,' Francesca eventually said, 'here in Beaufort West. You want to go?'

'Not really,' I said.

'Day One-Hundred tomorrow,' Marco rejoined. 'You must be excited.'

'Not really.'

For the truth was that I wasn't excited, not at all. This was the source of my unease: Day 100 marked the original finish date for this long and arduous and enlightening and stupefying expedition. It was where the journey was supposed to come to an end. And that left me feeling far from excited. It left me, rather, feeling sad. Not because we hadn't made it on time, but because it made me think of the end of the expedition – an expedition, I realised, that I didn't want to ever end.

And so I awoke on the morning of Day 100 not with the adrenaline I had anticipated during those planning days back in London that seemed a lifetime ago, but with a barrage of negative emotions. Chief among them was that lingering wish that South Africa was not the southernmost tip of our journey, not the end of the landmass we had chosen to cycle across, that there could somehow be a way to *keep going*, even on to Antarctica and then around the bottom of the world, spat out somewhere in the far south of Patagonia, where we could restock our supplies and then pedal all the way to Canada.

But there was more to it than that: more doubt; more fear. This expedition had consumed my life to such an extent that it had *become* my life. One hundred days of cycling, and before that two years of planning, had all been directed towards the moment we arrived in Cape Town, which stood less than 48 hours away. Yet I had come to understand that, in reality, the journey itself had been the real prize and that journey was about to end. The prospect left me mortified. What on earth was I going to do? I had nothing to go back to: no job, no security, no girlfriend, not even a place to live. I had thrown it all away for this, this expedition, and then I had raced through it in chase of an arbitrary record I had not even achieved.

Which left just one final thought, a thought I could not wrest myself from as I climbed back on to my bike on the morning of Day 100. And the thought was this: *was it all worth it?*

———————

Our cameraman for the close of the journey, Grant, came to meet us in the late morning. Each time he asked us to stop and film a commentary, I did my best to get into the spirit and describe the landscapes we were passing through. Yet I could never seem to find the words. When I climbed back on to my bike and set off again after another failed attempt, I felt ashamed at my verbal incapacity. But too much doubt and reluctance and insecurity was running through my head, and it seemed that if I gave voice to it in front of the camera it would only make things worse.

We ended the day at Laingsburg and ate dinner at a steak restaurant. Francesca, knowing that something was wrong, soon gave up on the questions I could not answer and we dined under an awkward silence. Back in our rooms – Steve and I sharing one while Francesca and Marco shared another – I completed our logbook and then fell heavily into my bed without undressing.

'Everything all right?' Steve asked.

'No,' I admitted.

'Didn't think so. When it was up to me to suggest we should stop for some filming, I knew something was wrong.'

'I didn't have anything to say.'

'Exactly,' Steve laughed. 'Something must be wrong.'

I closed my eyes.

'It's the record, isn't it?' he said. 'Today should have been the day we got it. But now the day's over, and we didn't.'

I sighed. 'I gave up on the record a long time ago. It's nothing to do with that.'

'Would it cheer you up if I told you we just received a thousand-pound donation from one of my clients today?'

'A little,' I said. 'But it also makes me remember that you still have clients, that you've still got a job. And I don't.'

'Is that what's bothering you? About what's going to happen when you get home?'

'Partly. But not totally. I'm just feeling a bit down. About everything. I can't help thinking one question.'

'And what's that?'

'Was it all worth it?'

Steve jumped up in bed and bounced on the mattress. 'Was it worth it?' he cried. 'Fucking right it was worth it! Have you ever before done what we've just done? Has *anyone* ever done what we've just done? We shouldn't just be proud about all this, mate – we should be over the moon!'

'I get that, I really do. But that doesn't answer the question. We might have done something out of the ordinary... but... *was it all worth it*?'

'I can't answer that for you,' Steve said, turning off the light and settling back into bed to signify that the conversation was almost over. 'But tomorrow I'll show you exactly why it's all been worth it for me.'

I struggled to rise in the morning, but Steve bullied me out of bed with his repeated cries of: 'Day One-Hundred-and-One! Cape Town tomorrow!'

'What are you going to show me?' I grumbled as I dressed.

'You'll see! Day One-Hundred-and-One! Cape Town tomorrow!'

Francesca, Marco and Grant met us for breakfast. I remained quiet, though it did not matter so much as Steve did the talking for both of us.

'He's on good form,' Francesca said as we paid the bill, Steve already mounting his bike outside and shouting into Grant's camera: 'Day One-Hundred-and-One! Cape Town tomorrow!'

'He's going home,' I said.

'Is that it?'

'I don't know. He said something big is happening today.'

'Well then,' Francesca said. 'Let's get on and find out what it is.'

Steve hit such a pace that I struggled to keep up with him. Morose and lacklustre as I was, the car kept level with Steve instead of me, filming him as he whooped and hollered all the way to Matjiesfontein. Once there, he took a sudden turn into a petrol station and I watched as he homed in on a parked hatchback with its tailgate wide open. Five people stood outside it, and when they saw Steve approach they leaped up and down with effusive joy. He stopped, and two of them pounced upon him with such force that he fell from his bike. He managed to get back to his feet before they did the same again, soon joined by the other three, and when I came to a halt beside them all, Steve introduced me to his mother, his girlfriend and three of his closest friends. They took turns shaking my hand and asking how I was before bundling back on to Steve, who stood in the middle of all this jubilation, wiping his eyes and beaming. I had never seen him look so happy.

I peered into the boot of the car, which was piled to the brim with food and drinks.

'Help yourself!' Steve's mother cried out to me from somewhere under her son's arms. 'You must be famished! Eat! Drink! We're so happy to see you!'

It took perhaps 20 minutes for Steve to extricate himself from the tangle of embraces, and when he did he came to me, wrapped his arm around my shoulder, and said: 'This is it. The expedition's nearly over. It has to end. But this is what happens when it does. This is what it's all about. Not a job. Not money. Just being with the people you love. After such a long journey. This is what makes it worth it.'

Steve left me with a chuckle and returned to his pack. His mother kissed him on the cheek, his girlfriend kissed him on the lips and his friends berated him with exaggerated impressions of his anglicised accent. They all smiled, never stopped smiling, and as I watched them I realised I was smiling, too. Steve was right. The expedition was coming to an end. But that could mean celebration rather than despair. There was none of the latter in the group of people who entwined Steve into themselves, not even the merest hint of melancholy. There was only exultation.

I suddenly realised that I wanted that for myself. And it lay only a day away, in Cape Town.

———————————

Day 101 ended in Worcester. Seventy miles lay between us and the finish line. Marco bought us all pizza for dinner and then we checked into our guesthouse, where I stayed up late into the night checking my emails, our social media and the donations page. Francesca had updated everyone that we would be arriving in Cape Town on the 102nd day, and a flood of supportive and congratulatory messages had poured in, along with a swathe of new donations. I checked the total, £21,000, and swelled with pride. In a matter of days, that £21,000 would be funnelled deep into Madagascar and I only wished I could be there with the Malagasy children when they were told.

On the morning of our last day, Day 102, Steve and I woke, rose and dressed in silence. Such silence was not uncomfortable. It was more that we simply had nothing left to say to each other. We had exchanged all the jokes, memories, stories and secrets we each held in our personal stockpiles over the past 101 days and now we were both conversationally spent. What was there left to say?

Instead, behaviour replaced vocabulary and we were content with that. We smiled and laughed at each other in a manner almost akin to shyness, and when we recognised the peculiar timidity we smiled and laughed some more, yet still said nothing. Francesca, Marco and Grant met us outside with the car ready. We performed a brief piece for the camera, swapped a few hugs and then there was nothing left to do but ride.

One final mountain separated us from Cape Town: Bainskloof. Ignoring the highway tunnel that burrowed beneath the Hawequas range, we chose the old road that would lead us high up on to and over the Bainskloof Pass. It meant one last arduous climb, but after that it would be downhill all the way to Cape Town, and the notion of one final up and down felt appropriate on this conclusive day of our expedition.

And so we rode up: up through the myriad springs and luscious meadows; up along meandering hairpins and beside treacherous drops; up into thinner, cleaner air, which I sucked into my lungs with carefree abandon. Once at the top, we pulled over and the car stopped beside us. Grant asked for one final piece, and once it was filmed, he, Francesca and Marco piled back into the car and drove on to Cape Town to man the finish line. Steve and I stayed. Once more, there was no need for words. Instead, we sat back in the browning grass, closed our eyes and lifted our heads to the sun. I felt the heat sink into my cheeks and then glow throughout my body. I leaned back on to my elbows, and then went further, laying my shoulders across the earth and then my head. An overwhelming peace enveloped me. I could have fallen asleep.

And perhaps I did, for when Steve said, 'We should probably make a move', it jolted through my consciousness like electricity and I sat up with a start.

'I could stay here,' I said, 'for a lot longer.'

'Me too. Shall we?'

'Yes.'

And so we did, sprawled out on that African soil together like two old dogs, exhausted after a long walk, and finally back home in front of the fire. I felt suddenly very sorry for all the flare ups that had occurred between Steve and me, for all the extreme reactions that had come down to the extreme emotions of extreme circumstances. I wished they had never happened, but I also knew that they were an intrinsic part of the journey: a journey that had tied us together and produced a wonderful form of brotherhood. In fact, it was *more* than brotherhood, what Steve and I shared. I could never have endured the same expedition with my own brother. Yet, with Steve, I had not only endured but flourished. So had he, and that was because, at the end of it all, we had worked together. Despite the arguments and the bitterness and the resentment, we had always succeeded in coming out the other end of it and continuing. We were a team. When I thought about the staggering distance we had covered and the sheer enormity of the obstacles and travails that had been a part of it, I understood how fortunate I had been to have Steve by my side. I could not have done it without him and that surfacing truth was a beautiful one.

When it was time to leave, we both knew and there was no need for either of us to cajole the other. We set off down the mountain at a breakneck speed, plummeting towards the vineyards of the Western Cape and, behind them, Table Mountain. It rose before us in all its symbolic glory: this vast monument of Cape Town, of South Africa and of the end of our own long cycle towards it.

———————

Cape Town came on so quickly it swallowed us long before I noticed its presence. Our arrival seemed too swift to be believable. Everything about this expedition seemed too swift to be believable.

With the sun at its peak and unobscured by the high-rises all around, with palm trees growing from gardens and the scent of full-bloom barbecues ever present, with road signs no longer pointing towards 'Cape Town' but instead pointing towards 'Centre', and with the road itself a teeming mass of congestion and exhaust fumes, we crossed a junction and suddenly saw it. The finish line. The exact spot within Cape Town where we had agreed with GWR that our journey would end. It seemed impossible that we had made it.

A trail of stationary cars came first: their drivers bemused and curious, some stepping outside to find the source of the hold up and then gazing at us as we coasted past. Beyond that, a collective of bounding and hollering and waving individuals coursed beneath the wide Koga banner held aloft by Marco and Paula. Teasing brakes with our hands, we came to a stop just below the banner, and were immediately surrounded by the scores who pocketed their photo-opportunity cameras in favour of a hug or kiss or shaken hand. We knew every single one of them, and surpassed their joy of seeing us with our own ecstasy of seeing them. A troop of Zulu dancers leaped into the fray to spin and kick in time to their drummers.

Champagne was produced, shaken wildly and then spurted everywhere. Grant asked us for our thoughts for the camera. We had so many, but could find none of the words that might ever possibly do them justice. And so we grinned, and made incomprehensible noises, and then fell into the arms of our friends and family, revelling in their understanding that we had no need to speak, and that our smiles and tears and giggles and whoops revealed more than words ever could, and that our incoherence was right, was justified, here, at the end of the road.

EPILOGUE

BEGINNING AGAIN

The end of a journey is a peculiar and somewhat dichotomous time. On the one hand, there is elation: elation that you have endured and survived; elation that you are with people you know and love once more; elation at the easy intimacy that flows between you and them. On the other hand, there is emptiness. For the journey is now over and, with it, an immense slice of your life. I felt both on that Cape Town finish line, overjoyed to be in the arms of my friends and off the saddle, and yet simultaneously wishing myself back on to it.

Steve and I parted company later that day. Francesca, Marco and Paula stayed with me, and together we spent a few blissful days in South Africa, sightseeing, basking in the warmth of the weather and each other, indulging ourselves with good food and wine. Soon, they too had to leave, to return to their homes and their jobs, but I was reluctant to do the same. I had neither a home nor a job. I checked into a small Cape Town bed and breakfast, and wondered what on earth I was going to do with myself.

The truth is, I had let my expectations get the better of me. Over those 102 days riding from the Arctic to South Africa, I had passed much of the time regaling myself with fantasies of broadcasters, agents and publishers meeting me at the finish line, of sudden bidding wars erupting over the rights to my TV series and book. I had played out those fantasies so many times in my head that I had genuinely come to expect them to happen. But the reality was far different. There were no knocks at my door, no emails or messages press-ganging me into a series commission or book deal. There was nothing, and that nothingness began to overwhelm me.

One day, I took a walk to the beach and, staring out over the waves, a realisation came to me. I could sit and wait here for days or weeks or months on end with no joy, or I could start making things happen for myself. And so I made a plan. First of all, I would write my book, this book, the story of Kapp to Cape. Once that was complete, I would take the vast amount of footage I had from the journey and turn it into a film. I would still need the investment of publishers and producers, but if they were not going to come to me, I would be sure to have a viable product to take to them.

After so long with only Steve and my own thoughts for company, I felt a tremendous urge to surround myself with people I loved while I worked, and so I flew to California, where my mother and brother and his family lived. It was a beautiful time. Being with my family gave me the base of love and familiarity which I craved, and the hard work I endured bent over a laptop for 12 hours each day writing my book and emailing production companies, broadcasters and publishers was offset by good family meals, by long conversations with my mother, by evenings playing with my nieces, and by Sundays surfing and cycling.

Then something remarkable happened. An Italian production and distribution company called Samarcanda Film got in touch with me. They were interested in turning Kapp to Cape into a television series. After reaching an agreement, I flew to Rome to work with them.

Those next four months passed in a blur. Life was supreme. I woke up each morning excited to be going to work that day. That had never happened in London. I fell in love with the creative process. Adventure travel was a spectacular way to live, but this was something else. I was not just experiencing and enduring. I was *creating*. And I adored it.

We finished making the TV series in November. December came and went, taking Christmas and then the New Year with it. No one, it seemed, wanted the series. January passed in the same manner. Meetings with Samarcanda took on bleaker and bleaker tones. In spare moments, I finished the second draft of my book and began to tout it around publishers and literary agents. None were interested.

With my savings depleting swiftly, I was forced to make a decision. I could no longer afford to stay in Rome or fly back to California. With options running out, I called my aunt in Kent, and she kindly offered to put me up in Tunbridge Wells for as long as I needed. As grateful as I was, I could not help but feel utter despondence when I arrived at her house in early February. Fifteen years earlier, I had come to the UK for university and she had hosted me. I was 25 back then, and now here I was, in exactly the same place, yet with fewer prospects and far less money. Despair settled in. I loved my aunt, but the knowledge of being back on her couch, only this time 40 years old and scratching my head wondering what on earth I had done with my life, was almost too much to bear.

Weeks passed. With just £500 left of my savings and only a gaping overdraft below it, I began to think of work once again. That meant London, and when a friend of mine moved abroad and asked around for someone to move into his property and maintain it until he could find a paying tenant, I snapped up the opportunity, kissed my aunt goodbye and made my way back to London. Where it all started. Where, if I was going to be realistic about things, my old life would have to begin again. Although I loved London and always will, I dreaded what the return to it would likely entail.

If you've read this far, you no doubt know what happened next. I can ramp up the tension and the drama as much as I like, but, by virtue of reading this book, you already know it has a happy ending.

And it does.

But I'll tell it anyway.

I'll skip the monotonous days sitting in greasy spoons and coffee shops scouring the classifieds for job vacancies; I'll skip the long dark nights of the soul when I lay awake and questioned what it was that had driven me to end up homeless and unemployed at the age of 40 with my credit cards exhausted and my overdraft limit reached. Instead, I'll just get straight to the good stuff. Because, as it happened, it came not long after my return to London.

First: an email from Samarcanda. On the same day, two networks bought the TV series of *Kapp to Cape*.

Second: Summersdale agreed to publish my book.

Third: Samarcanda gave me the green light to begin my new project, an expedition I had long dreamed of – a deep and immersive journey through the Amazon rainforest. Not only would they co-produce it with me, but they would do so to such an extent that I could begin work on it immediately. All I had to do was say yes.

Which, of course, I did. I said yes. I said it so many times and to so many people that the word itself began to sound strange to my own ears. I no longer walked but bounded; I no longer stood still but floated. I spent the next week proclaiming everything in an excitable shout, laughing at the thinnest of jokes and whenever I greeted someone I did so with a smile so wide that my jaws began to hurt. In fact, I say I only did that for a week, but the truth is I'm still doing it.

It took me a long time to get here, and it took hardships that I never would have thought endurable in that London office so many years ago, but I would go back and endure them a thousand times over if it meant that I could get to where I am today. Because I'm still immersed in this life that I've always wanted to lead: adventuring, creating, raising awareness, writing, making films, building schools and, most of all, *living*.

ACKNOWLEDGEMENTS

This book is all about going, and then keeping on going. I learned the going from my father. He was a TV director, a man full of interesting ideas. He taught me that, if you have an idea, you should just go and do it. Don't sit around and talk about it. And I learned how to keep going from my mother, a woman who never gets tired of pressing ahead. She was a TV producer and I feel I have inherited her producer genes. She is relentless and works hard to achieve things. Giving up is not an option for her. And so, as my mother and father's son, I go and I will keep going. Thank you both.

My brother has definitely inherited our parents' genes, too. He supported me all the way and he never gave up. From the minute the Kapp to Cape idea was born, he went out and campaigned for it in the US, attracting sponsorship and donations, and always continuing to support me.

Once in a while, every person comes across someone who will change their lives. When I met a tall, bearded man – a friend of a friend – in a London bar, I had no idea that he would be one of these people. I knew then that I wanted to change my life and make a living from travelling and adventure, but I really didn't know how to do it. Meeting Arash set the path for me. I met him just before setting off on my Sahara expedition. We talked and Arash was amazed by the expedition and encouraged me to make a film from it. He gave me a camera and said: 'Just put the setting in automatic and shoot.' I had no idea how to film and what to do. I just shot whatever I could. Fast-forward to *Kapp to Cape*, and together we produced a four-episode documentary that has so far been broadcast in 12 countries by eight separate broadcasters. Arash's passion is cinema, and he helped me because he loved my idea and saw the passion I had for it. Thank you, my friend.

From the minute the idea was born, Francesca became the backbone of the expedition. This dear friend of mine not only played an important role as the logistics manager – planning the route and so much else – but she also lived the entire journey minute by minute with me. Throughout the post-production of the series, she hosted me and made me feel at home while in Rome.

Acknowledgements

Like Francesca, none of this would have been possible without Paula. Not only did she join me for the first and last sections of the expedition, but I wonder if, without her, the film ever would have seen the light of day. It was Paula who networked in Italy on my behalf and put me in touch with Samarcanda Film.

I have a dear friend who not only flew to the finish line to see me but also drove 620 miles north from Cape Town to spend the last couple of days with me before the close of the journey. Since I started my adventurer's lifestyle, Marco has never stopped supporting me.

The result of the expedition wouldn't be as significant if I didn't have Andy managing our social media and writing our blog. Andy is a genius writer and social media expert. His effort, combined with amazing web support from my cousin Bahman, helped us raise enough funds for SEED to build two schools in Madagascar. I would like to thank my cousin Amir Hossein, who helped me lots with turning my daily emails into brilliant stories for the press.

Thank you to Jacopo, Francesco, Leonardo and Luca at Samarcanda Film, who believed in me and decided to invest in the project. During the five months we worked together, they gave a novice like me so much creative freedom and we experienced an amazing time together in the studio in Rome throughout the whole process.

My relationship with Steve was a tumultuous one, but now I'm pleased to say that our friendship is solid. Although there were really tough moments between us and although we had different opinions about things, we always managed to focus on our common interests and leave the differences for later. One of Steve's mantras was 'Let's ride it off'. I learned from him exactly how to do that. We went through a number of hardships together, but they only made us stronger. I have to admit that I'm a bit of a faffer, not the quickest person to get going early in the morning, and if it wasn't for Steve pushing me hard we would never have got to Cape Town in 102 days.

Being on the road for a while gives you a lot of thinking time. During my journey, I realised how important family is to me. My aunt Mahin, my cousin Susanne and her husband Jeremy provided me with much needed support before the journey, throughout the production of the film and after. A big thank you to them.

When I finished the production of the film in Italy, I was so broke I couldn't even afford a room. I was hopeless and barely surviving. However, in that moment I realised the value of friendship. I am ever grateful to Mike, Rassa, Azadeh and Amirpasha, Maryam, Kourosh and Chloe and Ashley, who opened their doors to me and offered me hospitality when I needed it the most.

I met Paul Mill in 2011 before my Sahara expedition. He shouted something at me while we were training and it got stuck in my head: 'Reza, do whatever you want to do! Don't give up!' Paul made me believe that I can do things beyond my capability, so long as I believe in and don't give up on them.

To my friend Helen – do you remember that time, in Stanford's in London, when we were browsing through the travel books? You said to me then: 'One day, your book will be on these shelves.' That seemed to me such a stretch of the imagination at the time. And yet, two years after you said that, I got my book deal. Helen, thank you for all your involvement from the minute the idea of Kapp to Cape was born. You helped me with so much, from arranging for packages to be delivered to me in Nairobi to helping me write sponsorship proposals and documentary treatments.

A big thank you to Mark, Jo, Tegan and Mal at SEED Madagascar for their help and support throughout the expedition. These selfless people are out there helping the people of Madagascar, educating and developing on the front line. Hats off to them.

A big thank you to my friend and co-writer Charlie Carroll. Working with him has been nothing but a pleasure. The first time I met him, I felt a very strong bond between us, and realised that we have many common interests, especially travelling and music.

Massive thanks to all at Summersdale, especially Debbie Chapman, who took the risk and actualised my dream of becoming a published author.

Last but not least, my thanks go to Roy Varner, Annie, Ivan and Katya, Hedi, Ghazal and Chris, Amirali, Sanam, Kamyar and Afrooz, Midhat, Grant, Shirin, Peiman and all the people who helped me to get this expedition off the ground and get to the finish line.

Throughout the whole writing process, a very special person entered my life. Jaleh, the love of my life, gave me her unconditional support and love, and enabled me to finish this book. I am ever grateful for that.

ABOUT THE AUTHOR

Reza Pakravan is a traveller, adventurer and film-maker. He holds the Guinness World Record for crossing the Sahara Desert by bicycle: his preferred mode of transport. He has also cycled the Annapurna Circuit, the length of the planet from Norway to South Africa, and through the Amazon rainforest along the Trans-Amazonian Highway. In 2012, he was listed amongst the world's top 20 most seasoned travellers by *Men's Fitness* magazine. Reza is a patron of NGO SEED Madagascar and has received a prestigious Lloyd's Charity Award for his work building schools and fundraising for Malagasy children.

You can follow Reza's adventures at **rezapakravan.com**
or on Twitter at **@RezaPakravan**

Find out more about SEED Madagascar's work at **Madagascar.co.uk**

12/18/18

Have you enjoyed this book?
If so, why not write a review on your favourite website?
If you're interested in finding out more about our books,
find us on Facebook at **Summersdale Publishers**
and follow us on Twitter at **@Summersdale**.

Thanks very much for buying this Summersdale book.

www.summersdale.com